THE

LIGHT OF THE CONSCIENCE

BY THE AUTHOR OF

"LIFE OF S. FRANCIS DE SALES;"
"THE SPIRITUAL LETTERS OF S. FRANCIS DE SALES;"
"THE HIDDEN LIFE OF THE SOUL;"
ETC., ETC.

With an Introduction

BY

THE REV. T. T. CARTER, M.A.
Rector of Clewer, Berks
And Honorary Canon of Christ Church Cathedral. Oxford

RIVINGTONS
WATERLOO PLACE, LONDON
Oxford and Cambridge
1876

TO THE

REV. T. T. CARTER, M. A.

Honorary Canon of Christ Church,

AT WHOSE SUGGESTION IT WAS WRITTEN,

This Little Book

IS AFFECTIONATELY AND GRATEFULLY

DEDICATED.

PREFACE

A MONG the many aids to the spiritual life issuing from the press, this little book has an aim and purpose peculiarly its own. It is not a regular treatise, nor does it profess to exhaust the subjects it proposes for consideration, nor enter into the principles underlying them. It does not touch on questions of a novel kind, nor will it gratify mere intellectual curiosity; but it supplies valuable advice on common topics, and is eminently practical in the very best sense of the term, as giving only what acknowledged spiritual guides have recommended of their own experience, and what personal use has tested and approved.

Moreover, it is not intended to deal with cases of grave fault, or touch the springs of lives wholly disordered and abandoned. It assumes the existence of a real honest purpose, a true faith, and purity of intention. It seeks to raise those who are well disposed, and sincere in desiring to lead a higher life, and advance more and more unto perfection. To such persons the book will suggest matters of real practical import in the way of self-discipline and patient effort, with the view of making life, in "its trivial round, its common task," disciplined, devout, and conformed to the orderings of God's Providence and the expressions of His overruling Will in the love of our ever blessed Lord.

It is not unfrequently observed, how in proportion to the grace of spiritual discernment the value of little things is the more highly appreciated; how the momentous issues depending on a faithful use of common events, of ordinary duties and uneventful trials, is increasingly felt. As we are taught that "he that contemns small things shall fall by little and little," even so the truest saintly experience shows, that whoever diligently employs earnest thought and prayer in sanctifying small things in the quiet order of daily life, with a deepening sense of their importance, ever trying to live in recollection and patient self-discipline under the Eye of God—most surely advances, as "the shining light that shineth more and more unto the perfect day." The reason of this is evident. A spiritual life depends, under the grace of God, on matured habits and regulated impulses. But such a chastened state can be attained only by constant exercise in matters of detail, a succession of acts and endeavours continually, though it may be silently, renewed. Striking events occur but seldom. Great trials are not the common lot. They cannot therefore be the occasion of forming habits. Equally important is it to note, that the only hope of rightly meeting those greater trials, lies in the previous preparation gained through "patient continuance in well-doing" in the minor details of life. The mind duly set on making use of common and little things, as the opportunities of perfecting holiness, is at the same time, unknown to itself, acquiring a strength which will come forth in the hour of need to be "more than conqueror, through Christ strengthening" it.

The undersigned does not suppose that his recommendation can add weight to the writings of one so well known and appreciated as the authoress of this work; but he is glad to be associated with her in bearing witness to the value of the assistance she has sought to supply out of the varied stores of experience collected and embodied by her in the following pages.

T. T. CARTER.

CLEWER RECTORY,
  January, 1876.

CONTENTS

xii   # Contents

I.

Light is Love

ALL who are seeking to advance in holiness and the grace of the hidden life will readily grant, that in order to this we need to be ever aiming at an increasing purity of heart, at a greater tenderness of conscience, and a fuller light therein. Light in the conscience is essential to any real spiritual growth; but our own indolence, faint-heartedness, and self-love tend to avert the searching Light, which must often cause our earthliness to shrink, when its full scorching blaze falls on the hidden corners of the heart; and the world is ready to deceive us into accepting the glare of its false light instead, and Satan will use his every wile to keep away the purifying rays, which he well knows will overthrow his reign within our heart. There are hindrances on all sides besetting the conscience that would fain come to the Light; but to this there is one all-satisfying answer. As it has been beautifully said, " Every light is

B

love;" and it is in and through love alone that we may
seek that Light which, rightly used here, will admit us
for ever into the land of light, where the King of Beauty,
who is also the Light of the world, has promised to be
our Light for evermore—a Light which then will only be
needed to give eternal brightness and gladness, there
being no more sin to search out or purge away beneath
its pure life-giving rays.

Love, then, is Light; God's love of us, our love of
God.

"Love is a great thing; yea, a great and thorough
good.   By itself it makes everything that is heavy light;
and it bears evenly all that is uneven; for it carries a
burden which is no burden, and makes everything that
is bitter sweet and tasteful.

"The noble love of Jesus impels a man to do great
things, and stirs him up to be always longing for what is
more perfect.   Love desires to be aloft, and will not be
kept back by anything low and mean.

"Love desires to be free, and estranged from all
worldly affections, that so its inward sight may not be
entangled by any temporal prosperity, or by any adver-
sity subdued.

"Nothing is sweeter than Love, nothing more courageous, nothing higher, nothing wider, nothing more
pleasant, nothing fuller nor better in heaven and earth;

because Love is born of God, and cannot rest but in God above all created things.

"He that loveth, flyeth, runneth, and rejoiceth; he is free, and cannot be held in. He giveth all for all, and hath all in all; because he resteth in One highest above all things, from Whom all that is good flows and proceeds. He respecteth not the gifts, but turneth himself above all goods unto the Giver.

"Love feels no burden, thinks nothing of trouble, attempts what is above its strength, pleads no excuse of impossibility; for it thinks all things lawful for itself, and all things possible. It is therefore able to undertake all things, and it completes many things, and warrants them to take effect, where he who does not love would faint and lie down.

"Love is watchful; and, sleeping, slumbereth not. Though weary, it is not tired; though pressed, it is not straitened; though alarmed, it is not confounded; but as a lively flame and burning torch it forces its way upwards, and securely passes through all.

"If any man love, he knoweth what is the cry of this voice; for it is a loud cry in the ear of God, the mere ardent affection of the soul, when it saith, 'My God, my Love, Thou art all mine, and I am all Thine.'

"Love is active, sincere, affectionate, pleasant, and amiable; courageous, patient, faithful, prudent, long-suffering, manly, and never seeking itself. . . . Love is circumspect, humble, and upright, not yielding to softness or levity, nor attending to vain things; it is sober, chaste, steady, quiet, and guarded in all the senses.

"Love is subject and obedient to its superiors, to itself mean and despised, unto God devout and thankful, trusting and hoping always in Him, even when God imparteth no relish of sweetness unto it; for without sorrow none liveth in love."

So says Thomas à Kempis, and most surely all holy souls have ever found that it was through such love alone that they grew in light; that their conscience became first perceptive, then enlightened, then purified. In the light of that love let us look into some of the hidden corners of our own hearts, strive to clear out that which cumbers and darkens them, and so by God's Grace make some progress towards the path of the just, which shines brighter and brighter every day.

The one thing then that first and above all lies at the root of all holiness is the Love of God. "A demon believes, yet loves not," says St. Augustine.* "None loves that believes not." And again: "Our fruit is charity, which the Apostle defineth, *of a pure heart, and a good conscience, and faith unfeigned.* . . . Whence also,

* Hom. in St. John lxxxiii. 2.

when with the works of the flesh he would contrast the fruit of the Spirit, put this as the head of all : *The fruit*, saith he, *of the Spirit is love*, and then strings the rest together in their connexion as all rising out of that as their head ; namely, joy, peace, long-suffering, kindness, goodness, faith, meekness, temperance. In fact, who rejoices aright that loves not the good whereof he rejoices ? Who can have true peace but with Him Whom he truly loveth ? Who is long-suffering, by perseveringly continuing in that which is good, except he be fervent in love ? Who is good, except he be made so by loving ? Who savingly faithful, except by the faith which worketh by love ? Who serviceably gentle, that is not támed by the discipline of love ? Who continent from that which debaseth, except he love that which ennobleth ? With good reason therefore doth our good Master so often insist on Love, as if it alone needed to be enjoined, as that without which other good things cannot profit, and which one cannot have without having the other good things by which a man is made good."*

So again, "There are two loves—of the world and of God ; if the love of the world inhabit, there is no way for the Love of God to enter in ; let the love of the world make way and the Love of God inhabit, let the better have place. Thou lovedst the world ; love not the

* Hom, in St. John lxxxvii. 1.

world. When thou hast exhausted thine heart of earthly love, thou shalt drink in Love Divine, and thenceforth beginneth charity to inhabit thee, from which can nothing of evil proceed."*

The Spirit of Light then is a Spirit of Love, and if we can but attain to a real and true love of God, we shall therein attain to the whole science of religion. This love, which must be the very foundation of all light of conscience, of all spiritual life, has been classed under three divisions—as regards God Himself, a love of preference; as regards His law, a love of fulness; and as regards the service of Christ, a perfect love.

By a love of preference is meant a love which constrains one to love God more than anything created, "to love the Lord thy God with all thy heart, and with all thy mind." Not necessarily a love always consciously warm and sensitive, for that is not within our own control; not with a defined measure of fervour; not after a vague, shadowy, speculative philosophy, but with a deliberate and practical preference, which will make one ready to lose all else rather than forfeit God's Love; a preference which will make one strong to resign and forsake all, however attractive or precious, which is in any way contrary to His love. It was of such love

* Hom. in Epist. 1 John ii. 8.

that St. Paul said he knew that neither "tribulation, nor distress, nor persecution; neither death, nor life, nor angels, nor principalities, nor powers, nor things present, nor things to come, nor height, nor depth, nor any other creature"* could separate it from God. Surely it behoves us who think we love God from time to time to examine ourselves very closely whether there is anything so dear to us in the world, or that we so greatly desire, as to come between us and Him, were He to require it at our hand in proof of our love. Supposing I were to bear the brunt of some persecution, such as the world knows how to inflict on those who choose rather to obey God than its exacting laws, and that I could easily escape by some act, some consent, which the world would justify, perhaps applaud, but which He would condemn, what then? Is my love. that strong "love of preference" which no persecution can separate from God? Or again, a man is plunged into poverty, his fortunes are broken, ruin impends; but he could regain his position by dishonesty, by a distinct and conscious violation of God's commands. Is his love of God such that he will prefer to accept the temporal loss rather than offend his Lord? It may be very true that all these things are hard, but nevertheless, unless our love is strong enough

* Rom. viii. 35-39.

to bear such tests, it can hardly be called a love which "prefers" God to all else. Yet this is the measure by which we shall one day be measured, and then (awful as the thought is, we must face it) the mother who has loved her child more than God, the wife who has made an idol of her husband, the bridegroom who has preferred his bride to Christ, and not only those who have bestowed their "love of preference" upon guilty objects, will be told, "Ye are not worthy of Me."

So as to the fulness of Love. "In theological language," says Bourdaloue, "when I tell God that I love Him, I, so to say, specify my voluntary acceptance of and obedience to His every commandment. This one act is a pledge of my submission to His law in every detail; for Christ has said, 'If ye love Me, keep my commandments,' and 'He that hath my commandments, and keepeth them, he it is that loveth Me.' Do we, then, love God because we obey Him? or do we obey Him because we love Him? Be sure that whosoever loveth God heartily has already fulfilled His law in his heart, and when outward occasion ariseth, he confirms in act that which is the very life of his soul."

And the same author says, "Men deceive themselves cruelly as to the great precept, 'Thou shalt love the Lord thy God.' Nothing is easier than to say, I love Him; but nothing is more practically rare than such

love, because we deceive ourselves, and fail to discern
between a true and a false love of God. We deceive
others, it may be hypocritically; but we also deceive
ourselves by a voluntary blindness. So long as we do
but feel the slightest emotion of love towards God, we
are satisfied, and imagine ourselves filled with His holy
love; whereas often we mistake some merely natural
emotion for a stirring of grace, and a moment of grace
we reckon to be a proof of our own faithful love; we
confuse the gracious inspirations which draw us on to
love with Love itself; that which God works in us we
attribute to ourselves, and rest satisfied as though we
had done enough. But all this is error. To love God
really is to refrain scrupulously from whatever His love
forbids, and to do all it enjoins; it implies continual
self-renunciation, a continual war upon our earthly
passions; it means humbling one's spirit, crucifying
one's flesh, with all its lusts and evil longings; it means
resisting the world's delusions, the stream of this world's
ways and customs, the allurements of evil example. In
short, it means a will stedfastly set to please God in all
things, a resolution to displease Him in nothing." Is
not such love in very truth a light of the conscience
before which no dark corner can remain uncleansed?
And how else, save by such diligent searching love,
casting its penetrating light in everywhere, and helping

us to drag out every adverse thought or habit, can we
hope to attain to that perfect Love which is "the fulfilling of the law"?

Guided by Love then, let us each look carefully upon
our own conscience, and see how far we are loving our
dear Lord with all our heart, all our mind, all our soul,
and all our strength, not only in avoiding great and
obvious sin, but in the diligent cultivation of all those
virtues and graces which are as precious flowers in the
Lord's garden, pleasant and acceptable in their fragrance
to the Master of the vineyard.

II

Recollection

THE first aim of Love will always be union with the object of its affection; and where such union is effected, the inferior is sure to be drawn into and made like to the superior. Watch the sun drawing up the mists into its own brightness; watch the river as it flows, absorbing all lesser streams; watch the flame as it stretches forth and kindles the fuel it meets with. More than all these does God absorb into Himself, into an ineffable, unspeakably sweet union, the soul which really loves Him. It is a union, not bodily, but spiritual; a union to be obtained by seeking God with the under- standing and with the will. St. Bernard says that there are four principal means of attaining this union of the mental faculties with God—spiritual reading, meditation, prayer, and contemplation. These he calls the steps by which the devout soul rises to God; and he adds, read- ing walks, meditation runs, prayer flies, and contempla-

tion attains the end of the whole, and rests in God
Himself.

Saints have ever told us that no prayer is so fruitful as
that which perpetually seeks an increase of God's love,
earnestly craving to be answered. St. Augustine says
that they are blessed of all men whose life is a continual
prayer. But he does not mean a continual *visible* act
of prayer; rather that recollection of the heart which
keeps up a constant fear and loving thought of God, and
insures a perpetual desire to please Him in all we do.
All habits, whether of thought or act, are formed by use,
and the more men practise an act or a craft, the more
perfect they become in it; and so the more we strive to
live in a habit of constantly realising God's Presence,
constantly referring to Him and His holy Will in every
thing we do, the closer will become our union with Him,
the deeper our love.

Recollection then, what is it? David tells us over
and over again in the Psalms—from Psalm i., where he
speaks of that blessed one "whose delight is in the law
of the Lord, and who exercises himself in it day and
night," to Psalm cl., where he bids "every thing that hath
breath praise the Lord." St. Paul tells us that it is to
have our "conversation in heaven;" and our Blessed
Lord has told us that it is to have our hearts fixed where
our treasure is. Earthly cares and claims may draw our

thoughts to the things of this life, but they will revert to their true rest in a recollected spirit, even as the bent bough springs back when loosed, or the iron follows the magnet. St. Teresa made, as she said, a little oratory within her heart, where she could always keep up the service of her dear Lord, and to which she could per‧petually fly amid the disturbing activity of the outer life. Was not this what David meant when he said, "I have set the Lord always before me"? And if the natural levity and instability of our mind lead to endless distractions, if we are continually losing hold of this precious recollection, there is no need to be disheartened; only let us recollect ourselves anew, and turn once more to God. Let a man but once acquire the habit, and that habit will become as a second nature to him; and so far from finding it wearisome, he will crave after the rest of a recollected spirit. Only we must never forget that we can neither acquire nor retain it of ourselves. We must have God's help for this; but it will never fail those who do their own part humbly and stedfastly.

Gather yourself up then; withdraw into the depth of your hidden self, and dwell there. This is Recollection; and it is thus that you will find God. Of course He is everywhere, and in all things; but nowhere is He so present as within the heart which seeks Him. It may be that needful occupations, and the unavoidable claims

which surround us all, will hinder you in maintaining the
settled recollection at which you aim. But beware of
thinking it useless to persevere. Whatever else comes
across you, you can always keep one avenue clear for
God, and so it will be easy to return to Him as other
claims drop off, and by degrees you will become more
and more rooted in Him, and in the consciousness of
His Presence, so that nothing can for long or greatly
disturb you. The danger to many of us is, that we
imagine it to be an undertaking beyond our strength,
and because it is not easy at first, we turn from it as
impossible. But perseverance and habit will do wonders.
God may have shortened the road to the Land of Promise for some few of His chosen servants, but most of
us have to journey along it slowly and painfully in the
spirit of patience and perseverance.

One great help to recollection is having a store of uplifting thoughts ever at hand. To this end it is good
to learn by heart Psalms, Canticles, passages of Holy
Scripture, and hymns, wherewith to kindle and refresh
one's spirit when it flags and droops, and seems unable
to excite any spontaneous good or holy affections in
itself. It is surprising how much help the spiritual life
gains from a habit of learning by heart, not only such
as the above, but prayers, collects, and even sometimes
special passages of other books. There are many

moments, such as when dressing or undressing, waiting for others, going to and from some (it may be) irksome duty, lying awake at night, &c., when such stores in the memory both keep away the evil or unprofitable thoughts which Satan would excite, and help to maintain the soul · in that blessed attitude of Recollection which so specially promotes union with God.

Louis of Grenada advises those who seek to advance in the spiritual life to fix two periods in every day at which to inquire how far they have preserved a recollected spirit, and to quicken their endeavours by a brief prayer for its maintenance. However much you aim at a perpetual practice of Recollection, he says, these special moments, short as they may be, will serve to intensify it. He also warns us not to allow Recollection to become an intellectual exercise, which would probably hinder the cleaving of affections and will to God. It should be a simple stretching forth of the heart in love to God. A celebrated Spanish writer says that men are wont in their folly to strive to know God rather by study than by love, and therefore fail to find Him, Whom to know without loving were pure misery. At best our knowledge of God will but be according to our feeble earthly capacity; but the measure of our love need know no bounds, save what He is. Nevertheless these daily efforts at Recollection must not be made languidly,

mechanically, or perforce. Nothing so done will serve
to strengthen love and holiness in the heart. We need
to bring all the attention and devotion we can to all
such practices; at the same time, there is no good in
forcing ourselves, or endeavouring to kindle piety with a
strong hand. All warmth and devotion come of God's
grace, and are granted rather to diligence and humility
than to vehemence and impetuosity. A short prayer,
made in a diligent, humble spirit, is far preferable to
many religious exercises in which that is lacking. A
great philosopher has said, that the "just man" is not
he who performs many just deeds, so much as he who
performs them all in a just spirit; and it is quite possible
to go through a routine of religious practices without
any spirit of recollection to vivify and make them profitable. To take a homely illustration: if your window
is filled with coloured glass, you will see all outer objects
tinted with its hue; and so, if your spirit be recollected,
you will see and do all that comes before you through
the day in the light of the Love of God.

Again, a pure intention in all we do both fosters Recollection, and is fed by it; and such intention is, in
fact, a continual prayer. It dedicates every act of daily
life to God, whether the ordinary acts which seem
altogether unspiritual and secular, or those which have a
direct reference to Him. Nothing that a Christian

rightly does need really be apart from Him and His glory. If one is called on to perform some good work for the general or special welfare of our neighbour, it is desirable to fix one's own mind less on the general advantage of the work than on God's Will, so that it may be the main point in view to the intention, and then all will be safe and restful, and there will be little danger of self-seeking in what one does. Moreover, he who does this will find himself marvellously undisturbed as to the results of what he does, and that whether he succeed or not in his external object; whereas a busy, restless spirit of doing good for the sake of visible results makes one troubled and careful, sometimes impatient and desponding, if one fails, thereby proving that it was more self than God we sought.

And if a pure intention is one of the greatest helps to a life of Recollection, purity of heart is no less so; necessarily they react one upon the other. Purity of heart banishes the self-love, the earthly longings, the overrunning cares which distract the heart from God; it clears away the impediments which prevent the soul from cleaving to Him, and keeps the temple from being polluted by idol worship. But a pure heart can only be maintained by watchfulness over the senses, through which earthly and unholy thoughts and desires enter in, and so we come again to the necessity of devoting all

c

our members, eyes, ears, tongue, hands, and head, to
God; and to form or to keep up such devotion, we need
a continual and careful searching of conscience, lest the
little foxes steal in and spoil our vines, as also a steady,
patient, persevering rule of life, for these graces cannot
be won fitfully, or kept without painstaking—it may be
sometimes wearisome—labour and voluntary submission
to the yoke of Christ's law in small things and in great.
Let the Light of Conscience in then freely, and examine
your own hidden life by it. And first, consider your
habits of devotion.

III.

Prayer

PRAYER. Let the first act on waking be to place yourself, your heart, mind, faculties, your whole being, in God's Hands. Ask Him to take entire possession of you, to be the Guide of your soul, your Life, your Wisdom, your Strength. He wills that we seek Him in all our needs, that we may both know Him truly, and draw closer and closer to Him; and in prayer we gain an invisible force which will triumph over seemingly hopeless difficulties.

There should be very frequent self-examination as to how we pray. If we suffer our prayers to grow slack, the whole foundation of the spiritual life within us is shaken. Yet who has not felt at times as though the spirit of prayer was paralysed, or at least asleep within them? A poor man asking relief of one who can supply all his wants does not fall asleep while presenting his petition; on the contrary, he urges, he persists, he presses his claims, his needs. Examine yourself whether your prayers are as earnest and eager as the requests of the street-beggars you have just passed.

True devotion does not depend upon feeling. Sometimes we are disturbed because we have no devout feelings; but what we want is a devout will. We cannot always control the imagination, and it may be distracted and beyond our power, but we can always do that which is our duty carefully and patiently, with a view to pleasing God, and proving our love to Him. We may feel cold and mechanical, but we cannot fulfil our appointed duty without an exercise of the will, and therefore all duties diligently performed testify a desire to love, and prove our love. Sensible devotion is not necessary, and perhaps too much of it would scarcely be a real help to us. There is an energy only to be won at some cost, and perhaps when we have made a diligent, faithful effort to be devout, God may reward us with some conscious sweetness. But He sees how often it is our own satisfaction that we seek in devotion rather than Himself, and then He chastens this imperfection of the intention by dryness and dulness of spirit. If we could be less pre-occupied, many of our religious duties would be better performed; if we went to confession, to communion, to prayer with more simplicity and good will, we should gain more by them. In the *Gloria in Excelsis* God promises peace, not to the

high and spiritually-minded, but to "men of goodwill."*
What we want is to be blind, deaf, and dumb to all that
is of the earth—to see, hear, and speak to our dear Lord
only.

How often do we repeat the most wondrous prayers
mechanically, without any living sense of the weight of
the words we use, or any true feeling of what they mean !
How often have you called yourself a "miserable sinner,"
without thinking that you are really such in God's sight !
We are all apt to want to feel comfortable in our devotions, to dress our souls so as to appear confidently before
God ; sin makes this impossible, and thus it is often self
that we are really seeking when we ought to seek God.
It was not in this spirit that David cried out, "Have
mercy upon me, O God, for Thy name's sake ! Be
merciful unto me ; for I have sinned against Thee."
Careless people do not sufficiently feel their need of
God, or the real value of simplicity and confidence in
prayer. You would not be bound by mere outside form
in your intercourse with any one you really loved, why
then with God ?

Sometimes the heart shrinks up in fear, and becomes
restless and timid. You can never put too much trust
in God. It may be that recollections of the past hinder

---

* As is well known, the true rendering of these words in the
Gloria is not "goodwill toward men," but "to men of goodwill."

you, but you must reject them; anxious thoughts may
arise, put them away; your faults seem to raise up a
barrier, but no past faults can separate a loving heart
from God. Prayer and trust are always fitting. Our
dear Lord became man on purpose to bring us nearer
to Himself, and it is not possible to trust too entirely in
Him. How full the Gospels are of His welcome to
sinners, the prodigal, the woman taken in adultery,
Magdalene, Peter; and if any marvel at this, let them
remember His own gracious words: "I came not to
them that are whole, but to those that are sick."

Habitual prayer is speaking to God as one speaks to
one's father, one's friend, one's guide; it is the outpour-
ing of want, of lamentation, of love to the beloved one.
It does not wait for convenient seasons or for appointed
forms; everywhere and anyhow the heart speaks, or if
not, its silence may be the most expressive prayer.

If there are times when you feel specially drawn towards God in love and confidence, and when something
within seems to suggest that it is mere presumption on
your part, be sure that this suggestion is a temptation.
Open your heart gladly to confidence and love, and
reject the doubt as a wile of Satan's to disturb you. You
might indeed well be afraid because of the multitude of
your sins, and sink into discouragement, if you come
before God in your own strength; but if your trust is

wholly in Him, if you are leaning solely on His Mercy, and Goodness, and Love, you need not fear being over bold. Is He not your Father?

All daily duties, even your ordinary household cares, if done for His sake, may become prayer. Remember that everything helps or hinders us towards perfection; above all, the surrender of self, of self-will, and self-pleasing. Be diligent in seeking for all such opportunities. There is no surer way of attaining to union with God than giving to Him freely of all that touches our self-love; but all such offerings must be freely made, without any looking back, and with a simple desire to grow in the love of God. Such a spirit of sacrifice, if won, will bring untold peace, and a marvellous progress in the inner life.

So again with suffering. Remember our dear Lord in the garden of Gethsemane, how amid His anguish He continued to pray, using the same words, " Not my will, but Thine;" and be sure that if in suffering you can but cast all your pains into your Father's Hands, you are really uniting your prayer with His, and take comfort, even if pain and distress hinder you from any more detailed acts of devotion.

Sometimes we are disposed to murmur, and be discouraged, as though our prayers were not heard, because we cannot see their visible answer. Perhaps you have for long asked that some soul which is very precious to you may be turned to God, and you see no change in that soul. But never doubt for one moment that any prayer in the Name of Christ is heard; believe rather that God in His Mercy is trying your faith, your confidence, your fervour. Perhaps He is checking what would become an overweening presumption in you; perhaps He is training you to make some sacrifices such as you have not yet contemplated, "not knowing what you asked," on behalf of that which is dearer to Him than all else—a soul to be saved. Or it may be that He means to lead you to a far higher degree of trust in Him. Could you resign yourself to die without seeing your prayer granted, and that beloved one turned to God, believing with a full faith that in His own good time it will come to pass? It may be that He is leading you to this.

We must strive never to lose faith in the efficacy of prayer, even when we do not see the fulfilment; we must rest lovingly in our Father's Hands, Who knows to the full all we desire, and how best it may be accomplished. We see such a little way, and He looks through all time and eternity for us. Let us leave it all to Him. "What I do thou knowest not now, but thou shalt know hereafter." We must not be in a hurry; we must take the work, the pain, the amount of satisfaction, which He bestows at this actual moment, certain that it is precisely that which will most entirely further our real spiritual good, and striving to believe, as well as say, "I KNOW that all things work together for good to those that love Him."

It is sometimes helpful to dwell awhile upon the difference between the perplexities and complications in all earthly affairs, and the simplicity of the one great matter of eternal life. That alone really matters, and that rests with each one of us for ourselves to gain or reject, and every trouble and trial forwards it. One of the most powerful means of sanctification is simply to leave all to God's Providence :—

> "Never so safe as when our will
> Yields, undiscerned by all save God."

It is not an uncommon form of temptation to feel, that after having prayed long and earnestly to know God's Will, everything seems, as we say, to go amiss. But you did not pray that all might be smooth and clearly demonstrated to you. You asked, did you not? that God's Will might be made plain to you, and that you might be led in His way. You need more confidence, a fuller giving up of yourself into God's Hands, and less fear of drawbacks and hindrances. When one has come to a decision after due prayer and taking counsel, one must refuse to give heed to any "buts" and "ifs;" and simply saying, "Behold the handmaid of the Lord; be it unto me according to Thy Will," one must accept that Will, even though it be not as ours. We are apt to be so impatient if God does not take *our* way of doing things. We fancy that we know the right time and the right manner for everything, and we are disappointed and discomposed when He sets aside our plans and works out His own. Depend upon it, the hour of success is that which He appoints, often coming only after a long and, it may be, painful waiting. But "it will come; it will not tarry."

Keep this in mind every time you make the sign of the Cross. It is the token, the memorial of the pains and humiliations which our dear Lord bore for us; and each time we make it we ought to mean thereby that we take up His cross, accept it willingly, clasp it to our heart, and unite all we do to His saving Passion. With this intention, let the Sign of the Cross be your first waking act; dedicating your day to Him as a soldier of the cross, let your last conscious act before sleep be that precious sign, which will banish evil spirits from your bedside, and rest upon you as a hallowing safeguard till day returns. Begin your prayers, your work, with the Sign of the Cross, in token that they are dedicated to Him. Let it sanctify your going out and your coming in; let it hallow your conversation and intercourse with others, whether social or in the order of business. Who

could be grasping, overreaching, false; who could give
way to unkind words, harsh judgments, uncharitable
gossip, unholy talk, who had but just stamped the cross
of Christ upon their lips, in token that they are pledged
to use the gift of speech, like all else, in the service of
their God? Let it consecrate your food, so that eating
and drinking, instead of the mere indulgence of earthly
cravings, may be "to the glory of God." Let the Sign
of the Cross soothe and stay you in sorrow, when above
all you are brought near Him Who lays it on you, but
Who also bore it for you; let it sober and steady your
hour of joy or pleasure; let it calm your impulse of
impatience, of petulance, of intolerance of others, of
eager self-assertion or self-defence; let it check the
angry expression ready to break forth, the unkind word,
the unloving sarcasm; let it purify (as the hot coal laid
by an angel on the prophet's lips) the light, or careless,
or irreverent utterance, the conventional falsehood, the
boastful word of self-seeking. And be sure that if the
Sign of the Cross is thus your companion and safeguard
through the day, if in all places and seasons you ac-
custom yourself to

> "Softly make
> The sign to angels known,"

it will be as a tower of strength to you, and the power of
evil over you will become feebler and feebler.

Some persons have found it a great help in conquering a besetting sin, as *e.g.* hasty expressions, unholy thoughts, exaggerated words, to make the Sign of the Cross in direct recollection of their baptism, when that holy sign was made upon their forehead, in token of the fight they were then pledged to make against sin, the world, and the devil, and as a renewal of that pledge. Or again, in overcoming indolence or self-indulgent habits, to make the sacred sign in special union with our dear Lord, rising up and going out to pray "very early," "before it was yet day," or working in the carpenter's shop at Nazareth, or sitting weary and spent by the well at Sychar.

Probably no one ever used the Sign of the Cross devoutly and reverently without gaining great strength and blessing from it; but then it needs, like all other spiritual helps, care and watchfulness, not to let it become a mere external · thing, a mere matter of habit, which surely must be distinctly irreverent. Perhaps one who finds himself growing careless or mechanical in the use of this holy sign would do well to leave it off for a while, not as simply omitting it, but as an act of privation, of penitence—a more active remembrance really than the use of it—saying inwardly, "No, to-day I must be deprived of the privilege; for yesterday I used it carelessly. Lord, I am not worthy. Yet not the less

do Thou sanctify my goings out and comings in, my
work, my rest, my food, my sleep. And when the last
great day shall come, and Thy cross appear as the
standard, be mine a place at its foot, and may its sacred
figure be found stamped upon me, heart and soul, forehead and breast. Thine for ever."

IV.

Meditation

So much has been said and written about meditation, and yet, I suppose, most of us still have our own peculiar difficulties and troubles concerning it. All spiritual writers agree that it is a necessity, indispensable to the life of growth in holiness. But it must vary in many respects, according to the capacities and dispositions of different people; and while systems and minute plans help some, they do but hinder and perplex others. Every one, says an old writer, should more or less make his own book, and adapt the subjects of his meditations to his own soul's needs, his own mental requirements. And so all books are good as a help, though probably no one ever finds any one book that exactly supplies all he wants. It is impossible to fit every case alike, but each can take what helps him, and leave the rest. It is well however not to change the book one uses too often. Keep to the same for a year; read over the points at night, and the next morning, after having placed yourself in the Presence of God, and offered all your faculties to Him, begin slowly to meditate and pray. You must use, but not strain, the will and intelligence, and beware of being discouraged because the appointed subject of your meditation does not kindle your soul. This may be because it is very familiar. Anyhow, be sure that obedience and faith will cause it to bring forth an abundant nourishment to your spiritual life. It is often well to exercise the will much more than the intelligence in meditation. Truths which have long been familiar will fail to excite the imagination, but then there is the more need to fill the heart with them, and to lie in calm trust before God, asking to live by them. Avoid simple inactivity, but set some plain thought before your mind, and strive to let your heart feed upon it. If, for instance, you are meditating upon one of the mysteries, call to mind the facts, thank God for what He has done for us in and through that mystery, and humble yourself because you have not hitherto used the grace it brings to better purpose. One object of meditation is to touch the heart, and if you can do so without much mere intellectual labour, so much the better.

If, when meditating, thoughts on the subject in hand do not flow readily, it is not well to be disturbed, but rather to abide quietly in God's Presence. He sees you,

and knows it all. It may be that the truth you seek to
meditate has dropped like a seed into your soul, there to
germinate, and some time, when you least expect it, it
may expand, and the light it sheds upon you may prove
that it was not lost, but that God was keeping it back
for His own time. Only persevere in remaining patiently
in God's Presence, in proof of your obedience and good
intention, and even though you see no definite results in
the shape of a well-thought-out meditation, or good resolutions, you may be sure that your trust in God, the
submission of your will, and your renewed strength, will
prove that the time has not been wasted. But try always
to be simple, trustful, calm : excitement is worse than
useless.

We very often feel in meditation that our heart is as
cold as a stone. Then we may pour out our complaint
to God, who can "raise up children to Abraham out of
the stones." It is often well at such a time to take a few
words from the Bible, a single verse perhaps, or to go on
reading some narrative until something fixes the attention,
and kindles the affections. But if even this fails, and one
feels perfectly empty and dry, we must wait on humbly,
ask God to speak when He will to the soul, and be
patient. The mere making such an act of humility, and
of waiting upon God, is a gain.

There are times when one is so restless and distracted

that it seems impossible to fix one's mind on anything. Then the only course is to humble oneself before God, crying out, "If Thou, Lord, art extreme to mark what is done amiss, how can I do anything?" Then wait patiently. When you are told not to trouble about a lack of *feeling* in meditation, it does not mean that you are to give way to a voluntary indolence or mental torpor. While bearing patiently with such dryness as God permits, you should at the same time seek for food for your soul, either in some book, or by calling to mind spiritual advice given at some former time, which helped you, or by repeating some prayer in which you have found comfort; and also make acts of humiliation because of your coldness or distraction. Sometimes the self-knowledge gained in this way will be as profitable as a well-made meditation. Sometimes, when the mind cannot collect itself at all on the appointed subject, it is best to take a favourite book and read a little, and to say a familiar prayer, the *Anima Christi* (Soul of Jesus, sanctify me) for instance, pausing on each sentence until the mind has recovered a certain power of fixedness and attention.

Some people find it a help to represent to their minds our Lord teaching His disciples, and imagine themselves listening; others put themselves into the attitude of a beggar asking alms of a rich friend who never refuses aid. If the weakness caused by illness distracts

D

you, say, "Lord, he whom Thou lovest is sick." No subject will so help the sick as our Lord's Passion.

Try to do what God requires of you exactly, and with precision, and then do not dwell upon what you do or do not think, or upon your sense of interior emptiness. If even a book wearies you, put it down; accept your incapacity humbly, and be content with using ejaculations, or an Our Father devoutly said. It is a great matter in the spiritual life not to be always craving after something you have not; always imagining that if you had the natural fervour of such an one, or the intellectual force of another, you would do great things. Take what you have, and use it conscientiously, and as in God's sight. He will not ask you to give account for gifts with which He has not endowed you, but He will ask for an account of those you have, and no one is entirely without good gifts from Him.

V.

Ejaculatory Prayer

WE must strive to be filled with a consciousness of
God's Presence everywhere and in everything; to
realise that He is as truly present in His immensity as
we are actually present to ourselves. · If once any one
can confirm himself in this habitual sense of God's
Presence, the shafts of the evil one will be powerless to
harm him. It is our levity, and our absorbing interest
in earthly things which surround us, that hinder our
realising it. We cannot keep up a perpetual thought of
God, but renewing it by a momentary glance at each
thing we do will result in a constant and lively sense of
His Presence. The very essence of the Christian life, the
main-spring of it, is a continual reference of the soul to
God; each uplifting of the heart, each ejaculation as it
darts upwards, touches the sacred Heart of our dear Lord,
and brings a fresh supply of His grace to us.

St. Francis de Sales strongly urges ejaculatory prayer,

as not only a powerful preservative against great faults, but a very special safeguard against carelessness and laxity, which are the natural tendency of our earth-bound hearts, and against our constant disposition to look at things as the world looks at them. If we believe that God is always at hand, always ready to hear, surely we should take delight in telling Him all our little cares, and woes, and hopes, as they flit by. It will not do to wait for great things to tell Him. Who does not crave to pour out all his little anxieties, and hopes, and wishes, to the earthly friend he loves and trusts in most?

It is a good thing to have fixed seasons for lifting up the heart to God, not merely the appointed hours of prayer, but a momentary act before and after meals, beginning any occupation, entering into society, leaving the house, &c. Especially it is a help to make such brief acts after having said or done anything either wrong or foolish, after any trifling vexation or disappointment, when the spirit feels (it may be) wounded and desolate, or when one's vanity is annoyed at having been guilty of some little folly or unseemliness. Sometimes we are more really troubled and sore at trifles of this sort than at far weightier things, and the devil is quick to take advantage of the little earthliness and self-seeking. But if all such things were met with a momentary uplifting of the heart to God—"Without Thee I can do nothing;"

"Keep Thou my feet;" "I am Thine, save me," or the like, all these little frailties and worries would tend to mould the character more and more to God's pattern, and they would assuredly lose their sting; for he who thinks much of God will daily think less of himself.

VI.

Particular Self-examination

ONE of the most helpful practices of the spiritual life, and the most tending to let light in upon the conscience, is what is technically called "particular" Self-examination; that is, beyond the daily general self-examination, taking some one special point, either one's besetting sin, or whatever subject our confessor may commend to our concentrated vigilance and effort, or whatever may seem hardest and most difficult of attainment, to oneself in the ordinary course of daily life, and making a careful examination as to that. It is often recommended to make a brief examination of this at midday as well as in the evening. Most people, if they watch, will find themselves reviewing what has been said and done to them during the day. So-and-so said a disagreeable thing to or of me; another inflicted some petty slight; and a third bestowed certain praise, open or covert, which fed my vanity and self-complacency. All this should be, so to say, reversed. Have I said nothing that could offend or displease my dear Lord? Was my intention in this or that to please Him, or win praise to myself? Is He satisfied with my work to-day? Has everything been done to His glory? "When anything wounds you," it has been said, "do not shrink up, but rather expand. Instead of concentrating yourself inwardly, lay yourself open to God; pour out the overflowing of your heart to Him, and thus let the first sharpness of mortified self-love pass by." A special self-examination on our little sensitivenesses, jealousies, suspicions, complacencies, and the whole tribe of self-seeking pettinesses, which we sometimes neither seek out in self-examination, nor tell out in confession, for very shame's sake of acknowledging them even to ourselves, would go far to cleanse the conscience of many a cloud, which, though it be small in the beginning, may grow on until it break forth in a heavy storm, laying waste the spiritual life within us.

VII.

Holy Communion

STRIVE after earnest recollection, both while going to church and on entering. Think of your Saviour Christ coming down from Heaven to give you audience, to hearken to your needs and desires, and Himself to present them to His Father, with the merits of His own one adorable Sacrifice. This is what you really go for. If you find recollection difficult, take a book and follow it, but try not to get disturbed and anxious. If you can follow the whole service with the intention of uniting your heart and mind to Christ crucified for you, now set forth upon the Altar, it will be most helpful.

Make an act of humiliation for your faults in the Confession, specially accusing yourself to our Lord; think of the Mount of Olives, and of your sins helping to weigh Him down there. Offer yourself as well as your gifts, adore Christ present after the Consecration, and try to go up to the Altar to receive Him calmly, and without listening to troublous thoughts that may assail you.

Nothing will help you more at that sacred time than perfect calmness and stillness. Whatever form of devotions you may use, or with whatever intention you may assist, never omit to offer the Holy Sacrifice to these four ends: 1. As a devout act of adoration. 2. As a thanksgiving for all that you have received—creation, preservation, redemption, down to this very Eucharist. "What hast thou, that thou hast not received?" 3. Asking forgiveness of your own sins, of the sins of all you love, of your country, your Church, of all men. 4. Asking for all that you need, whether for yourself or others. And do you not need everything? It is at the Altar, above all other times and places, that God gives freely, abundantly, beyond all we can ask or desire. Never come away but with full hands.

Make some special resolution before you leave the Sacred Presence, to abstain from some fault or failing, to do some act, or carry out some intention. As far as possible, let your resolution be something concerning the present day, something that you can do while the freshness of your Communion is upon you; general resolutions, or resolutions affecting the future, are apt to become very unreal. It is often found a great help to offer both your resolution and all that you are about to do that day in union with all the celebrations offered up throughout the Church on that particular morning.

Give great care to your thanksgiving. It has been said by those experienced in the spiritual life, that half the Communions made are spoilt for want of earnest, devout thanksgiving afterwards. Gather up the special causes you have for thankfulness since your last Communion, and offer them together with your thanks for this, the greatest privilege of all, the being made one with Christ—and He one with you. If you cannot say many prayers, never mind; lie in rapt adoration before your Lord, content to say, "My Lord and my God." But do not hasten back to the world, and forget Who you bear in your heart; rather strive to keep a sweet, tender thought of that Presence throughout the day. Probably no devout communicant but would infinitely prefer to receive his dear Lord to merely assisting at the Sacrifice. Yet, as there must be seasons when for various reasons he cannot receive;—such as health, the advice of his spiritual guide to abstain, or even where these causes do not hinder communion (though where within reach of daily celebration they probably must do so to all at times), it is a great benefit to be present at another celebration, either after having received, or when unable to receive. Who but would feel that this is a very precious and a very special approach to his Lord, though not the nearest of all?

The "visible form, notifying His Presence," is a great

help and blessing; and "when we behold those outward signs, Himself is proved to be there, we are at once filled with this consciousness, and the mind is satisfied and absorbed as at no other time, and this may be independently of the Communion which follows. He is there, and the assurance of the visible symbols is enough; it is the certain pledge of our sacramental relation to Him. Communion is necessary for the actual felt embrace of Himself within one's own self; but without this we may have the satisfaction of the feeling of our being near to Him, and He being near to us. To be thus near to such a Presence, even though we do not actually receive Him, cannot but be fraught with blessing. We read how they brought sick folk, and laid them down where the apostles passed, that even the shadow of Peter passing by might overshadow some of them, and become the source in some measure, at least to them, of healing power. Our Lord, as the crowd pressed upon Him, let pass through the very hem of His garment the virtue which healed the sick woman who touched it. An effluence was shed abroad around Him, emanating from Him, and passed upon those prepared to receive it. The savour of the sweet ointment is diffused beyond its own substance. The Sun of righteousness was to arise with healing in His wings. Around Him, wherever He reveals Himself, effluences of light, and peace, and joy are shed abroad—the indirect effects of His nearness—over and above the fulness of life which from His Divine Person, possessed and possessing us, becomes our abiding joy. We can hardly but be stirred to quickened faith and tenderer love as we pray before the consecrated signs of His Presence, His coming near to bless. Nor can we suppose that the soul, which has thus approached with its longing of desire and pleadings of its need, can go back from that Presence wholly empty and unchanged. Then, too, we may meetly prepare ourselves for the reception of our Lord, if unable at the time to receive Him. To be breathing the atmosphere which His Sacramental Presence breathes; to cheer and gladden the soul with the brightness that surrounds the shrine of His abode; to be drinking in fresh resolves, quickened desires, purer aspirations, and more vivid faith, where angels and archangels are folding their wings to adore Him in His earthly sanctuary, leaving even heaven awhile to do Him honour—this cannot but be to catch at least something of the grace shed abroad by His Person, and to gain a deepened love, making the soul more worthy when the time of actual reception is come."*

Whether, then, as an act of preparation before, or of

* *Spiritual Instructions on the Holy Eucharist,* p. 144, &c. Rev. T. T. CARTER.

thanksgiving after, or of simple worship and adoration of Christ hidden under the veil of His Blessed Sacrament, the soul craving after closer, ever closer union with Him will find all Eucharistic devotion a source of strength and blessing. Nor where real love and real craving for that union exists need we fear that the lesser privilege will ever be made a substitute for the greater, but only a supplement and stimulus to the greatest joy and gift the Christian can win on earth—of eating and drinking that Body and Blood, without which, our Lord Himself has said, we can have no part in Him. Let it be seen in the lives of those who love to frequent His Altar that "they have been with Jesus," that their presence at celebrations without communicating is but a means towards more and more devout communions, that their frequent communions make them gentler, truer, meeker, humbler, more Christ-like in word and deed, and the opposition raised against such attendance, either by those who dislike it as (to themselves) a novelty, or dread it, lest it diminish the higher and better actual Communion, will fade away, and all will learn to go on ever seeking more and more for that Blessed Presence, in which one day we hope to wake up, SATISFIED with it—Christ.

The holy Eucharist is the very centre-point of heavenly love; nothing can so surely kindle its flame in our heart

as that precious food which God has Himself given as
the memorial of all that He has done for us. On the
Altar our blessed Lord offers His very Body and Blood
for Love's sake, and gives Himself to be our Food and
Drink. There He becomes one with us; He infuses
somewhat of His own very life into us His weak
creatures, in order that we may give it back in love to
Him, in order that we may have strength to overcome
the tendencies and lusts of our earthly nature, and that,
filled with a somewhat divine, we may be able to submit
our thoughts and feelings, and longings, and actions, to
His Law of Love. It is hardly possible to conceive the
closeness of union established between our dear Lord
and us in Holy Communion; and when love calls us to
accept such union, who could turn away? Frequent
Communion should surely transform the heart into a
very furnace of love to God. It was therein that martyrs
found strength to glorify Him in their death; therein
that saints have learnt to lead a life harder to endure, it
may be, even than death. Who among us has not known
what it is to go to the Altar sinking in heart, weighed
down, all but crushed under some burden, some grief,
visible or invisible, which seemed almost beyond their
power to bear, and then has come back from it so
strengthened, so refreshed, so filled with that gracious
Presence, that the heavy burden seems to have grown

light, the intolerable grief endurable, the whole soul raised, and strong to bear and suffer!

Yet all must more or less also have experienced at times a deadness, an impossibility of feeling any sensible joy in approaching the Blessed Sacrament, which is very harassing indeed, if one allow it to sadden us, or look upon it as a sign of chilled affection. At such times we must more diligently than ever offer our longings after the love of God, and our earnest desire to realise it; we must offer Him ourselves, our whole being and faculties, our every thought and action, and not give way to the feeling that we are doing it all coldly and mechanically without reality. A persistent offering to God, amid dryness and deadness, will not fail to meet its reward. It is easy to pour out warm, glowing feelings, excited love; but to persevere when all seems cold and lifeless within us is a surer test of real love, which thinks only of the object of its affection, careless of self-satisfaction in return.

Christ came to be our Way to Heaven, and in the Sacrament of the Altar He vouchsafes to be our companion on that way, to lead us on our often wearisome path. Day by day He offers Himself, bringing home to the heart of each that it is for every one of us that He came upon earth, and that He feeds us continually with His own Body. He tries, if we may say it reverently, how close, how binding a union He can establish between

us and Him.   What can we do on our part but try how
entirely and devoutly we can make Him our delight, our
stay, our hope, our strength?   Surely the blessed Sacrament is the very greatest marvel of the world, as well as
of angels.   We shall never fathom its blessed mysteries
until we attain to the fulness of joy on the other side of
the veil.

Those who are blessed with a continual opportunity of
seeking Christ on His Altar need to remind themselves
very frequently Who it is that invites them—their Lord
Himself.   It is He Who bids us come with confidence
and loving hope of finding relief there from all our
troubles.   Our part is to accept the invitation gratefully,
trustfully, and in all humility.   The privilege of frequent
Communion comes of His free benevolence, not of our
merits; and lest any should be tempted to think highly
of themselves because they are frequent communicants,
it is well to submit this to the direction of our spiritual
guide, and let him determine how often we may approach the Sacred Feast.   "Obedience is the best preparation for Communion," it has been said; and if a
self-complacent thought crosses the mind because we
are more frequent guests at our Lord's table than others
around us, it should be checked with the remembrance
that the privilege is not a reward of our merits, but an
indulgent application of the Merits of our Lord to us,

which, so far from exciting any self-sufficiency, ought to kindle greater love, trust, and humility towards Him Who gives us this as all other gifts.

Those who communicate frequently will find it profitable to take a brief period—say ten minutes—for special recollection of God's mercies and their own ingratitude, and want of correspondence thereto, on the evening before; and a like brief season for meditation on the particular needs to be taken to the Altar, and gifts sought in the morning before going to Communion. Strive before Communion to keep yourself *in hand*, not to let yourself act or talk carelessly or heedlessly, to maintain a very calm spirit. Half our distractions arise from our own neglect in cultivating a calm tone of mind. Some devout people trouble themselves greatly with the fear that their preparation is insufficient, and their thanksgiving cold. This often arises from a mistaken idea of what preparation is needed. The most experienced spiritual guides say, that for frequent communicants the usual course of devotion is sufficient preparation. Their meditation and prayer will be made at home as is wont. On entering the church an act of love and sorrow for sin may be made, especially for any faults committed since their last confession. One may hope that there would not be any mortal sin in the case of a frequent communicant, but venial sins there must ever be. From

E

these we must rise up trustfully and lovingly as often as we fall, saying, "Lord, I have sinned against Thee; but Thou knowest that I love Thee. I am weak, help Thou me." If we fall a hundred times a day, a hundred times must we rise up thus and turn to God, so saints tell us, believing that He will listen and accept us as lovingly the last as the first time. He never yet rejected the feeble soul which clung to Him in love.

If at times you feel constrained and hampered by the vocal prayers and acts which you commonly use before Holy Communion, put them quietly aside, and seek only a silent union of your heart with Jesus, letting Him guide you without any forced effort on your part. Written acts and prayers are meant to help those who need them, not to hinder those who want to go straight to God. If one feels utterly cold or distracted, it is often best merely to lie at our dear Lord's Feet, and tell Him that it is so, and cleave to Him for warmth and recollection. If one feels weary and spent, it is a help to picture oneself kneeling on Calvary at the foot of the cross, with the mother of Jesus, spent with her sorrow.

The common causes of imperfect thanksgiving after Communion are—first, want of time; and next, want of care,* though sometimes indeed we hinder ourselves by trying to do too much; we want to say, and feel, and

* "The spirit of prayer is the fruit of prayer."

excite more than our heart is equal to, and it becomes
an effort rather of the brain than the heart. The remedy
for this is more calmness, a more listening heart, a willing-
ness to abide patiently, even in the desert, if need be.
There is no need for self-torment: rather let us rejoice
quietly in possessing our dear Lord.

We have several great examples of thanksgiving set
before us; *e.g.* Our Lady, when the angel announced the
coming of God within her, and she broke out with the
sublimest thanksgiving ever uttered, which the Church
continually delights to raise, "My soul doth magnify the
Lord, and my spirit hath rejoiced in God my Saviour." It is
the same Saviour Who comes to us in the holy Eucharist,
and we may well break out with the same song of praise,
not forgetting blessed Mary's self-abasement: "For He
hath regarded the lowliness of His handmaiden." Our
thanksgiving must be mingled with humility if it be real.

Again, Simeon, who at length saw all his longings
fulfilled, and held the Saviour within his arms,—his
thanksgiving declared that all earthly things were as
nothing to him. Once possessing his God, he asked no
more—"Now lettest Thou Thy servant depart in peace;
for mine eyes have seen Thy salvation." The soul which
receives Jesus detaches itself from all else; it contains its
God, or rather is contained of Him, and now it only
desires never to lose sight of Him again, to behold Him

for all eternity. Here below, there is ever a risk lest we
lose Him; therefore let us more and more stedfastly
fix our gaze on the land that is very far off. Earthly
things cannot satisfy us; the Presence of Jesus once
enjoyed must detach the soul from earthly treasures.

Again, Zaccheus, when he had enjoyed the privilege
of receiving Jesus into his house, was eager to give all
he had to the poor, caring for nothing save the honour of
so beloved a guest. Has the blessing we have enjoyed
of receiving Christ led us to give more freely of our
worldly goods? And is not a liberal free-offering of all
we have to Christ the best thanksgiving for His gift to
us? He withheld nothing. He has given us His Body,
His Blood, His Heart. What can we do but with absolute
generosity give Him ourselves, and all we possess?

So too we may take the sisters of Bethany as an
example for our thanksgiving. Jesus loved them, He
abode with them, taught them, ministered to them. One
showed her gratitude in active, zealous, busy service; the
other sat listening at His Feet, ready to receive still more,
and He told her that she had chosen the better part.
It was their brother Lazarus of whom Martha said,
"Lord, he whom Thou lovest is sick." And so we may
amid our thanksgiving say to Jesus, "Lord, he whom
Thou lovest, he to whom Thou hast but just given Thyself, needs Thy pity and help, for he is sick;" and then

we may lay before Him our cares, our troubles, our difficulties—"I am proud, passionate, self-seeking.". In the
very strength of gratitude for past mercies seek more.
That is a thanksgiving which Jesus loves; or if you can
sit with Mary at His Feet, wrapt in silent love and adoration, heedless of all outer things, take her for your model
of thanksgiving, only do not deceive yourself, there must
be calmness and detachment from earthly things, and
from self, to make that thanksgiving real.

The beloved disciple St. John made his thanksgiving
leaning on Jesus' Breast, absorbed in Him he loved, in
perfect, unquestioning rest, although on the eve of great
troubles such as he had never yet known. So if we
possess Jesus, if our heart is one with His Heart, we
may lie upon His Breast, not fearing sorrow, temptation,
care, trial, pain, not even fearing the assaults of sin;
since He bears us and all our troubles, He can heal,
sustain, soothe, and strengthen us.

The celebrant in Holy Communion may afford us
another example of thanksgiving. After receiving the
Body he takes the Cup into his hands, to himself saying,
"What shall I render unto the Lord?" and then receives
the precious Blood. Even so the best thanksgiving for
one Communion is to make ready for the next; and the
best preparation for Communions to come are those which
are past.

These suggestions for thanksgiving might be gathered into a week's scheme, thus:

Sunday.—Gratitude: the *Magnificat.*

Monday.—Aspiration after heavenly things: the *Nunc Dimittis.*

Tuesday.—Self-oblation, generosity: Zaccheus, "Behold I give," &c.

Wednesday.—Offering of cares and troubles: "He whom Thou lovest is sick."

Thursday.—Silence, recollection of heart and soul: Mary at Jesus' Feet.

Friday.—Absolute confidence: St. John lying on Jesus' Breast.

Saturday.—Thanksgiving and preparation for the next Communion: the Body and the Blood.

Even after the actual thanksgiving has been made, and we have left the church, a spirit of thanksgiving may be kept up through the day—better still, until our next Communion. His Presence within the heart will surely enable our eyes to see further into heavenly things, our ears to catch divine sounds to which we were deaf, our mind to enter into thoughts which were a dead letter to us. One while we may mentally place ourselves before Jesus as a beggar, needing everything, and asking of one ever ready to give. From time to time it may help to cross the hands upon the breast, where He has vouch-

safed to dwell, and ask that every thought and word may
be conformed to His likeness, Who was meek and lowly
of heart, so that all men may know Who it is that dwelleth
in us. As we go about our ordinary occupations, we may
keep up a memory of that blessed Communion, and ask
to have a faith, a hope, a love, a Christian bearing, to
lead a life worthy the gift we have received. Perhaps
sometimes a living act of gratitude, which restrained an
impatient or uncharitable word, an unkind or self-complacent thought, because of the privilege we have just
received, would be even a more acceptable thanksgiving
than a long office most precisely said. Every action
through the day might be moulded by this spirit of
thanksgiving; and nothing surely would tend more to
keep up a consciousness of that blessed Presence, than
to find it influencing the will, the affections, and the
outward deeds.

A thankful spirit towards God will induce a generous
spirit towards man. One very true element of thankfulness is to desire that "His way may be known upon
earth;" and your thanksgiving will be all the truer and
more fervent, if in it you commend, not only Christ's
Church, but all those who have not yet known Him, to
His Redeeming Love. Probably the *Anima Christi* makes
part of most people's thanksgiving, and it is well to use
it with intention for all one loves, living and departed,

for all commended to one's prayers, for all who are in sorrow, temptation, and who have none specially to pray for them. Many find the *Te Deum* a great help in their thanksgiving, using the first part in acknowledgment of mercies received, and the latter part asking for their continuance.

It is sometimes too profitable to make a very brief examination (two or three minutes at most) before leaving the church after Communion, as to whether one has been recollected, calm, and the like; and whether our intention, resolution, &c., have been properly heeded. At the same time we must be careful not to let ourselves be disturbed at finding how imperfect all our devotions are, or the great need there is of patience with oneself. Thoughts that disturb and trouble us seldom come from God. It is generally best to put them away, and throw ourself, with increased trust in Him and mistrust of self, at His feet. And never forget, amid whatever may befall you,—dryness, coldness, desolation and disappointment, consciousness of many faults, and of great weakness and want of faith,—that where love is, there God is sure to be. He never yet has suffered any soul to fall wholly from Him who, amid all its frailties and falls, clings to Him in love.

Some people are sorely tried by feeling themselves so cold and lifeless even at the very moment of Communion.

Perhaps this is partly that we think so much of ourselves, and of the personal comfort or pleasure we find in our acts of worship. But if it be a real grief, we had better only commend our heart, with all its imperfection and infirmity, to God, confessing ourselves wholly unworthy of any consolations or privileges; crying out with David, "Lord, I am as a beast before Thee!" but trusting our whole condition to Him, and believing that out of our darkness and coldness He can bring warmth and light. Nor is it well to be weary and anxious because we have not found sensible pleasure in our Communions. If we are trusting ourselves patiently and trustfully in God's Hands, He will take care of us. A religious man, who was once complaining to a holy person that he felt as a mere log of wood before the Altar, was met by the answer, "Well, and what is fitter wherewith to kindle a fire? You only need that our dear Lord should apply one spark of His love." Be at rest, and strive to calm your spirit.

Of course such counsels must not be perverted to encourage an indifferent or careless habit of mind. Any one who is troubled with this sense of internal deadness and coldness will do well to be very careful as to all outward reverence and devotion, paying even a more special reverence to holy things, and fulfilling all appointed religious duties with more than usual punctuality and care, as a proof to himself that it is not from slackness or sloth that his coldness arises.

People often ask whether they ought to abstain from communicating when they are disturbed by some trouble or infirmity. To this experienced guides have replied, that if the disturbance comes from yielding to the never-ending pettinesses arising out of self, it may be well to defer a Communion, and look upon it as a punishment for carelessness, resolving to practise greater watchfulness. But if the trouble is real, if the heart has been grieved, wounded, upset, then, above all times, it needs the strength and consolation of the Bread of Life, and to abstain is as though the sick man cast away the medicine that would heal him. But as a rule, if possible, no one should adjust these matters for themselves. It is far better and safer to act under the advice of one's confessor; the mere fact of obedience in itself is helpful and strengthening; and if we once begin to deprive ourselves of Holy Communion, there is a danger lest Satan should turn what we meant for humility against us, and suggest frequent abstaining to our great spiritual loss and hindrance.

After all, the one great result we seek in Holy Communion is union with Christ, and the imparting of His Holy Spirit; and no formal rules or instructions for doing this can be given. On our knees, in earnest,

trusting faith, and in heartfelt appeal to that Holy Spirit
to guide us, we shall learn more probably in a few
minutes than through long years of theological study
without that faith and love.

It has been said to some, "Talk to our dear Lord as
you would to your director; tell Him all that is in your
heart, *as though He did not already know it.*" Such a
close, loving intercourse will tend greatly to increase
your humility, trust, and straightforward simplicity.
Oftentimes you will feel sick and weary of yourself, and
all your petty wilfulnesses, and self-seekings, your voluntary self-deceit, and mean subterfuges; but never mind,
be sure that as you throw all these troubles upon Him,
He will take them away, and make you more like to
Himself. This is surely what is meant by "putting on
Christ."

The heart of Christ is drawn closer to us by love, by
suffering, by humiliation; and we shall draw closer to
Him by faith, by submission and trust. We can be ever
clinging thus, but the choicest moment for it is in the
Blessed Sacrament. Come away from it, saying many
times in the day, "Lord, what wouldest Thou have me
do?" Do as perfectly as possible what you know to be
His Will, and wait for His further manifestations. No
surer path can be found, and in it He will let you want
nothing. But we are so restless; too often restless even

in our aspirations after what is good. We are too fond of seeking something fresh, and while, of course, mere routine is to be avoided, that restless desire for somewhat new is a great snare to many. To lie still at Jesus' Feet, and remember how rapidly the things of this world pass away, that will often be our best spiritual exercise.

VIII.

Confession

CONFESSION would be a greater help to many, if they could more definitely keep before their mind the thought that the priest is simply God's representative, that what they say to him is really said to God, and that God uses him as His channel to convey instruction and forgiveness. We approach the sacrament of penance in order to be cleansed and fortified, and that none save God can do. But what we know men cannot, faith tells us God can effect through His appointed minister; and the trustful, hopeful obedience we render to our confessor is directly rendered to God.

Some persons, if thwarted or restrained, are ready to declare that it is because they are "not understood." This is a mere excuse. There is less difficulty than we may imagine to one accustomed to deal with souls in understanding the characters and needs of those to whom he ministers; and moreover God gives His servant grace as he requires it for his ministry. Trample on your alarms and apprehensions; come out of yourself; let others see for you. The will, and not the feelings, are our real test of faithfulness to God. He would not have you troubled or harassed; He wants you to go on in all peace and liberty. Excited feelings are not necessarily real penitence; and sensible fervour (as it is called) does not depend upon ourselves, even in sorrow for sin. It is enough to go on stedfastly and patiently in the path pointed out to us.

Do not be over-anxious because you think you are not remembering or profiting as much as might be from the counsel and instruction you receive. Our Lord says, " He that *doeth* My commandments, he it is that loveth Me." St. Francis de Sales says that all misgivings which tend to hinder us should be treated as the Israelites treated the bones of the Paschal Lamb, which they were ordered not to break,* but to cast away at once. And even so he would have all troublesome thoughts, which only hinder and vex the soul, set aside at once, without questioning or dallying with them. While we fancy we are refuting the devil, he often gets a hold on us which he would not do if we simply turned away.

If your self-love is humbled or wounded by anything said to you in confession, beware of seeking a false consolation, or fancying that if you were better appreciated

* Numbers ix. 12.

it would not be so. This is a mere temptation. Probably
our dear Lord sees a still deeper cause for humiliation in
you than His ministering priest sees. On the other hand,
do not be wilful in refusing to receive comfort when it is
given you. Take the message, whether of peace or of
warning, as from God. Submit your judgment, as well
as your will, to obedience, and you will never find reason
to regret it. Do not talk about what has been said to
you in confession. If God has spoken a word to you
through His priest which has touched and helped you,
cherish it and follow it; but remember that it may not
be suitable to others, although it has helped you; and
anything approaching to religious gossip over such
matters must do harm. If you feel convinced that
something given for your special guidance will help
another in some difficulty, or in conquering some
temptation, impart it very reverently, and not till you
have prayed over it.

Confession is one of our dear Lord's best gifts to His
struggling, often weary, children; and because it is one
of the very greatest helps to a holy life and stedfast
perseverance unto death, therefore, as might be expected,
the devil exhausts his inventions to deter people from it,
and to place every possible hindrance in the way. How
skilfully he adapts his objections, his difficulties, and
sophistries, to the various minds he tampers with, often

setting up the most delusive and treacherous pleas, taking indeed upon himself the outward garb of an angel of light. And even when men are convinced, in spite of him, that confession is a blessed thing, and one likely to promote their salvation, he finds fresh ways of hindering them. Sometimes he suggests that confession is so very difficult. Not to those who seek it with a will simply set to obey God, to cast out their sins, and win His pardoning grace. It is only difficult to those who are not in earnest, and have this or that reserve, this bit of pride which they cannot bring themselves to humble, that occasion of sin they would fain not give up. But one would suppose that where confession is voluntarily sought there would be few feeling this difficulty. Another way in which the devil tries to keep people from the blessing of confession is the same he often applies to Holy Communion—suggesting that they ought to bring a perfect preparation beyond what they feel able to attain. Of course, the answer to this is plain. Do the best you can. God is not a hard or exacting Master. Never mind about a perfect confession; do the best you can.* If you are (1) sincere, (2) contrite, (3) humble, the Great Absolver will look tenderly upon all your imperfections, and they will not stay His grace.

* There is an old French saying which St. Francis de Sales used to quote on this subject—"*Le mieux est l'ennemi du bien.*"

The devil is always on the look-out to keep you from confession. He knows full well how much less power he has over the soul which has come back from its penitential discipline purged from sin, strengthened for fresh and more earnest efforts after holiness by the grace of absolution, cheered and encouraged by counsel and admonition, refreshed by the precious Blood sprinkled over it. He sees how that soul goes back to its daily task with new energy; how prayer and meditation are more devout, self-examination more diligent and searching, communions more loving and real; how temper and tongue are more guarded, thoughts more controlled; how work is better done for Christ's sake, and as a thing to be given account of to Him; how self-indulgent habits are checked, and punctuality, regularity, diligence, cultivated; how humility and recollection are encouraged; how the Presence of God is more remembered, and the day of Judgment more looked to. And so seeing, who can wonder that the great enemy of souls, whose special aim and desire is to draw men from all that brings them nearer to God, should at once set to work with all the subtlety that his eighteen hundred years of experience in perverting mankind has taught him, and dissuade them from what he knows is a choice weapon for his overthrow.

He will tell them that confession is a mere super-

F

stition—alas! has he not told them the same of Christianity itself?—that it destroys self-reliance. But is it not through self-reliance that men have fallen into deadly sin, from the day when Eve took the fruit from his hand to that when Peter's self-reliance led him to deny his Master; to the hour just past, when some poor child, confident in her own strength and self-reliance, has lapsed into deadly soul-destroying guilt? He will tell them what a noble thing independence of character is: independence, that is, of God, mind you, not of Satan. Then he says, "All these things will I give thee, if thou wilt fall down and worship me"—submit your independence of will, your knowledge of right and wrong, to me. He will tell men and women made for eternity, and meant by their God to win heaven, who are losing it through sins of the flesh, sins of the intellect, pride of life, through the accumulative sins of unchecked habit— the hardening surface of it may be what we call "little sins," choking up conscience, and leaving no place for God's light to enter in;—all such he will tell that confession is a good thing for deadly sinners, good for the murderer or the adulterer, (perhaps even here he may whisper, "if he be found out,") good for the great crime before which men set legal punishment and temporal disgrace; but forsooth, needless, if not harmful, to those whose sins are lighter, more universal, less onerous.

As of old He Who was tempted of this same tempter answered him out of God's Word, so let us answer him now, even if he speak to us through the channel of lips we love or revere. Who was it that said—"Whosoever shall break one of these least commandments, he shall be called least in the kingdom of heaven," or, as His apostle adds, "he is guilty of all"?

Who was it that put the angry word on a par with the murderous blow, and the impure glance with the adulterer's crime? Would He have told any single one of His struggling, ofttimes falling servants, that they need not seek to wash in His precious Blood until they had somewhat heavier on their conscience? Would He have told them that instead of seeking pardon and renewal "seventy times seven," once was enough?

There is an old superstition in some of our hilly countries which seems to have found its counterpart in spiritual things. Many untaught, unreasoning persons believe that a man's life may be *once* saved, but once only, by bleeding; and consequently, however urgent the need, they will steadily refuse the leech, which would bring immediate relief and safety, rather than "use up" the charm!

Surely, surely, until the *habit* of sin ceases, those who would fain seek to have their conversation in heaven, and to attain that place where no sin can enter in, will best defeat the evil one's attempts to keep them out by letting their repentance and their application to the precious Blood for absolution and renewal be a habit too.

Another hindrance which the devil makes use of with scrupulous minds is to beset them with fears that their confessions have not been properly made, that they have omitted something, or softened rough edges. Of course, if this were true it is a great fault, and needs the most determined reparation; but in such a case it would be God's Voice speaking to the conscience that stirred the sinner, not Satan tempting him. To the latter the answer is plain. If you have honestly confessed all you remember, and have not intentionally concealed or distorted anything, God has accepted your confession, be sure; and you should put away all anxious and scrupulous thoughts. If you really recall some fault hitherto forgotten, tell it at your next confession; but do not be troubled, or make way for Satan's doubts and hesitations to come in. A great saint long ago used to say that he had much more satisfaction in hearing the confessions of humble, ignorant peasants than those of well-educated and often so-called spiritual people, because the former were so much more simple and to the point, not seeking to define or analyse, but calling things by their right names, without pretence or evasion in self-defence.

Many of the holiest men, both of our time and earlier

times, have advised each person to be ruled by their own
spiritual guide as to the frequency of their confessions.*
To one a longer, to another a shorter interval may be
most helpful. Even the same person may at one time or
another need a varying rule. Some special temptations
are best met by immediate application of the Sacrament
of penance; other scrupulous frames of mind, or persons
addicted to self-dissection, may be the better for a longer
interval between their confessions. No priest could *refuse*
to hear a penitent; but he might and would advise some
to delay their confession, or to make them sooner, according as he saw need. You trust your doctor as to the
frequency with which the quinine or steel with which he
is treating you should be taken. Cannot you equally
trust the spiritual physician?

The following instructions have helped some persons :
Before Confession. It is well the day before, in medita-

---

* The late Bishop Gray, of Cape Town, says, in a letter to one
consulting him on this point: "You will do much better to refer
the question as to how often you should go to confession to your
own Confessor than to me. I think it is a little bit of pride which
makes you ask me rather than him. . . . The person who is dealing
with your soul must know best how often you will be the better for
the discipline. To some it is a great help to be frequent in confession, especially in conquering a special sin. Only, don't leave it
to chance, or you are very likely to shirk, and go longer without it
than is wise or safe."

tion (and if you are present at a celebration), to ask God's help to make a good confession. Lift up your heart to this end. You might practise some small act of self-denial with the same object.

The direct preparation. This means self-examination, contrition, and deliberate resolution to do better.

Examination. 1st. Place yourself in the Presence of God; make an act of faith in His Presence. "I am before Thee, good and merciful God, Who willest not the death of a sinner, but his conversion and salvation; before Thee, Lord, Who came not to save the righteous, but sinners; Who bade us forgive our brother seventy times seven, and Thyself forgivest yet more; Who tarried for the woman of Samaria, and received Magdalene; Who didst not condemn the woman taken in adultery."

2nd. Invoke the Holy Ghost—*Veni Creator.* All this will only occupy two or three minutes. Then begin your examination, making it with such precision as you would use in ordinary business of importance. God asks no more. It should be adapted to your knowledge of God, of religion, and of duty. Self-examination is a relative matter; you would expect it to be differently made by a peasant and by a learned theologian. A good confessor will himself bear this in mind while helping his penitents, otherwise he will puzzle them.

You will examine yourself as regards God, your neighbour, and yourself, going through the duties of your individual condition. One very important point is to let no mistrust, no fearfulness of God, creep in. Do not be over severe upon yourself. There must be full and deliberate consent to make a mortal sin. By God's grace, those who frequent the Sacraments, and aim at an habitual love of our dear Lord, do not often fall into mortal sin. Ten minutes ought to be enough for your examination. Do not torment yourself about the precise number of your faults, but note pretty nearly what it is. The important thing is to go back to the root of them, and pluck that up. Your besetting sin will of course always receive special attention. Do you say that ten minutes is too little, your attention wanders so? Never mind; the time is over—stop! Next time you will be more attentive.

Contrition. This is not so difficult as some people imagine; the difficulty lies chiefly in our own mistaken ideas. God knows our weakness, His goodness is ever prone to forgive. What more need we?

When your examination is done, make what Mgr. de Lamothe, Bishop of Amiens, used to call his three stations. The first, in Hell: "This is what I deserve; hither sin was leading me. My God, I repent." The second, in Heaven: "This is what I lost through sin. How good Thou art to restore me to such blessings. I

love Thee. I will cease from sin, and enter heaven."
The third, on Mount Calvary: "Here I behold the
result of·sin. I ask forgiveness, my God, because of
Thy Merits and Thy precious Blood; through Thy Death
I attain to life." A brief prayer to our Lord, and you
are ready for confession.

Resolution for the future. This is in a measure involved in contrition. But to make it more specific,
while resolving generally to amend all your faults, make
particular resolutions as to the one or two special failings
you have determined to correct. Five minutes is enough·
for this. To test your good resolutions, examine how
far you have resisted temptation since your last confession; how speedily you have recovered yourself after
falling, and whether you are increasingly anxious to
amend.

In Confession. Do not be afraid. See only our Lord
Jesus Christ in the priest. You will soon acquire the power
of this abstraction. People who make unreal confessions are apt to suppose that the priest dwells greatly on
what is told him; but in truth he only heeds it so far as
is necessary to fulfil his ministry. That done, he forgets
all. When you kneel down, say, "Lord Jesus, keep my
lips in sincerity and humility; speak one word only,
and my soul will melt." Let your confession be humble,
simple, as short as possible, and consequently precise

and thoroughly honest. Accuse yourself as to our Lord. Avoid all exaggeration. Call what is certain, certain; and what is doubtful, doubtful. When you have done, listen quietly to the priest. While he is giving you counsel, do not let your mind wander back to your faults; by so doing you will lose the benefit of what he is saying to you.

At the time of Absolution. Resist all temptations to think that you are not duly prepared. Bow down as at the foot of the cross, as though waiting for some drops from the wounded side of Christ to fall on you. Humble yourself, and make a fervent renewal of your act of contrition. If you foresee any difficulty in performing the penance laid on you, simply tell your Confessor.

After Confession. Spend five or six minutes in an act of thanksgiving to our Lord. Go over the advice you have received, and the resolutions you have made ; and then admit no further questioning as to what has been done, but be confident of God's Blessing on what you have done to the best of your powers.

Do not go back to the faults of your past life, even if you fancy they have not been thoroughly confessed ; they probably have been virtually comprehended in other previous confessions, and there must be some halting-point, or we should be perpetually renewing our general confessions. If Satan tempts you to dwell on circumstances of past sin, turn resolutely away. Do not be discouraged because you fall again into the same sins. It is a great matter if you make some progress gradually.

One remark it may be worth making as to spiritual direction; namely, that people are apt to expect too much in the way of spiritual consolation, and then to be disappointed, injured, and discouraged because they have not got all they want. Sometimes people fancy that they are not understood, not sympathised with, not sufficiently helped, merely because they have a preconceived idea as to what they want; and if the confessor does not take that line, or does not minister to what is perhaps really a self-seeking spirit, they at once decide that he is hard and unsympathising, that he does not care about them, perhaps even that he is not "spiritual-minded." But if, instead of complaining, these people would calmly think over the advice given them, and strive to apply it to their needs; if—as Bossuet says to a person complaining thus—they would break the shell and get at the kernel, they would probably find that the help they really needed was there. The object of direction is to lead the soul nearer to God, to strengthen it where it is weak, to make plain what perplexes it, to discipline and correct it where it is faulty. But human nature seeks more than this, and sometimes strives to turn all that which is matter of fact, dry, it may be severe, work, into a soothing, self-indulgent luxury, an opportunity for pitying itself, and claiming a sympathetic indulgence from the confessor, a means for evading part of its burden. And then direction loses its value. Bossuet says that a good director's aim will be less that the soul he guides should walk according to his own direction than to lead it to God, and make it ready to receive His direction, so that He may be all in all.

IX

Spiritual Reading

NO one will question the immense benefit of reading, and especially spiritual reading, or how valuable a taste for reading is to the Christian. It has been truly said that such a taste is a great defence against the evil one, who takes possession of unoccupied minds with terrible rapidity. So that to occupy and garrison the mind with thoughts, directly or indirectly bearing upon God, is a very important matter. Moreover, as has been happily said, "it is by this occupation of our thoughts that reading hinders castle-building, which is an inward disease wholly incompatible with devotion. Perhaps it is speaking too broadly to say that reading hinders it altogether; but at least it makes it much less likely, and confines it within much narrower bounds. In temptations also it is a twofold help, both negative and positive; negative, because all occupation involves the non-existence of a great many temptations, and positive, because it furnishes an actual distraction while we are under temptation, as well as gives us light in our warfare with them, and a beating of the heart which prevents our being chilled by their icy touch. It also delivers us from listlessness, which is a dangerous enemy to devotion, especially to those who live in the world. To sit down in a chair without an object, is to jump into a thicket of temptations. A vacant hour is always the devil's hour. When time hangs heavy, the wings of the spirit flap painfully and slow. Then it is that a book is a strong tower, nay, a very church, with angels lurking among the leaves as if they were so many niches."*

The sins of the tongue, into which all are more or less apt to fall in society, are greatly lessened when the mind is stored with subjects of greater interest and importance than petty gossip; and reading must tend to lessen the ignorant narrow-mindedness which so often makes people uncharitable, censorious, and even irreverent. It has been truly said, that those who read become useful missionaries in ordinary society, by imperceptibly raising the tone of those they mix with. "How many a narrow mind has it made broad!" Faber writes: "How many close, stifling, unwindowed hearts has it not filled with mountain air and sunshine, so making room for God, where He had no room before! It also heightens our whole

---

* FABER, *Spiritual Conferences*, p. 324.

spiritual standing, by making us more free from human
respect. When we have a taste for reading, and reading
approved religious books, we acquire the sense of standing under the eye and at the judgment-seat of great and
holy minds. Their judgments give the law to ours. They
introduce us into another world, where right measures
and true standards prevail. Hence the judgments of
that little inefficient circle immediately around ourselves,
which we surname the world, are less important, less all
in all in our eyes than they used to be. We have got
accustomed to higher things, to wider prospects, to
greater worlds."

And if general reading has so healthy an effect, surely
spiritual reading will not be found less helpful. Only,
like most other good things, it needs certain safeguards
and rules. First, then, it should be regular. No day, if
possible, should be allowed to pass without feeding the
mind with some nourishment by reading, and of all
books the one to be most studied is of course the Bible.
"Religious books are profitable," an old French writer
says, "but the best of them do not contain the juices
and marrow which you will find in every word of Holy
Scripture. One sentence will often suffice to fill the
mind, and uphold and strengthen it through the day.
Who cannot return over and over again to the Gospels,
especially that of St. John, or the Epistles, or the Books

of Wisdom, finding continually new delight? whereas
most human writings grow tedious to us after we know
them well."

But spiritual reading should be slow and deliberate,
not as we read to acquire information, or amuse a passing
hour. It is well to pause on what is read, often lifting
up the heart to God, and to gather up some thoughts
which may serve as ejaculatory prayer, or assist our
meditations. One book, often gone through, will help
people more than a great many hastily read. St. Francis
de Sales always carried the *Spiritual Combat* about with
him, calling it his "dear book;" while his own *Devout Life*
has filled the same office to many others. We have known
more than one saintly heart which rarely passed a day
without refreshing itself with some paragraphs from the
Imitation of Christ, and probably the number of those who
have learned to love the *Christian Year* as an endless
friend of helpful spiritual reading is beyond reckoning.
Many other books will fit in to individual minds : Bishop
Taylor's *Holy Living and Dying*, the *Confessions of St.
Augustine*, Isaac Williams's most devout books on the
Passion, and many more, have become the constant
companions of souls seeking to dwell more and more in
communion with God. But it is a wholesome counsel to
seek guidance in such reading, especially in our days,
when the supply of spiritual books is so abundant. All

are not equally suited to the wants of every one, and
sometimes positive harm may be done by ill-adapted
spiritual reading, just as invalids sometimes hurt themselves by the study of medical books. One has seen
people living a self-indulgent, luxurious life, unbraced by
discipline or hardness, lying on a sofa, reading ascetic
books, and imagining themselves capable of entering into
them. Or again, highly imaginative, visionary people
have fed upon mystic writings, to the great detriment of
their practical duties. Scrupulous people have terrified
themselves into mistrust by reading chiefly of the terrors
of the Lord, and the like. It is hardly needful earnestly
to deprecate the reading of sceptical or doubting books
by those who have no call to do so (as *e.g.* clergy have
who must be prepared to meet the difficulties they raise
in men's minds); many a person has begun to read such
books out of curiosity, as an intellectual gratification, or
because it was convenient to be prepared to discuss them
in society, confident in their own strength, sure that their
faith could not suffer, and then, bit by bit, they have
found speculative notions, doubts, sceptical assertions,
cleaving to them; till if they do not altogether lose their
faith, there will be much pain, much uneasiness, and
many a struggle with the evil one to be undergone
before they will be free from the pollution. Old Fuller
says somewhere in his *Good Thoughts for Bad Times,*

that he never heard a bad or profane thing without feeling that it had left some uncomfortable impression on his mind, as mud thrown on a wall leaves a stain, although it be wiped away.

Perhaps we sometimes need to be reminded that *spiritual* reading is not the same as theological or exegetical reading; that the former may really be considered a part of our religious exercises, having as its object the cultivation of a spiritual mind, and a closer approach to God, in the knowledge of Him, and communion with Him; whereas the latter is with a view certainly to increased knowledge of God, but of a different kind; its aim is to acquire information which may be useful in forming and cultivating the mind, to strengthen habits of thought, and set forth the glory of God, according to the vocation of the reader.

X

Common Faults

PEOPLE who really aim at a holy life ought, both for their own sake and for the sake of God's glory, to pay great attention to their natural and common faults and frailties, which are apt to bring discredit on religion, and often to be a hindrance to our neighbours. It is humbling to have to own that one's character is over-bearing, impatient, intolerant; and how can habitual pride exist in the heart of one who has been long sitting at Jesus' Feet? But so it sometimes is, and we shall do well to study disagreeable facts, and look our evil tendencies fairly in the face. It does not follow because we see more faults in ourselves than we did awhile since that we are guilty of more. They were there, but now God has given us a clearer light by which to see them.

People who live together in close intimacy often jar one another considerably. There is no need to be disturbed because you cannot help perceiving your neighbour's weak points; God does not require you to think anybody perfect, only be thoroughly considerate and kindly towards those you are thrown with. Perhaps you are too sharp and energetic in tone, too decided in manner. The thing in itself is not amiss, but your manner is wrong. Perhaps you overlook your own little peculiarities, your *uppish* tendency, your little egotisms, petty vanity concerning rank, fortune, or means, trifling impatience, unworthy recriminations, exaggerated complaints when anything annoys you, and a crowd of the like imperfections to which we are apt to be very blind in ourselves, though we see them with wonderful distinctness in others.

Self-love generally taints what we do heedlessly. Your natural temperament leads you to find fault with everything that differs from your own view; well then, having found that out, strive to acquire a habit of more mistrust of yourself, and greater humility. It is a positive duty to seek to use the numberless opportunities which God supplies to us of conquering self and helping others. Ask God to show them to you, and help you to meet them. A habit of prayer, and of realising God's Presence in all we do, will go far to make us see many things plainly, which else would escape us, and to give true courage in well-doing and humility.

Do not fret because of the jars which you feel to exist between yourself and those you live with. If you ever do wrong in consequence, be penitent, but do not be disheartened. It is no sign of contrition to be disheartened by a fault; on the contrary, that often is merely the result of wounded self-love, vexed at its own weakness. True contrition grieves at having displeased God, but it goes hand in hand with a brave resolution to begin again and do better with His help. When you have done all you can to meet such difficulties, accept what discomfort still remains as a cross, a trial to be meekly borne. Something may be gained, if it is only a deeper sense of your own weakness; for all self-knowledge is a grace. When you feel humiliated, give God thanks, and try to be glad that others should see you as you know God sees you.

Amid contradictions, try to acquire the habit of not dwelling on the immediate cause of vexation, but look beyond to Him from Whose Hand it really comes. A stone has fallen and bruised you, but do not murmur against it; God allowed the bruise for your good, though you see it not. When the devil was permitted to overwhelm Job with blow upon blow, he did not accuse Satan; he said, "The LORD gave and the Lord hath taken away." Do you the same; be sure that God overrules all things, be it ours to submit lovingly. Great patience in bearing with a constant succession of petty trials and vexations is very acceptable in His sight.

It may be said that as a general rule religious people have an excess of activity, and need to study how to moderate it; that is to say, checking haste, and curbing their inward impetuosity by the thought of God. Excessive activity is fatal to the soul's health. It may not prevent piety, but it will prevent piety from standing on a solid foundation. When you are conscious of this superabundant activity and energy as needing to be checked, try to speak little, to compress your words, to be less eager to know and do everything, to give yourself up more passively to be led by God's Holy Spirit. It has been said that perfection consists less in action than in a complete yielding up of self to God, suffering His Holy Spirit to guide one wholly. This would restrain and subdue all our eagerness. It is a good habit sometimes to check yourself just as you are about to say something clever or *telling* in society. It is a blow to vanity and self-love. Wait a little, and if there is any real good to be gained by speaking, you can say what is necessary later on more quietly and with less display. If an active, energetic spirit does not seek always to keep up a sense of God's Presence, it is sure to forfeit much of the blessings won in sacraments.

XI

Irritability

ONE can hardly suppose that any one aiming at a
really Christian life would wilfully indulge in
irritability towards those around him. One may differ
from them, and put forth and maintain one's own
opinion kindly and courteously; but failing to convince,
it is well to let it alone, and not persist. Above all, strive
to be quiet and not constrained with those whose opposition irritates you. Constraint arising thus has separated
people who really loved each other. One of the first
duties of a Christian life is to be kindly, and religious
people ought not to have to turn to the worldly to learn
this lesson from them. Yet we often see that mere
worldly courtesy and love of popularity make men
smoother and more amiable in manner than those who
ought to act on higher motives. A person professing to
be devout, and yet habitually giving way to impatience
and irritability, cannot fail to be a source of scandal to
others. It is a very real act of adoration, or of the Pre-

sence of God, to check for love of Him some angry or
petulant impulse, or some dislike or repugnance. How
many roughnesses would be smoothed out of life if we
each resolved, even once in every day, to check some
trifling act, or word of unlove, as a direct act of love to
God. The habit would probably so grow on us that
unkindness would become a rare thing to the person
who adopted the practice for a season. When one is
very sensitive, very easily jarred, very fastidious and
open to annoyance, it is a great help to think of our
dear Lord on earth, with His delicate, sensitive, refined
frame, so much more alive to all annoyance than ousr
through its exquisite nature, and touched as He must
have been by many a slight thing which we might scarce
perceive. Yet where can we find a trace of impatience
or irritability in His intercourse with men? Rebuke,
tender compassion, loving pity, but never scorn or impatience. "Wear velvet gloves in family life," it has
been said ; in other words, touch all who come near with
a soft, unirritating hand, seek to avoid vexing any, strive
to - promote unity and concord with all. Pascal says
somewhere, that while most people would take care not
to knock up against a man they know to have a sore or
tender limb, hardly any one takes the least pains to avoid
touching or vexing the sore or irritable temper which they
know their neighbour possesses. The same philosopher

remarks, that while we are not irritated by one who has a bodily halt, we are irritated by a halting mind (*un esprit boiteux*), and accounts for it by saying that the lame man admits that his neighbour walks well, while the limping mind affirms that *he* is right and his neighbour halting.

 Probably no thought would tend more to repress irritability than the remembrance that by it we lose some measure of God's love for us, and tend to efface the likeness to Him in which we were made ; for our dear Lord was meek and lowly of heart. After all, life is very full of contradictions and vexations ; but they glance lightly off him who treats them as a further means of lifting up his heart to God.

One help amid annoying circumstances is to look on from the visible cause of our annoyance, not dwelling upon the fault of those who inflict it, to God, and seeing His Hand inflicting, or at least permitting, the lesser as well as the greater trial. Many people are ready to refer great trials, bereavement, severe illness, and the like, to God, who refuse to see His Hand in the little troubles of daily life ; but therein they lose greatly. A quaint old writer says : "The way to learn a real blessed submission is to know how to profit by little daily trials. A hundred trifles contrary to our wishes and likings must inevitably occur to most people from day to day, either through our own incautiousness and folly, or through the malice and carelessness of others, or through the unforeseen course of events over which men have no control. Life is full of these troublesome briars, which give rise to all manner of bitterness, hatred, envy, fear, impatience, disappointment, anxiety; which disturb the soul's peace. For instance, you say something for which you are directly sorry, and an angry retort is made; your servant is careless or forgetful, your child is troublesome, a horse passing by splashes you all over, the weather inconveniences you, your work does not get on as you want, some piece of furniture is broken, some article of dress torn or soiled. Well, I don't pretend to say that any of these are openings for the practice of a very heroic virtue; but I do say that they are the sure means by which you might acquire it, if you choose. I do say that if any one would make a stedfast habit of watchfulness, and offer all such petty vexations to God, accepting them as coming in the course of His Providence, he would advance marvellously in the spiritual life and in nearness to God, and he would be as strong again to meet the weightier troubles of life."*

It is very good for one to be forgotten and overlooked when one is self-absorbed and anxious to be prominent. There are some who so sincerely desire to be unnoticed

* _La Voie de la Paix Intérieure_, PÈRE DE LEHEN, p. 80.

that it is a real trial to them to be put forward. It is hard to keep vividly enough before one that we deserve nothing but to be humbled and set aside. Who, if suddenly called to appear before God, would feel that he had anything in his hand whereof to boast? Such a thought would help to keep up a spirit of penitence and humility. There will always be a double self within each of us. One day the Bishop of Calcedon asked St. Francis de Sales (his brother) how he could listen unmoved to the insults and offensive remarks lavished upon him by some opponent. "Ah, you don't hear what mutters within," the saint replied; "but then I answer, Am I willing to lose the fruits of forty years' toil?"

When you are vexed or put out, try not to let your countenance express your annoyance; let that be a secret between you and God, not told to the outer world. Tell Him what troubles you, and then let your outward manner be calm and gentle, as if nothing were amiss. An even temper is really the victory over self-love; and there is no more valuable means of promoting the sanctification of those around you, nothing gives greater weight and influence, than the impress of your religion on the ordinary matters of life. To people not themselves of a religious character it gives a marvellous impression of reality, and the outward manner is generally taken by them (and not untruly) to be an index of what is within.

A serious manner is all very well, but let it be also accessible and gentle, free alike from haughtiness and harshness. Be very careful, too, never to use any expression or action indicative of temper or passion. We might all with advantage follow the example of one who writes: "In my own family I try to be as little in the way as possible, to be satisfied with everything, and never to believe for a moment that any one means unkindly towards me. If people are friendly and kind to me, I enjoy it; if they neglect me, put me aside, leave me, I am always happy alone. It all tends to my one only aim—forgetfulness of self, in order to please God."

XII.

Calmness

R EAL calmness is that temper of mind which knows
how to check first impulses, and only to act after
they have been modified and over-ruled by reference to
God. This is the weapon wherewith to destroy the over-
earthliness of our minds, and by the help of which to
live as a true disciple of Jesus Christ. Thomas à Kempis
says of compunction, "I had rather feel it than understand the definition thereof;"* and we may say the same
of calmness, it implies doing whatever is for God's service
quietly, stedfastly, and without self-seeking. The best
way of attaining to an inwardly calm spirit is habitually
and silently to keep up a sense of the Presence of God,
and when you become conscious of the throes of natural
activity to watch carefully over them. Calmness does
not mean that you will not have many a struggle with
the impulses of self-love; but the closer you hold on to

* Book I., chap. i.

God the more emphatically these will be subdued. Never allow yourself voluntarily to consent to anything whatsoever that you know to be wrong. One might almost say of a calm spirit, that where it is given all else will follow, as when King Solomon asked for wisdom, and all other gifts accompanied it; yet even this gift of calmness should itself be calmly sought. If you are naturally eager, impulsive, restless, begin with aiming at one thorough victory over yourself during the week; if God strengthens you for more, be thankful, but at all events, in this way you will go far towards self-mastery. If you know that your life is liable to be disturbed, excited by unavoidable circumstances, make ready to meet the difficulty. When you wake, and in your first morning prayers, offer all that may arise to disturb you to God. Renew this intention from time to time, and then, when some troublesome claim upon your time, or any other annoyance arises, you will be able to go forth calmly and meet it; your soul will be stayed on God. It may be that you will not have altogether won the day, but will be still striving for victory when your last hour comes. Still be not afraid, eternal calm and rest will be your portion then. "The blessing of peace" is spoken of very earnestly in Holy Scripture. The soul that seeks it knows that it is only in quietness and confidence that it can hope to receive God's grace and light, therefore it will seek habitually to still all the storms which rise within it, and humbly to await His holy inspirations. This is a sure way to quench the troubles and excitements in our intercourse with others which self-love creates. St. Augustine says that love of self is our greatest enemy. Probably no one leads so calm a life as he who thinks but little of himself.

Our restlessness and anxiety show that we have more to do yet in self-control. Over-activity is a hindrance, and the only remedy to a crowd of perplexing thoughts is resignation to the Will of God. Do not give way to a restless, eager longing, even for the saving of souls; rather work, toil for it; but not to the neglect of your own salvation, your own co-operation with God's intentions concerning you. This can only be done in quietness. As you gain a calm spirit you will be less harassed with temptations and with self-love. You will soon find that self-love is concerned in almost all your little daily sacrifices, and all your spiritual progress will be advanced as you grow calmer; but you must not be eager in the endeavour to be calm. When you are very much disturbed, instead of pouring out your grievances in talk, tell God; ask Him to show you how to act wisely and rightly in whatever may be the subject of your disturbance. Do not stop short in *wishing* to be calm, try to become so. Perhaps the most perfect model of calmness (except, of course, our Lord Himself) is the Blessed Virgin. From

the moment of the Incarnation, and her calm reception
of that astounding mystery with " Behold the handmaid
of the Lord," to the last moment of her life, in the care
of the beloved disciple, what a perfect stillness and calmness there seems to have been ! And yet, to say nothing
of the sword which pierced her soul, how continual the
trial must have been to see her Son rejected, despised,
tortured, slain, knowing as she did that He was all-per-
fect, knowing that with one word He could overwhelm
all who molested Him. We are not told how much
Mary knew of what was coming ; but it does not seem
presumptuous to imagine that Jesus may have told her
much of "what-should come to pass," yet she remained
calm. We fidget and fret, and try to peer into a hidden
future, dread troubles which perhaps never come, while
we fail to meet with what is sent to-day to prove us, and
thus a worldly spirit of fear and calculation destroys our
peace.

How often people fret at themselves for fretting. It
requires a great effort of loving trust to be content even
to make, as it seems to us, small progress in that which
is good. But it is the will, not the measure of progress,
that matters. Very restless, eager people have found it
a help sometimes to pause amid their work, and for a
moment or two to place themselves more immediately
in the Presence of God. This may be done even in the

bustle of society or business, and it has a marvellously calming effect. All real steady work, when excitement and undue hurry is banished, has a calming influence upon the mind. Perhaps to some it is even more difficult always to speak than to act calmly. Make a rule to yourself not to repeat the same thing over again eagerly and unnecessarily, whether it be an order, a remonstrance, or a request. Continued reproaches for some evil done are useless, and the moral force of reproof when really needed is weakened. Always remember, too, that if reproof is a duty in certain positions, it is a still more urgent duty to set a good example. Do not be too ready to find fault. There are often times when it is better to say nothing about trifles, at all events for a season. One valuable way of practising self-control is in checking grumbling, and an unnecessary display of vexation at petty inconveniences. A workman has fulfilled his task imperfectly, some order is wrongly executed, some one keeps you waiting unreasonably; people are careless or forgetful, or do what they have in hand badly. Try not to be disturbed; be just, and show the persons to blame where they are wrong, even (if it be needful) make them do the thing over again properly; but refrain from diffuse or vehement expressions of displeasure. A habit of quick, hasty speech grows so quickly upon people, especially upon those in authority. A naturally quick, impetuous person will find that to cultivate a calm external habit is a great help towards gaining the inward even spirit they need. An experienced spiritual guide once wrote to one of his penitents, " I rejoice to hear that you are learning to walk slowly ;" and saints have not thought it unworthy of their care to dwell upon the benefit of *festina lente.* One can hardly bring the idea of bustle and hurry into compatibility with great holiness; and yet in these busy, eager days there is great need to beware of what has been cleverly called "the idolatry of bustle."

Of course every one must be liable to be disturbed and surrounded by excitement and confusion over which they have no control, but this will not affect the really deep-down, calm spirit; and such an one will fall back naturally into his quiet, orderly, external ways when the accidental pressure is removed. It is not the outward disturbance that need shake the firm inward will to be in all things conformed to the Will of God. Thus it may happen that you begin the day, expecting to have your usual hours for prayer (public and private), for reading and study, or for the good works you have undertaken ; then comes some unexpected claim upon you—people call to whom you must be kind and courteous; one hindrance and interruption occurs after another, and your time is gone, and your appointed religious duties are unfulfilled.

H

Never mind if the interruptions have been accepted for God's sake, and used after His Will; they will take the place of acceptable devotions. A very lovely legend is told of some medieval saint, who was the wife of a rich nobleman in the north of Italy, full of duties and domestic cares, which she strove not to neglect, while giving the best of her heart to God. One morning when, as she thought, her household cares were over, she retired to her oratory, and began to say her office; but just at the third verse of the Psalm she was saying the saint was called away to some commonplace duty, and without hesitation left her prayers to fulfil it, returning as soon as free. Three times following this happened before the saint could get to the end of that Psalm, and when for the fourth time she began to recite it, behold the verse at which she had stopped was illuminated in letters of gold!

One can hardly imagine a sharp, hard word coming from the lips of our Great Example; and one whose temptation is to be over-decided, abrupt, incisive in manner, careless of wounding others' feelings, will find it a help to remember that if he would "put on Christ," he must get rid of the natural man and its asperities.

Over great anxiety about trifles, or a brooding, injured manner, are great trials to those we live with. For such and other like troubles, it has been suggested simply to throw oneself either actually or mentally at the foot of

the cross, and ask to be strengthened against them for
the rest of the day, and then to go on with our duties,
refusing to dwell upon our own mistakes and follies, or
those of others. Forgetfulness of self is a sovereign
remedy for all such troubles. "Do not be so self-
occupied," a director writes; "you are like a woman of
the world, who is for ever looking at herself in the glass.
Look more at Jesus Christ, think more of Him, that is
the *real* thing that matters.

XIII.

𝔉𝔞𝔪𝔦𝔩𝔶 𝔏𝔦𝔣𝔢

NOTHING is so sure a sign of God's reign being established in the soul, and of the love of Christ, as a great perfection in all the daily duties of home-life. Holy Scripture sets this before us in many places, notably in the characterising of a "virtuous woman" in Proverbs xxxi. Christian women (and men too) might take this as a test whereon to frame their rule of life. The active orderly habit, rising early, seeing to all common-place duties, great and small; industrious, thoughtful, considerate for others, foreseeing responsibilities and claims, compassionate, charitable, not self-indulgent, cheerful, wise, and kindly in speech, not despising a due attention to personal nicety: altogether it is a wonderfully comprehensive picture of what the head of a family should be. One would think that King Solomon's "virtuous woman" was never pettish or worried, unduly depressed or selfishly irritable. A deliberate purpose to make the best of one's condition, whatever it may be, to seek to fulfil all its duties loyally, and to bear with its necessary trials patiently, without fretting at them as undeserved, trying to see them as God sees them, as a means of disciplining the character, of seeking closer union with Him;—such a purpose would make many a home far happier than it now is.

To this end spiritual writers recommend what is called "a holy indifference" to all created things, including things inanimate, place, time, and the like. Try as far as possible to be indifferent to all things, not apathetically, but in entire submission to the Will of God. Do not allow yourself to be overcome by that nervous irritability which it is so hard to repress. We say, "we know that all things work together for good to them that love God," even when they seem most adverse. Not unfrequently we are less tried by what is really difficult and hard to bear, than by the difficulty of deciding in trifles, or the disagreeable side of things. But here, as elsewhere, a humble, trustful, persevering prayer will be our great safeguard against giving way to the errors of our natural judgment. Sometimes, when we think that we have planned and arranged everything so cleverly, all our arrangements are upset, and yet the undertaking succeeds !

Do not be too keen about obtaining or using influence, and beware of letting your object be the carrying out of your natural likings, or your tendency to rule. Let the real good of souls, the good guidance of your family, and the fulfilment of God's Will, be your aim. If your position is one without authority, still you have no doubt a right to express your opinion, either when it is asked, or when God moves you to do so. But having done this simply, do not revert to it. This is a rule which would prevent many angry recriminations.

Try to win those whom you want to influence for their own good; try to get an entrance into their hearts, and seek to be guided by God's Holy Spirit in all you say. If you do this, be sure that out of a hundred times when you feel inclined to speak you will be silent ninety-nine. Give advice very quietly. There are some characters indeed to whom it is better to say as little as possible, even when you are consulted. If you have to say what is unacceptable, let it be said very firmly, but quietly and briefly. Appeal to the faith, the reason, the better feelings of those you deal with, and avoid all appearance of displeasure in your manner. If you know that you will not be heeded, and that the person in fault will not receive your counsels, it is better to wait; God may make the way plain shortly.

Do not be afraid of giving advice, but choose both time and manner. Then say what is right calmly, and without being alarmed at little difficulties; let yourself be guided by God, and always remember that while He requires you to do your best for any He has placed under your care, He does not require success. Your part is to take measures, His to bless them; and nothing will more surely draw down that blessing than patient endurance of contradiction, disappointment, and humiliation. It would be a weary thing indeed, if we were responsible for the success of all which, however rightly done, fails in its result. We must be prudent; but he who wants never to give advice, save when it is to be thoroughly successful, may as well take a vow of perpetual silence!

Your solicitude may do much for those you love, but your prayers will do more; not long prayers said on your knees, but all through the day acting and bearing with that intention. One great act in influencing those around is never to persist *with them;* keep all your persistence for God. Let the suggestion or counsel drop which you see annoys or irritates; it may bear fruit hereafter; but, at all events, no good will come of it while it produces vexation. Beware of letting a worldly spirit fill you with little susceptibilities and an exacting tendency, which are very damaging to a Christian life. Never allow yourself to brood over deficiencies in the respect, or affection, or consideration shown to you by others. You can never be the living image of Christ so long as you listen to the murmurs of self-love and egotism; the rays of His warm sunshine will not penetrate the chill which selfishness produces. You should look upon yourself as a channel of God's goodness to those around; but this you will never be until you forget yourself. Do not let your over-caution or prudence keep you from doing what you see plainly to be God's Will; but let yourself be moulded and led by it wholly and entirely.

If you are thrown with any one whose character is very trying, but in whom you cannot hope for a change, try to believe that God has some wise purpose in letting you be disciplined by a constant contradiction to your natural inclinations, and *do not argue with Him.* We are so ready to put away at once whatever is disagreeable or unacceptable to ourselves; and if we cannot do so, we are profuse in lamentations and self-compassion. But surely this is to forget that we are sinners in a world of sin, and moreover disciples of a crucified Master. We should do more credit to our religion, if we accepted the disagreeables patiently, and tried to turn them to our soul's profit. Do not talk about the troubles of your home, or of the annoyances, real or imaginary, which you experience from any in it—above all, from husband or parents. Let your complaints on all such matters be made to God only. Even if you need counsel as to your own actions under such difficulties, do not speak of the personal failings of others to your spiritual guide. If you try, you will find it quite possible to represent your difficulties and needs without speaking unkindly of individuals. Sometimes we hear people complain that they are not appreciated, that no one gives them credit for the sacrifices they make, and that their best deeds are turned against them. It were well to receive such humiliations silently, asking oneself whether one had acted to please God, or to win the praise of man?

If you have others under you, be very ready to impute good intentions to them, and be very indulgent to their deficiencies. You will attach your dependents to you very much by dwelling more on their goodwill than on their faults. Every Christian ought to be growing gentler as he grows older. God allows us to experience sundry little vexations and trials in our intercourse with our inferiors, as a means of increasing humility and patience. These little crosses may be golden opportunities to you, if you accept them; but if you trample them down or shun them, they will be as thorns, and pierce you. When you are very keen about effecting some change, take time to consider whether the matter is really as important as it seems to you just now while you are excited; and if the thing is in itself unimportant, do not be too eager in seeking perfection.

XIV

Contradiction

WE are all very much disposed to contradict, and it is a tendency which needs watching. It is so much better to let numberless matters drop. If you are bent on setting everything about you to rights, you will never be able to attain a quiet mind. Do not get into a habit of criticising, except where there are matters of real importance to be rectified; and while in no way encouraging what is wrong, do not be eager in your opposition. Try to train yourself in a spirit of real compassion for wrong-doers as for those who are moral invalids, and you will have much more power to help them.

It may be that those with whom you live are the cause of perpetual trial and vexation to you, so that from morning to night you must be on your guard, and that all your life. But do not be afraid; life's day at longest is brief, and but as a short winter's day. Bow before God's Will, and strive to co-operate with it to your utmost. Such a deliberate purpose will tend more than anything else to soothe the irritation which naturally arises from an habitual contradiction from those around you. Amid your annoyance you will feel that God is watching you, and that He is saving you from the disastrous effects of indulged self-love. You have no idea, until you have tried, how the sting of an unkind or rude word, or of some other vexation, is drawn by accustoming yourself to feel "God permits this; it is His Will; it shall be mine too." It has been happily said, that we ought to learn how sometimes to go boldly *through* our troubles, and at other times to go alongside of them. A man who is travelling through a snow-storm does not stop to count the flakes; he pushes on as steadily as he can; and though the journey may be wearisome, sooner or later he comes to the end of it. Patience is the truest strength.

If you would have God's blessing even upon your aspirations after what is good for the souls of others, you must aim at quietness and calmness. Think of our guardian angels and their calmness whatever goes on among men. I know you will have *buts* and *ifs* to bring forward; but depend upon it, this is a true maxim. If you are firmly convinced in your heart that God over-rules everything for good, you may be tempted to think the failure of your best endeavours very surprising, very hard; but you will be certain that He has some good

reason for not yet granting you that success which you
so greatly desire. Try to be sober in your longings after
what is good, whether for yourself or others, by which is
not meant indifference, or passive neglect, but rather
reflection, and a quiet mind, able to weigh and judge
discreetly. Wait patiently to see your seed spring up.
God's times are not always exactly what we might have
chosen.

If by God's grace you have found the key to any
heart, above all things remember that ever since locks
were invented they have often been strained or broken
by hasty, incautious opening. So expect but little, and
wait to see whether God will grant that little. When
you are perplexed and doubtful as to what it is really
best to do, try to be patient and wait; *e.g.* if you are
uncertain whether it is wise to give advice, be silent.
Those who are anxious to help their fellow-men may
learn a lesson from our fields. The farmer ploughs them
and prepares the soil, and then, when the seed is sown,
he leaves all the rest to God's Providence—storm and
wind, rain and sunshine, all bear their part in bringing
the crop to maturity. Sometimes it is His Will that we
go on toiling and praying year after year, without seeming
to bring about any result; and then, perhaps, when we
had almost ceased to look for any, and were well-nigh
out of heart, the seed springs up, we know not how,

reminding us that however we may sow or water, God alone can give the increase.

When you are very anxious about any one, consider from time to time whether you are not requiring more, being more exacting than God. He is often a more pitiful Judge than man. It is a great temptation to a certain class of mind to be painfully anxious to see the good works in which they are concerned prosper, or the persons they seek to influence grow in goodness; and then they take to themselves some merit because they are so anxious. But when one's wishes are not satisfied, the only safe course is to be still, and accept it as God's Will, certain that by so doing there will be more real gain, even to the work or person we have at heart, than in restless, fidgety dissatisfaction. It is a great trial to be disappointed in something undertaken for God; but if once we can adopt the principle of letting God go first, ourselves content to follow after, there will be no real disappointment in failure. "There are no disappointments," it has been said, "to those whose wills are bound up in the Will of God."

You will be surprised to find, on close examination, how often your disappointment and vexation about others, or in the failure of some pet scheme, arise more from the thwarting of your own tastes and likings, or from wounded self-esteem, than anything else.

XV

Sensitiveness

" A VERY marked feature in your character," a guide
of souls writes to a very sensitive person, "is a
certain self-love which makes you so susceptible to un-
pleasant impressions, and dissatisfaction when you do not
meet with as much external affection as you crave for. All
this may be turned to good account if it keeps you from
an excessive clinging to your fellow-creatures. Turn all
that craving for affection to God. Real submission to
Him lies precisely in this very thing for you. It is a
struggle between nature and grace. Our safest course is
to give ourselves up wholly to promote the happiness of
others, but without asking for any return. Then, whether
our affection is appreciated or not, returned or rejected,
we must go on for God's Sake, seeking only to please
Him. Be mistrustful of a treacherous susceptibility
which takes shelter in claiming what it considers its due.
All such sensitiveness is a dangerous thing. When anything is done to offend you, try to look at the act as

apart from your own share in it; be sorry, not because
you are wounded, but because God is displeased, and
offer your personal distress in the matter to God. . . . .
The continual mortifications endured by a very sensitive
temperament are a great peril, unless they are hallowed
by being offered to God. Feed your soul on the perpetual thought, 'God only;' and when the moment of
trial comes, say, 'My God, I accept it as a means of
serving Thee.' When you first wake in the morning,
offer your heart to God, however it may be tried,
wounded, or grieved during the day. A look at your
crucifix will often still its throbbings under some trouble,
real or imaginary. God is gradually loosening your hold
on earthly things; and while you are doubly diligent and
tender in all earthly relationships, He would have you
like the dove, which found no resting-place save in the
ark."

One form which the sensitiveness of self-love is apt to
take is so disagreeable, that we shrink from opening our
eyes to it; *i.e.* dislike to see others preferred to ourselves,
or enjoying greater advantages, or to hear their praises,
even sometimes to see them doing, it may be, better than
ourselves. A diligent practice of the Presence of God is
perhaps the only effectual remedy for this, and at the
same time a patient acknowledgment of the infirmity
and its deep humiliation. But it is not well to be angry

with oneself, or impatient. If a man's body is covered with sores, he will assuredly wince and cry out when touched; and the soul which is diseased with the ulcers of self-love will do the like. Be calm, be very humble, try to put aside and forget all these little cravings of a sensitive nature, not because they cause you pain or humiliation, but because they come between you and God, and you will find that they will dwindle, and at last die away.

XVI.

Decision

DECISION is a very valuable quality, especially in
those who are in a position of authority; but it
needs to be watched, lest it degenerate into abruptness,
harshness, or want of consideration for others. There is
a tendency in human nature rather to pride itself upon
decision, and to rough-ride others who are less decided.
Any one who is conscious of this disposition should
make a rule of being very slow in giving decisions, to take
half an hour, it may be, when a quarter would suffice;
and while ready to go straight to the point which is
clearly God's Will, yet to go so gently as not to overthrow
the weakest traveller at their side. Undecided people
have their difficulties too, and timidity becomes a great
evil in those placed in responsible situations. If you
have to come to an important decision, begin by trying
to be calm; place yourself in God's Presence; ask Him
for strength if you are weak, or for gentleness if you are

over-active; try to look at the subject in question as He sees it, and use your natural powers of sense and knowledge as to what you ought to do. And having come to a decision, with full reference thus made to God, do not suffer yourself to be disturbed, whatever the result may be. Results are not the true test of your course. The thing is to do right, and trust all consequences to God.

XVII.

𝕬 𝕭𝖚𝖘𝖞 𝕷𝖎𝖋𝖊

THE busiest life may be thoroughly Christian. There are many paths leading to Heaven, and he who commends all his business to God, and strives to serve Him in it, has found a safe road. St. Paul did not bid his disciples to have no cares; he bade them cast all their care upon God. Men grow to be saints, not through the importance of their deeds, but through the way in which they fulfil the duties He appoints them. "Whatsoever thou doest, remember thy latter end," the Bible says. This thought ever present would alike check negligence and vanity. There is great danger in giving too free rein to imagination; many a life is troubled, if not seriously hindered, by a reckless yielding to imaginary fears, wants, troubles. The one remedy is simple submission to God's Will.

Where you are brought into contact with others, try always to see your dear Lord in those with whom you deal; this will greatly help you to conquer what is faulty in your attitude towards them. "Inasmuch as ye have done it" (whether good or evil) "unto one of these, ye have done it unto Me."

Do not be positive or self-willed. The thing which you imagine to be altogether in conformity with God's Will may be less so than you think at first. If you are obliged to give up some plan which you thought to be His Will, learn to say with Job, "The Lord gave me this idea, He does not will that it should succeed, His holy Name be praised." Our ignorance and blindness are liable to deceive us; we must strive to go on patiently in the path of duty, satisfied that all will work together for good if we can but do God's Will, seeking to grow in trust and confidence. It is a wise saying, that men ought to act as carefully as if everything depended on their own wisdom, and then to await the result as depending wholly on God. We are apt to run into excess on the former clause. It may be a duty to forestall difficulties, but most of us need a more complete reliance on God's Providence than we possess. It is hard not to be over anxious about the future, not to be too eager to bring about just what in our blindness we think best. Then, too, failure is humiliating, and most of us are very much alive to a desire to have no cause for self-reproach, whether as to imprudence, awkwardness, ignorance, or anything else in ourselves which may tend to failure. But there is a great deal of self-seeking in this, and perhaps we should be more likely to succeed if we were more willing to see, and allow others to see, that we make mistakes; that our folly or weakness has hindered the result we sought for, and to put aside self, and let God work as He pleases.

When persons have learnt to look upon the daily course of their ordinary life, with its duties and troubles, however commonplace, as their offering to God, and as the safest school for themselves of perfection, they will have made a very important step in the spiritual life. Another step, so simple that it is often despised, is to do everything, however ordinary, as well as it can possibly be done, for God's sake. A third is to be always pressing forward; when a mistake is made, or a fault committed, to face and admit it freely; but having asked God to supply the deficiency caused by our own infirmity, to go on stedfastly and hopefully.

It is sometimes said, greatly to the discredit of professing Christians, that "religious people," as they are called, are just as eager after money and worldly advantages as those who are avowedly secular. Surely this ought not to be. A large-hearted generosity, together with a full recollection that money, &c., is a mere trust from God, to be used for His service, ought to possess all Christian people. "Having nothing and yet possessing all things," accepting God's gifts without cleaving to them, being ready to give up all for Him, such seems to be the only safe mind for those that are rich; but to be eager to accumulate, or anxious to save, tenacious about social rank and position, making the esteem of man a first object and the like, are surely grievous evils, and liable to come under our Lord's terrible denunciation, "Woe unto you that are rich! for ye have received your consolation."

When great troubles and trials come, it is needful, though hard, to keep in mind that, whether from the higher or lower point of view, it is a great evil to yield to discouragement, and thereby probably fail to learn the lesson which the trial is meant to teach. The trouble probably will soon pass away—at the longest, with the close of life; but its results are intended to abide by us for ever, moulding the heart for God.

It has been said, "Try to become a saint quietly;" *i.e.* by attention to little things, such as people sometimes despise. Watch carefully over your senses, so that they may all be used to God's glory only. Try to bring them all into close resemblance with Christ, remembering that even He "learned obedience, in that He suffered." Take whatever grieves and wounds you even in the tenderest places patiently; bear with the loss of natural

ties or friendship, with disappointment, lack of sufficient
return from those you love, and the like, without fretting,
and God, Who desires the first place in your heart, will
fill up the void with His own precious love. Be quite
sure that whatever you give up for His sake will be
restored to you tenfold—it may be even in this world;
most assuredly in the next. Some positions in life seem
to involve one incessant self-renunciation from morning
to night. But is there not a comfort in the thought that
even such was our dear Lord's life on earth? "Take up
your cross *daily*," He said; and if, as often happens, we
are too weak to take it up, His merciful Hand lays it on
us. Those whose circumstances throw them much into
society need a great deal of self-abnegation; and no
courtesy is so genuine or so refined as that which springs
from the highest motives. If you are thinking much
about pleasing God, you are less likely to think unduly
about pleasing men, while yet you will treat others with
almost unconscious gentleness and consideration. The
sacrifice of one's tastes and inclinations in society may
be offered to God like other things; and nothing done
for love of Him was ever yet lost. Do not be anxious
when in society to exercise any influence over others,
save such as promotes God's glory; and on the other
hand beware of being ever led to acquiesce in what is
wrong through human respect. Strive to put the best

construction on what those around you do; and if they
are obviously wrong, remember that their intention may
not be so bad as it seems to you. People who are
conscious of their own infirmities and deficiencies can
easily believe that they are a cause of trial to those
around, and so will be more tolerant of their neighbours'
infirmities.

. Sometimes visitors and social claims break in upon
habits we may be laboriously acquiring, or precious time
may be, as we think, wasted by unimportant interruptions. Of course every one ought to avoid as much as
possible really squandering time, or breaking through
real duties. But sometimes there is a great deal to be
learnt by quietly and patiently giving up an occupation we delight in for the sake of some unwelcome
interruption; by listening with a sympathising ear to
some long story of trouble when we would fain be otherwise employed; by giving up some religious practice—it
may even be some service—to devote the time to helping a neighbour. In short, as St. Vincent de Paul still
teaches his daughters, "to leave God for God." Only we
should be quite sure that it *is* for God that we leave—
for His service, and not from any secondary motive of
human respect or caprice.

To some persons one of the greatest snares of society
lies in the applause or admiration they receive in it,

whether for real attractions, such as personal appearance, talent, outward gifts, or because of position and fortune. There is one main safeguard against this—the constant reference of all such praise to God, and the remembrance that the accumulated praise of all mankind will not change our actual attitude in His sight, or win one particle of favour for us in the great day. "If you only saw me as God and my Confessor see me!" St. Francis de Sales replied to some one who was exalting his merits.

When conscious of the praise of men, and soothed and flattered by it, it is a help to remember that God sees something very different; and the sense of elation and self-complacency produced by the good opinion of others will melt away during a few minutes spent on our knees before God, striving to realise what we are in His sight. St. Francis of Assisi was wont to say, "What every one is in God's sight, that is he, and no more." A check placed on the words by one conscious of conversational powers; reserve in the display of knowledge, general or particular; great care not to indulge wit or the power of amusing people by turning others into ridicule, or disparaging them; avoiding such subjects as tend to show forth your own goodness, advantages, or the like; indeed, a general avoidance of self as a topic of conversation, and as far as may be keeping conversation from turning on individuals; these precautions will go a long way to preserve one from the perils of society. The real danger here, as in so many other matters, lies in self-seeking.

TO A PERSON ANXIOUS AS TO THEIR VOCATION.

" Place yourself calmly before God, and ask Him to shed the bright beams of His light upon you, and to fill your heart with earnest, simple straightforwardness. That is the daily bread you need just now. He will be light to your mind, strength and truth to your heart. Tell Him that you desire to resist Him in nothing, that you are ready to leave all at His word, and that you would know no will save His. Ask that His light may pierce and burn the inmost corners of your heart, that it may show forth every secret fold thereof, until He alone shall reign in it. Then follow the light God shows you to the utmost of your power, and let the earnestness with which you do so be the proof of your love. You must pray very much for the light you need. God will not fail to make plain to you both what He requires of you and how you can do it. But be very discreet in action, and prepare yourself, by recollection, prayer, and perseverance in your daily duties, for the future He may have in store for you. Let your continual ejaculation be, ' Lord, give me light.' We ought to beware in all decisions of acting upon our judgment on any merely natural impulses, through feeling, or prejudice, or human respect. Before coming to any decision, instead of obeying your own impressions, go on for long asking, 'Lord, what wouldst Thou have me do?' And while asking for light, ask also for grace to follow it boldly when given. Try not to shrink back when the light points out a path from which your natural weakness shrinks, but follow the Divine leading quietly and resolutely. Beware of bargaining with God. Vocation is a light, and it may be extinguished; it is a call, which may cease to be heard if unheeded; it is a way, and you may lose yourself, and fail to enter upon it. You may forfeit your vocation if you resist what God is saying to you."

XVIII

𝕽𝖚𝖑𝖊 𝖔𝖋 𝕷𝖎𝖋𝖊

A LMOST every one who is in earnest in the spiritual
life will have some kind of rule whereupon to
mould their daily habits. It is a great help to all, from
whatever point of view considered; tending, as it cannot
fail to do, to order, punctuality, method, diligence, stedfastness, perseverance, a due balance in occupations and
duties, recollection, self-knowledge, and patient earnestness in overcoming faults, and fostering the graces we
most need. For many the inevitable claims of home or
family almost shape the rule, and persons under direction
will not fail to get advice in this matter, the grace of
obedience adding so greatly to the benefit derived from
it. Some, who for one cause or another have not yet
found living guidance in this respect, may be helped by
reading a rule of life given long since to the mother of
a family living in the perilous days which preceded the
first French Revolution by an Archbishop, and counter-

signed by the Abbé Edgeworth, the saintly Confessor of Louis XVI.

"Seeking the glory of God, and the good of my soul, I will endeavour as far as possible to follow the ensuing rule of life :

"*Daily*. To give my first thoughts, my first feeling, my first word, and first act, to God. To rise, resisting sloth, at   o'clock; to dress modestly, and without wasting time, and to give half an hour to vocal prayer and meditation, concluding with such special resolutions as will best help me in the probable duties or cares of the day just begun.

"To go to Church, and during Celebration to offer my morning's resolutions to God, and ask the special graces for which I foresee need that day.

"To occupy myself diligently, and without allowing taste and liking to hinder me in my home duties, as wife, mother, and mistress of a family, remembering to act in each as a Christian above all.

"To say the hours, uniting myself with the Church and other devout souls.

"To take a few moments before meals for recollection in the Presence of God, for a rapid review of the way I have used my time, and how I have kept my resolutions, which I will renew.

"At meals, to consult my taste less than health, to

guard against mere self-indulgence, and to deprive myself from time to time of something pleasant.

"In society, to be cheerful and bright, but to watch against any thing like gossip, slander, illnatured criticism, questionable joking, and to be uniformly reverent in all that borders upon religion and morality,* and carefully and boldly taking God's side in all discussion.

"To say Vespers (or Evensong).

"To do some real work every day, whether by studying so as to be more competent to educate my children and guide my household, or some manual labour for Christ's Church or His poor.

"To take half an hour daily for spiritual reading, seeking really to profit by it, and ending with a brief prayer arising out of it.

"Family prayer at night, if possible with all the household.

"Self-examination; and on going to bed, to commend my soul to God as at my last hour, before falling asleep.

"*Weekly.*—To observe Fridays and other days of abstinence, and mark them in my household, with discretion.

"To say the Litany of the Holy Name or Passion on Friday, and the Rosary on Saturday.

---

* Those were days when the latitude and freedom of society admitted of what would shock at all events our refinement now.

"To be punctual in Confession and Communion.

"On Sunday to attend the services of my parish church, to extend my religious exercises somewhat, to provide or myself give some instruction for my servants, and to see that all my family observe that holy day fitly and devoutly. To make a brief review of my own doings during the past week, noting the faults to be avoided and the graces sought after.

"*Monthly.*—The last day of each month to make a review of my inner life, and to receive my next Communion as a Viaticum, in preparation for a holy death.

"*Yearly.*—To endeavour to follow the Church's teaching in her course of feasts and fasts, and adapt my reading to it.

"To make a Retreat, if circumstances permit of it.

"To endeavour everywhere, at all times and in all I do, to make God and my soul the first consideration."

The venerable Archbishop who gave this rule cautioned the person to whom it was given at the same time not to make herself a slave to it, saying that in such a position as hers a servile exactness would be a real fault, the claims of a mother and the mistress of a family being such as must inevitably break in upon any rule occasionally. It is quite another thing to see that indolence, disinclination, or self-indulgence, are not permitted to interfere with it.

XIX.

Retreats

NOW that Retreats have become so established and systematic a part of the spiritual life among us, the following suggestions, given to a person who was advised to keep one day's Retreat every month while living in the world, may be useful.

You should make three meditations of twenty minutes each. The first, early in the day, on the mental attitude in which you would desire to be found at your death hour, examining whether you are seeking to preserve it actually at the present time.

The second, about midday, on the virtues you would wish to have cultivated when you come to die.

The third, towards evening, examining how you would desire to have acquitted yourself of your ordinary duties, your wonted devotions, and your social obligations, when they are all ended, and you die. To this you would do well to add some examination as to how you bear ordinary trials and temptations.

About noon, take a quarter of an hour to consider how far you have kept your resolutions, and what benefit you have gained from your last Retreat.

In the afternoon, spend a quarter of an hour at least in Church, offering yourself, your whole mind, heart, and will, to our dear Lord in the Blessed Sacrament, preparing yourself to give up everything to Him.

In the intervals, study to maintain inward recollection, silence if possible, and at all events frequent interior Communion with God. The next morning let your meditation chiefly take the shape of self-oblation of all that is in you to the service of your Master, and a strong resolution to aim at ever-increasing personal sanctification. Go to confession, as if it were the last opportunity you would ever have, and ask God's special grace to use it rightly. Try more than before to attain that simple faith which enables one to receive and hear everything as coming from God; dwell upon the thought that it is the Precious Blood which is applied to your soul in Absolution; seek fresh courage through His Love and pity to persevere. If you have ever felt as though your confessor were dry and hard, and his words less helpful than they might be to you, this effort, earnestly and simply made, will go far to do away with the uncomfortable impression. Then make your Communion as though it were your Viaticum, as though it were the last time you expected

K

to receive your dear Lord in His own Sacrament, dwelling upon the perfecting of that union in the Eternal Life. Strive to be so united to Him that it would be all joy to know that in a few hours you were to enter His visible Presence.

In thinking of death, try to put away all fears concerning your last hours. Remember that either you will then be calm and peaceful, or if trials come they will be meted out to you by God's Hand, and His Grace will lead you safely through them. Do not suffer yourself to dwell on the thought of being lonely or desolate. Not all creation can protract your life by one second beyond what God has appointed, or give you one particle of consolation without His Grace; nor will that Grace ever be denied to those who ask it. Even if you were to be absolutely alone at your last hour, He would supply all your needs; in Him you have a sure Friend, the only one who can never fail you.

Do not ever omit your monthly Retreat, it is a great means of renewing fervour; for however stedfast a person may be in his religious duties, it is hardly possible but that he should slacken and become less fervent during the long interval of a yearly Retreat, and in our weakness we greatly need an often-renewed struggle against our besetting sins, and confirmation of good resolutions. It is very trying to feel oneself overwhelmed and disheartened, unable to arouse any conscious love of God, or real longing after perfection ; but steady perseverance in thus renewing the resolutions made during your annual Retreat will be a great help, especially when combined with the offering to Christ of all your daily thoughts, words, and deeds. If you will but persevere, through coldness and dryness, in these habits, you will so confirm and establish the life of Christ in you, that you will indeed be, as St. Paul says, "a new creature."

In preparing for your annual Retreat, it is well steadily to set before you the need of earnest efforts after salvation; the practical use of Retreats; mistrust of self; confidence in God; the importance of entering upon your Retreat in a free, generous spirit; of absolute obedience to rule while in it; of complete silence, not external only, but interior; of being as far as possible face to face, alone with God.

Remember that the one thing important above all others to you is the salvation of your soul. It is the great work of your life, far greater than your work as parent, child, husband, wife, or friend. All the duties belonging to those conditions are to be fulfilled relatively to the first point—God glorified in your salvation.

Do not trouble yourself too much about external help in your Retreat. You may have planned to get a great deal of counsel, to relieve yourself by pouring out your troubles, by asking many questions, &c. And God gives you only an opportunity of lying absolutely still in His Presence, in silent waiting for His word.

Mistrust yourself. Do not count upon lights you hope to win, sweetness in prayer and Sacraments, consolations to be found in spiritual advice. Ask, and look for nothing save from God's unlimited goodness. Try to fix all your hopes, all your expectations for this world and the next, solely on Him and His Mercy. Such trust in Him is the soul's true strength.

Strive to take a free, generous heart into Retreat; ready to give up all to Him; ready to make the sacrifices which He may point out to you as what He requires; ready to forego the consolations you so greatly desire and seem to need, if it be His Will. Yet all the while, ask fearlessly and boldly for all you want. God greatly loves to be urged and intreated : "the kingdom of heaven is taken by storm."

There is great profit in an obedient, faithful practice of the rule given you during Retreat. Never indulge little wilfulnesses· in rejecting this or adding that. If there is anything which your health renders unfit for your observance, tell the conductor, and ask to be allowed to leave that undone, but do not ask to add more or stricter observances to the rule given. The desire to do this comes of spiritual pride. Above all be very faithful to the rule of silence, and try to use the intervals of recreation profitably, either in writing out your notes, in such spiritual reading as may be recommended, or in physical rest, but carefully avoid whatever tends to distract your mind.

Between the meditations go over the principal points quietly in your own mind, impressing those results which come most home to your own heart; ahd think over any difficulties, or anything arising out of them, about which you may wish to consult the conductor.

It is well at these times (and indeed at others also) to confine yourself to the use of some one book, so as to concentrate your thoughts. A quiet, prayerful half-hour of spiritual reading daily will be found a great means of advancing in the spiritual life by most people. It is very important, however, to read little at once, and rather to seek our Lord's blessing on what you read by prayer and patience, than to run through a great quantity rapidly. Perhaps some single line of a book, instead of the several pages which you are in the habit of reading, read and meditated humbly—say the first sentence of the *Imitation* for instance—would do more to help you onwards in your interior life than the volumes you have run through so fast as, in a measure, to rub out the impressions made.

XX.

Suggestions for a Retreat

TAKE as your object to examine how you can best further the absolute reign of God's Will over your heart. To do this, calmness is needful: peace is the best guardian of mind and heart.

Begin by dwelling on your position before God, on all He has given you, all you owe to Him. Then think of our Lord, His Example, His Grace, consider what He asks of you, what will be acceptable to Him, and thus strengthen your will to seek entire conformity to His.

If you are so distracted, or in any way disturbed, as to be unable to throw yourself into the subject of meditation, have recourse to what is always within your power, and humble yourself profoundly before God, calling to mind His promise to "have respect unto the poor;" in other words, that His grace will never forsake the humble. It is precisely when clouds come over the mind, and we feel intellectually and spiritually dry and dark, that we need to lay our heart before Him, and wait in humble patience till He wills to brighten our horizon. However dark the sky, you can go on praying, though, it may be, you cannot find any pleasure or tangible relief in prayer. But wait humbly, saying, " It is the Lord, let Him do as seemeth Him good," and on that foundation of humility your spiritual edifice will be built in time. The publican probably did not find great sweetness in his prayer, but he humbled himself deeply, and our Lord says that he went back "justified."

The subjects given you in meditation will not be any- thing new; but if you seek to throw yourself into them heartily, though quietly, God will speak to you in them, and if He sees that you need any new lights, He will draw them out for you. Try to be as contented, if you are dry and dark, as if you overflow with consolation and light: He can give you abundant grace through either.

Hurry, confusion, anxiety, restlessness, any or all hinder the soul's vision, and prevent it from advancing; but if you can bring a calm humility and a humble quietude to your spiritual exercises, you will assuredly gain ground, even if unconsciously to yourself at the time. If, on entering a room long left in undisturbed dust, you begin to sweep vehemently, you raise such a cloud that you can see nothing; and if you want to distinguish your needs, frailties, and weak places, you

must try to do it by the light of God's sunshine, without
raising your own earthly dust to obscure your vision.

It has been said, " Humility comes with calmness, and
calmness with humility." God makes His Will plain to
us each in different ways. To some He speaks in
desolation, in loneliness, in urgent outward trials; while
others are called to hear His Voice by means of internal
conflicts. But the great point is for us to make up our
mind to accept His Will however it is brought to bear
on us. It may be very hard to feel that one is alone,
solitary, uncared for, and that in all human probability,
as years go on, such loneliness will press upon one with
still heavier weight. But the counteracting thought is,
that God alone chooses to possess my heart; He strips
me of other consolations, in order to bind me closer to
Himself. It may be very hard to feel oneself slighted,
neglected, unequal to those among whom one's lot is
cast. But it is the position He has assigned to me; He
knows what special grace He means me to win thereby;
and one day He will call me to "come up higher." It
may be very unrestful, very weary, to feel that one's life
is, and apparently must continue to be, a series of
struggles, contests, against evil—evil without and evil
within—and that one is often worsted in the conflict;
but there is rest and strength in the thought that He
watches over the battle, and that one need be afraid of

nothing. There is no stay so strong as an unreserved
abandonment of self into God's Hands. We risk nothing,
need fear nothing, in so doing. Friends in whom we
have trusted may fail us; coldness and neglect or
distance may loosen ties which once were strong; but
He can never fall short of His promises. Give all to
Him; keep back nothing; and He will give back such
an abundant overflow of love and blessing, though that
very love may at times seem to deal hardly with its
object for their greater good.

There are some who think they could more easily bear
outward trials and pains than the interior conflicts and
heartaches which often beset them. Perhaps this is partly
imagination. We are all apt to think the evil present
harder than any other. But grant that they are right;
and let them be assured, that even as martyrs have
found ease and joy amid their pangs through a perfect
obedience and trust, so we shall find the only real relief
to mental trials in the same. It has been well said, that
we can find our paths of obedience marked out for ourselves in patient acceptance of God's Will as truly as
in active compliance with His commandments. When
trouble, restless fears, anxious fretfulness, strive to overpower the soul, our safety is in saying, "My God, I
believe in Thy perfect goodness and wisdom and mercy.
What Thou doest I cannot now understand; but I shall

one day see it all plainly.   Meanwhile I accept Thy
Will, whatever it be, unquestioning, without reserve."
There would be no restless disturbance, no sense of
utter discomfort and discomposure in our souls, if we
were quite free from any—it may be almost unconscious
—opposition to God's Will.   But we do struggle against
it, we do resist ; and so long as that resistance endures
we cannot be at peace.   Peace, and even joy, are quite
compatible with a great deal of pain—even mental pain
—but never with a condition of antagonism or resistance.
The saints have always sought to will what God willed
only, and their whole spiritual structure has been built
on that foundation.   St. Paul says that patience perfects
spiritual work ; and hoping even where there seems no
hope, we must say with Job, "Though He slay me, yet
will I trust in Him."

Even when it seems lawful to change our position,
with a view to escaping from difficulties or troubles, a
thoroughly trustful, patient heart will pause long before
doing so, lest in putting aside a difficulty we also put
aside a grace.   It is well never to abandon an arduous
duty, or a post of wearing responsibility, or a troublesome
charge, until we have fairly endeavoured to be sure that
we are really fulfilling God's Will in so doing.   If any
one will take as a subject for particular examination,
how he bears, together with what is the prevailing cause

of his vexations and troubles in daily life, he will generally find that self-seeking lies at the bottom of a large proportion. The less we think of, or seek to please or flatter self, the less vexation, mortification, and disappointment will fall to our lot.

There are three manner of Crosses, it has been said, one of which we must each carry. We may not presume to aspire to the Cross of Innocence on which Christ Himself hung; we should shrink from that of the impenitent thief. Let ours be rather to seek that of the penitent thief, whereon in so brief a time he was purged from his past life of sin, and received the promise of Paradise. Only what he did in a few short hours is a life-work for us. Let us hang patiently on our cross. It is made up of all the difficulties, disappointments, anxieties, rebuffs, vexations, irritations, troubles, and heart-aches which beset the daily path of life in which God has placed us, including those which we often raise for ourselves in our hidden life; and he who patiently and meekly bears all these, saying, "It is my due," uniting his cross to that of His Master, will find pain and bitterness changed to sweetness and rest at last, and will for ever give thanks for what once seemed the troubles which marred and frustrated his ease and happiness.

XXI

The Privilege of Suffering

THE way of the Cross is not only the shortest way
to Paradise, it is also the surest, because it is the
one way by which our Father has pledged Himself to
lead us thither. Happy they who have courage to go
straight in this royal road, looking neither to the right
hand nor to the left.

All unworthy as you are, God has called you to become
a saint by means of the Cross, and there have been
moments when you could—so you felt—have accepted
whatever trial it might please Him to send. Our Lord,
entering upon His Passion, cried out, "Father, the hour
is come; glorify Thy Son." So do you say, "Lord, the
hour of trial is come in which Thou willest to give Thy
child a share in the Redeemer's glory; help me to do
and bear all with a view to eternal life and glory." Strive
to say with St. Andrew, "O sweet, O precious Cross!"
for it is of God. If it seems very heavy, strive to lighten

it by calmness and stillness. Take to yourself the consolation of knowing that you are under God's very special
protection; for it is He that thus lays it on you. Your
sanctification depends on bearing it. Do so, then, in all
trustful simplicity and quietude. Try to dwell less upon
the actual Cross than upon the Hand which lays it on
you; seek, ask earnestly, to know what He would say to
you by it, what lesson He means you to learn upon it.

Did you ever think how many temptations and faults
are averted by the little crosses of daily life; how the
graces of patience and forbearance, and sympathy and
lowliness, are fostered by the watchfulness they foster in
you? How often bodily weakness, or low spirits, or a
sense of disappointment, keep one from the mischiefs
attendant on exuberant life and energy; or poverty
from the temptations of the world; or depreciation and
coldness from those we love and wish to please, from
self-satisfaction and conceit? It is a helpful practice
sometimes at night to review the little crosses of the day
past, and to examine wherein they have been blessings.
Surely, if we knew how many graces are to be won from
our troubles, we should rather welcome than shun them
as we do. Sometimes people talk eagerly about holiness,
and their desire after sanctification; and there is often a
great deal of religious talk about ways and means of
seeking it, which somewhat savours of gossip. In truth,

there is no need to ask this or that person for new systems or nostrums; the surest way of sanctification is open to each and all of us; *i.e.* patiently to abide on our own Cross, never seeking to come down, or to put it aside until our dear Lord Himself removes it.

"Each on his narrow Cross to hang awhile."

But do not be disheartened if one Cross follows another. It does not rest with you to choose. Be sure that each cross exactly fits your need, is exactly that which to-day you need and can bear. If every day, every hope, every undertaking, seems to bring its cross; if there seems no outlet, no end, yet do not be disheartened. Let the Cross but do its work in you, embrace it readily and cheerfully, and you will find the end, the outlet, perhaps just when you least looked for it, assuredly in Paradise.

It is a great point to learn the reality of what we often say; *i.e.* that our Cross is a daily one. There would be less depression, less fretfulness, less disheartenment, among us if we kept this more in mind. If one could always accept the small vexations and worries, the petty contradictions and annoyances caused by ourselves or by others, as what we often call them conventionally —Crosses, they would mould and discipline, instead of irritating and fretting us. Some one has said, that while we owe a large sum to God, He allows us to pay in small instalments by patience under these trifling trials. Certainly the loving heart which seeks to offer all, even disappointments and vexations which touch the tenderest places, to God, will be more likely to grow in generosity of spirit than one who bears grudgingly what cannot be averted.   If we could really say, when thwarted, disappointed, or perhaps pierced through with wounded affection, "God wills it so, just that I may feel it deeply, that I may be crushed in worldly conceit or aspiration, that I may be led to put away what is becoming an occasion of sin, that I may find my true rest in Him only," the smart of the trial would be taken away, and, while feeling the wound, we should dwell chiefly on its healing result.   Some temperaments are naturally antagonistic, and these need a longer, stronger discipline than those more constitutionally plastic; but they too will find their best tactics those of submission.

It was doubtless pleasanter to lean on Jesus' Bosom than to struggle in the isle of Patmos; but our dear Lord often prepares those He loves by the one for the other, and when we experience great comfort or sweetness in Holy Communion, or in a more than ordinarily vivid sense of His Presence, it is well to remember that this may be our preparation for some trial, and while saying, "Thy kingdom come," to mean no general distant thing, but that His Will may reign absolutely and alone in our heart, our thought, imagination, and daily life.

It is very helpful to make a habit of offering, morning by morning, the troubles of the day just beginning to our dear Lord, accepting His Will in all things, especially in all little personal trials and vexations. Some persons have found great benefit from making, when first they wake, the act taught to Mdme. de Chantal by St. Francis de Sales, accepting "all things tolerable and intolerable" for love of Christ; then at midday, a moment's inward search to see whether there has been any voluntary slackening of submission, any deliberate opposition to God's Will, any hesitation in resisting the distaste or fretfulness, the impatience or discouragement we are tempted to feel when things go contrary to our own will and likings, making a fresh resolution to go on heartily; and at night, a quick review of the day's failures for which to ask pardon and strength to go on better anew. Some such habit as this is a great check to that terrible hindrance of the spiritual life, which, terrible though it be, is so apt to steal upon many good and earnest souls— a complaining, grumbling, self-pitying habit. It is a great matter to learn to look upon troubles and trials not as simply evils. How can that be evil which God sends? And those who can repress complaints, murmurs, and peevish bemoaning—better still, the vexed feelings which beset us when those around inflict petty annoyances, slights, &c., on us—will really find that their little daily worries are turning into blessings. It is a great gift though, it must be owned, a rare one, to be able to keep silence as to the various minor troubles and vexations which beset our lives. No doubt it is a great relief to tell these to a sympathising ear ; but are we not too shy about telling them to the dear Master who despises nothing that touches His servant's welfare, and too free in pouring them out to human listeners, whose kindness may often be injudicious, and tend rather to open than heal the wound of which we complain?

One thing we need greatly to learn, is not to try and make conditions with God. We are so ready to say, "I can give up all, save this one thing or that," to cling to some earthly stay, to some self-soothing belief that blinds our eyes. We do not like to take the way of the Cross just as we are, to go, as it has been said, "cheerfully over a path strewn with red-hot coals, or at least with broken glass!" We shrink from the maxim St. Francis taught his religious, "Ask nothing and refuse nothing."

"Your crosses will be of use to you just according to the way you accept them," a spiritual guide wrote to one much harassed. "Hitherto you have spoilt everything by your fidgetiness and wavering. But even if you have altogether wasted your time from A to B, if at B God

L

gives you grace to understand His purposes, you will reach C safely, and see the gates of Paradise opening to you."

Have you ever seen a good schoolmaster, or religious, saying his office amid the din and clatter of his school undisturbed by it all in his recollection? Try to do the like amid the clouds of dust which will sometimes rise up in your soul. Do not heed them more than you can help; shake your garments, and if need be brush them well, but never dwell on the hindrance.

A great point is gained when we have learnt not to struggle against the circumstances God has appointed for us. "Do you think you are only held in His Hand when you are among roses?" it was asked of one who did not read love in a series of daily troubles. Jesus Christ could have saved the world with less suffering to His Humanity, doubtless; but He chose to give up every member, hands and feet, pierced side, thorn-crowned head, and parched mouth, to suffer. You have often meditated on these details of His Passion, and perhaps tried to think how you would imitate Him under some great and sore trial; but have you tried to apply His example to your daily life? to offer hands and feet to the nails which pierced you? to "go up to Jerusalem," knowing that scorn, and weariness, and trouble await you? Again, some think that they could bear trials which, as they say, come direct from God; but they are not willing patiently to accept such as are visibly caused by men. But surely they are fostering a delusion. Both classes of trials alike come from God, though He chooses in the first to use a human agent, and in the other to show Himself without one. If, instead of revolting at the outward form in which the trial is clothed, such persons would in spirit kneel down at the feet of their Crucified Lord, and seek patience there, they would gain greatly in nearness to Him, and in detachment from earthly ways and clingings.

People of a naturally depressed mind are apt to add considerably to their own discomfort by continually foreseeing and forecasting troubles and cares. An old north-country proverb says, "Don't cross the bridge till you come to it!" and there is plenty of good sense in the maxim. Of course there is a wise and right looking forward by which we may arm ourselves against troubles and temptations; but a constant anticipation of evils which perhaps never will come, a foreboding which takes away life and energy from the present, will simply hinder and cloud the soul, and make it timid and sad. If troublous thoughts as to the future will press, darkening a bright present, or hurrying on coming clouds, the safest thing is to offer them continually as they arise to God, offering too the future which they contemplate, and asking for grace to concentrate our energies on the im-

mediate duties surrounding us. Many a one has dreaded
troubles which they thought must come ; and while they
went on ever expecting to make the turn in their path
which was to open out fully the evil, lo ! they found that
they had reached the journey's end, and were at the
haven where they would be. Who among us but has
good cause to say—

> " So long Thy power hath blest me, sure it still
>   Will lead me on."

Even for others it is not wise to indulge in overmuch
looking forward in fearfulness. Come what may to the
dearest ones we have on earth, God and His upholding
grace will be there, and He cares for them more than
even we can do. An earnest commendation to His love
will avail them more than all our fretting.

" Unquestionably your future looks very dark and
sad," a guide of souls writes to one much cast down,
" but we have no choice as to the nature of our trials.
He Who prepares them for each with wise and merciful
purpose must be adored in His impenetrable wisdom.
After all, provided we reach our true home at last, what
matters it how we journeyed thither?

> " ' When the shore is gained at last,
>   Who would count the billows past ?'

The position in which your Lord has placed you affords
precisely the means of grace and of succour adapted to

the duties, troubles, and difficulties which meet you there.
Give yourself up trustfully to God's Providence, which will
require nothing of you for which He does not provide
means. It is your part to ask and desire habitually that
His Holy Will may be fulfilled in you, and through you, for
those you love. However perplexing the way may seem
now, rest satisfied that He will gradually unravel so much
of it as you need from day to day, in order to follow His
leading. You will never be really left without guidance.
These trials are to you the royal road of the Cross; let
each one be to you as a station at which you prostrate
yourself in humble adoration of your Father's Will. The
last station will be heaven's very gate, and there you will be
able to joy over your patient, faithful, quiet journey. If
the path be sometimes dim, be like the little child, who,
half-frightened in a twilight walk, clutches convulsively
at its father's hand for protection. Consent freely that
your wishes, thoughts, intentions, affections, all that is in
you and of you, be reduced to the proportions of the
cross chosen for you by God; for it is thus only that
you can be made one with Christ, and in such oneness
with Christ Crucified you will find strength, light, comfort,
and cure for all your doubts and difficulties; your heart's
sore places will be soothed and healed. Fix your eyes
on Him hidden beneath the Sacramental veil, and be
strong in the assurance that these troubles, bravely borne

now, will be your great joy hereafter. He is looking lovingly upon you. Strive to keep yourself in an attitude of entire resignation, and for that end do not scruple to pour out to Him all the heaviness, and even bitterness, which in spite of yourself floods your heart, and He will give you a strength you never dreamt of. There are things sorely trying, almost unbearable, to human nature; but nevertheless our heavenly Father is both a good and tender Father. His powerful arm, and above all His tender love, will never fail you. 'Sufficient unto the day is the evil thereof.' Hope against hope, like Abraham; and while you take all reasonable means that are in your power, rest trustfully in His Bosom Who cares for the very sparrows. That was how the saints endured. Do you the like."

To one greatly beset with troubles the following short rules were given :

"When suddenly surprised by a trial, take your crucifix, and kiss it with a generous, joyful intention of heart.

" In very trying moments, pray and wait.

"When much pre-occupied and agitated, think of the peace promised to 'men of goodwill.'

"Accept the distress in submission to God's Will, and resist giving way to sorrowful thoughts. Do not argue with them, but cut them short, and say, ' I will only what Thou wilt.'

"Give yourself up anew into your dear Lord's Hands, not only for the present occasion, but for your whole life, and be certain that His grace will not fail you. Be stedfast in fulfilling your duties, and patiently wait till He gives what you need."

It has been said that the trial "bitterest to the lip of pride" is—

"When friendship scorns us, duly tried;"

and probably nothing is so hard to bear as disappointment or misapprehension in those we love. Yet an old spiritual writer has said this is a veritable mine of graces. Probably he means that such disappointments offer a large field for self-surrender, for giving up and crushing out self-assertions and self-conceits, for learning lessons of detachment, and freeing the soul from the cobwebs or nets which undue earthly affections are so apt to smother us with. It is cruel work, no doubt, to find ourselves less loved or cherished than we looked for, to feel our affection unreturned, or at least coldly met, to meet with ingratitude or (perhaps worse still) unconscious indifference, from those for whom we have poured out our heart's best treasure. But let us sit down awhile beneath the olive-trees of Gethsemane, or kneel before the Altar whereon our dear Lord's Body has lain, and the sting at least will be taken from our wound. Let us think of the ten cleansed lepers, of whom one only cared to thank

the Healer; of the young man who, though loved by
Jesus, turned away because he loved the world better;
of Judas betraying, St. Peter denying; of the disciples,
"every one," forsaking Him, and ask ourselves if He
cannot truly sympathise with wounded hearts whose
affections are ill requited.

There are some natures to whom earthly attachments
—albeit of the purest, holiest kind—are a peril. Their
strong clingings become too engrossing; idols are made
without meaning it; the intensified devotion, which is
God's due only, is offered to a lower object; and there
must be a rending asunder of ties which are full of
danger, if full of sweetness. But the idols are of clay;
and not unfrequently it is through what we call their
indifference, or ingratitude, or failure that the loving
Master, Who will have an undivided service, loosens the
earthly chains, gradually detaches us from all these
hindrances, and disperses the mists which have arisen
between the soul and Himself. Then He lovingly
draws the aching, sorrowful heart to Him, bidding it
taste and see whether He is not able to fill every void.
Surely it is a wonderful token of His Love for us when
He vouchsafes to speak of Himself as jealous. We all
know what an unsatisfied, craving passion jealousy is;
how it cannot bear the beloved one to bestow any
proofs of affection on others; how it would fain absorb

him entirely. And this is what our God deigns to say He is towards us.

It has been said that "women revel in sorrow, and feed upon it; but this is not Christian-like. God sends trials to train us in courage and generosity, not that we should let ourselves be crushed by them. People are fond of recounting their troubles, and thereby of fostering them; but they should put their fancies in quarantine, and sacrifice this self-indulgence to an effort after self-conquest. Imagination is a great hindrance to piety; indeed, it is one of the greatest dangers of our day. It attacks faith in one, practice in another. Be sure that feeling is worth absolutely nothing in devotion. You think yourself half-way to Heaven in the morning, because you have shed some tears; but you have no vigour in self-government, and at night you are still far away from the desired bourne. You would gain more by offering the disagreeable common-place duties of your life as they arise to God, and by resolving never to dwell in complacent self-pity on your trials. Without some dark days you will never reach Paradise."

It is a good rule to make for yourself, to speak rarely of your trials and troubles, save to God. To Him we may safely pour them out as fully as we will; but we rarely enlarge upon them to our earthly listeners without a large amount of self-seeking, exaggeration, and, it may be, self-complacent vanity. The compassion and sympathy which we exact is often really only a way of seeking praise and flattery in a less overt form, which deceives both ourselves and others. We sometimes see gentle, amiable people who really live upon this sort of perpetual plaintive moan, which inevitably weakens their spiritual tone day by day. How much better if they would try to "possess their souls in patience," to speak and look cheerfully, instead of with a pathetic depression which wearies others and injures themselves, and is—though they mean it not doubtless—a sort of perpetual murmur against God.

There are times and seasons when every one is liable to feel cold and spiritless towards God Himself, almost irritable, it may be. At such times what we want is not so much to make acts of faith as of obedience. "Behold the handmaid of the Lord; be it unto me according to Thy Will," is the safest prayer then.

Or perhaps you are fretting because you do not know how best to stir within the crucible where your Lord has cast you? Why should you fret? Lie perfectly still, and trust to His loving Providence. It is a great point to learn how, when we have done our plain duty in any set of circumstances, to rest quietly, and leave all results to God. There is only one really great trouble—not to love Him entirely.

"God has separated you from ——, and has allowed —— to grow cold towards you" (one versed in the spiritual life writes to a friend); "but be thankful. He is beginning your interior education. Let Him alone; He knows what you require. You fancied yourself very clever, very intelligent; you were full of self-satisfaction. And all this is bad; it is a crumbling wall. Let God overthrow it, and then with His grace build again in holiness. Accept the coldness of your near relations as your share in the cross of Christ. It is a path by which He leads many; tread it with humility and confidence, and you will gain strength. When God allows our natural ties to fail us, He does it in order to set us more free for Himself; and the sense of His love should overpower all else. Try not only to bear, but to prize, this heart's exile. You cannot help feeling impulses of sensitiveness and of self-love; but you will triumph over them by offering them to God. Not that you can do this of yourself; no supernatural graces can ever come of self."

Those seasons when we are wounded by the coldness of earthly friends are very precious, if used to forward detachment and a more entire devotion to God. In His love and holy jealousy He scatters thorns about our path that we may the more turn to Him for help and safety. The dove sent forth during the deluge was forced back to the ark, because she found no resting-place on the earth; and even so God lets us be surrounded with such circumstances as force us to turn to Him. Otherwise, if we met with entire satisfaction in our earthly relationships, we should rest content in them, and not look on to Him.

Some persons are very much more impressionable than others; and this fact tells both ways. Such people are more easily hindered; but, on the other hand, they have more to push them forward when the impressions offered are good. Impressionable people are apt to experience seasons of very great loneliness and desolation; and then there is no remedy, save in striving to unite all such trials with His Who trod the winepress alone, Who was so "sorely wounded in the house of His friends."

In all seasons of suffering—mental or bodily—it is a great help to try and dwell only upon the hour actually present. Bear or act for the best as in God's Sight for to-day, and leave to-morrow's cares absolutely to Him. They may never come in the shape you now imagine them; or if they do they will bring with them their own peculiar strengthening grace, which does not attend their contemplation to-day. Remember the fable of the discontented pendulum, calculating how many million times it had to tick, and striking work in despair, until the wiser dial-plate reminded it that at no time more than a second actually exists, and it had only to tick once in each second.

XXII

Cheerfulness

ST. FRANCIS DE SALES used to say that the greatest evil next to sin was sadness; and he never tired of teaching that all true piety is gentle and calm, but withal bright and cheerful. He had no patience with drooping, plaintive, depressed Christians, holding such to be ungrateful servants of a gracious Master, who loves a cheerful, happy service. In one of his letters he tells the "dear soul seeking God," to whom he is writing, that she is always so flurried, so troubled, that no wonder she never finds her way right. "You are always retracing your steps, catching yourself by your clothes, your hair, everything," he says.

He could not bear the fretful, scrupulous spirit which consumes itself in petty griefs and apprehensions; the minds which, as the Archbishop of Rheims says, "seem to fancy that in order to be religious they must needs be bandaged up like an Egyptian mummy, and are restrained and timid in their every movement like a person walking on pins."

St. Teresa used to tell her daughters that God is not so little-minded as they seemed to think, and that they would not serve Him well if they were fidgety and fretful in their efforts. "To walk cheerfully and freely in God's service" was her favourite advice. People who are always giving way to petty fears and scruples, and to infinite regrets, because they have done something that may perhaps be amiss, seldom grow in holiness; they fall again and again into the same faults over which they make their moan, and too often seem to think that their dismal looks and words are a sort of make-weight.

St. Francis advised people who were given to fret over scruples to treat all such first of all with contempt, nothing being so good a cure for a certain class of evils as letting them drop unnoticed. When you are disturbed by temptations, despise them. If people say hard things of you, or cast sly stones at you, why should you pick them up and put them in your pocket? Go home with empty hands, and when you have reached your own fireside, you will find that never a one hit you. Or your thoughts are buzzing about and hindering you: do not heed them. If you make a fuss, they will only beset you the more; rather try to seem unconscious of them;

remain at the foot of the Cross awhile, and you will wake as from a bad dream, and find them gone.

The saint used to tell how one day, walking in a garden where there were hives, the bees surrounded him, and he was about to try and drive them away. But an old peasant, who was near, bade him beware; because if he got excited the bees would pursue him, whereas if he let them alone they would soon leave him alone. And according to his wont, he saw a parallel in this to some of our spiritual troubles.

St. Francis and St. Teresa were of one mind as to what the latter used to call "holy melancholy;" and it is certainly in their spirit altogether that Faber asks, in his quaint fashion, "Was ever a melancholy man made into a saint?" "A downcast man," the same writer says, "is raw material, which can only be manufactured into a very ordinary Christian." It may sound at first a hard doctrine, but nevertheless it is true, that these melancholy, doleful people are rarely charitable in their judgments of others; they are generally stiff and unbending, and see everything through crape spectacles, tinted darkly. Wanting in geniality themselves, they measure their neighbours by themselves, and become (unintentionally perhaps) censorious. If good people would only study to make their religion attractive and winning, instead of angular and oppressive, how much

more good they might do. And, as a rule, kindness and
unselfish delight in the happiness of others are found
most active among cheerful people. "Her ways are
ways of pleasantness;" and I emphatically deny that
pleasantness can, under the most liberal interpretation,
be made to mean gloominess or melancholy. How
many persons have been driven back and repulsed by the
unattractive, sullen, grumpy, or tediously mournful manners of "good" people among whom they have been
thrown! Mgr. Landriot gives an apt illustration of this.
"Supposing," he says, "that your own mother had died
before your remembrance, but that you had formed a
most attractive ideal of her from all you had heard of
her sweetness, beauty, and goodness. Some one offers
to show you a photograph of her, and you eagerly accept
the proposal; but lo! when it appears it is so black and
blurred, so ugly and unattractive, that you draw back
with positive pain and disgust. Is this not what many
pious people do? They are commissioned to set forth
the image described by our Lord when He said, 'Be
perfect, as your Father in Heaven is perfect;' but the
copy which they produce has woefully little resemblance
to the original."

"Be cheerful, easy, affable, without timidity or shy-
ness," Fénélon wrote: "Ask God to help you to
conquer your shrinking, artificial manner; offer yourself

to God when you mix among people, but do not be dreamy and abstracted in society through attempting to keep up a consciousness of His Presence, which seems always slipping away; rather do what He would have you do, that is, be amiable and courteous. In course of time you will find it easier to keep up the lively sense of God's Presence. Do not try to seem pious by the help of a gloomy, constrained seriousness. 'Where the Spirit of God is, there is liberty.' If once you love Him with all your heart, you will always be cheerful, and your heart will always be free; but if you seek Him in a judaizing spirit of fear, you will not find Him, but you will find restraint and gloom. I would have you always innocently cheerful; for cheerfulness is very good both for body and soul."

And Madame Swetchine, who certainly made her religion attractive and loveable, says, "Let us try to be happy, as the best and most expressive homage to Him we love. Christians are too apt to forget that they owe to others not merely the example of goodness, but that of happiness. Why cannot we always preach Christ in the way which every one is sure to understand?"

The Archbishop of Reims, teaching an assemblage of women, tells them that if they are really religious, they ought to supply a large stock of comfort and brightness to their respective households. Prayer, Celebrations,

M

devout practices, union with God, ought so to fill the
hearts of those privileged to use them with joy, that it
should overflow upon all around, and bring cheerfulness
and happiness wherever they go. "It is a great error,"
says the Archbishop, "to suppose that the saints have
been dismal, above all as a consequence of sanctity.
Some among them may have had to contend against
constitutional depression, and have resisted it earnestly;
but in itself, holiness is what doctors call exhilirating;
i.e. joyous, and exciting joy."

It is very hard to some natures to be always cheerful,
especially to those sensitive temperaments which rise and
fall, barometer-like, with the influences of sunshine and
east wind, whether material or moral; for how intensely
east windy some people are! Yet this sensitiveness is not
a fault, if struggled against; rather an additional means of
seeking and serving God. Listen to Eugénie de Guérin,
that most loveable and attractive (albeit confessed a
trifle sad) woman: "I am not in the humour for writing,
or anything else amiable to-day, quite the reverse. There
are days when the soul shrinks into its shell, or puts out
its hedgehog prickles. Even prayer wearies me. This
is sad work. Happily though I remembered Fénélon's
saying, 'If God wearies you, tell Him that is is so.'
And I have told Him my folly very thoroughly!"

Cheerfulness is marvellously infectious. A bright,

happy soul, rejoicing in all God's gifts, seeing cause for thankfulness and gladness in everything, counting up mercies rather than trials, looking at the bright side, even of sickness, bereavement, and death—what a very fountain of goodness and love of Christ such an one is! I remember one who, worn with sickness and sleepless nights, answered to the question if the nights did not seem interminable? "Oh no, I lie still and count up my blessings!" That was surely worth many sermons on thankfulness, just as Mgr. Landriot says that those persons who are always even and calm in their brightness and holy joy (a character which is sure also to possess that "graceful courtesy which," as he says, "is the true perfection of an evangelic mind") are for ever preaching Christ, and drawing their neighbours to God, as by a heavenly loadstone. Such "holy joy" has indeed a very communicative property, and no wonder, inasmuch as it is a peace which comes because those in whom we find it are "stayed on God."

St. Bonaventura says, that he who possesses the grace of cheerfulness prays better than those who are sad, and is more readily united to the Holy Spirit of God, which is a spirit of joy; because like ever draws to like.*

* "Cor liberum et benevolentia jucundum aptius est ad devotionis gratiam recipiendum, quam tristitia et amaritudine constrictum: quia Spiritus Sanctus amor est, et benevolentia et jucunditas Patris, et similia similibus magis gaudent naturaliter."

"The voice of joy is praise. . . . Happiness is the temper of holiness, and if the voice of patient anguish is praise to God, much more is the clear voice of happiness, a happiness that fastens not on created things, but is centred in Himself. . . . They, whose sunshine is from Him Who is within them, worship God brightly, out of a blessedness which the world cannot touch, because it gushes upwards from a sanctuary which lies too deep for rifling. Sadness is a sort of spiritual disability. A melancholy man can never be more than a convalescent in the house of God. He may think much of God, but he worships very little. . . . There is no moral imbecility so great as that of querulousness and sentimentality. Joy is the lifelong morning of our souls, an habitual sunrise, out of which worship and heroic virtue come. . . . To the happy man all duties are easy; but he who lies down at full length on life, as if it were a sick-bed, poor languishing soul, what will he ever do for God!"

One more quotation, so beautiful that it needs no apology: "As under every stone there is moisture, so under every sorrow there is joy; and when we come to understand life rightly, we see that sorrow is after all but the minister of joy; we dig into the bosom of sorrow to find the gold and precious stones of joy. Sorrow is a condition of time, but joy is the condition of eternity.

All sorrow lies in exile from God, all joy lies in union with Him. In Heaven joy will cast out sorrow, whereas there is not a lot on earth from which sorrow has been altogether able to banish joy. Joy clings to us as the creatures of God. It adheres to us wherever we go. Its sunshine lights upon us, and gives us some sort of attractiveness above that which is our own. Joy hangs about everything which God has had to do with. . . There is an inevitable joyousness about all that belongs to God. There are souls in the world which have the gift of finding joy everywhere, and of leaving it behind them when they go. Joy gushes from under their fingers like jets of light. There is something in their very presence, in their mere silent company, from which joy cannot be extricated and laid aside. Their influence is an inevitable gladdening of the heart. It seems as if a shadow of God's own gifts had passed upon them. They give light without meaning to shine. . . . Somehow, too, all the joy turns to God. Without speaking of Him, it preaches Him. Its odour is as the odour of His Presence. It leaves tranquillity behind, and not unfrequently sweet tears of prayer. All things grow silently Christian under its reign. It brightens, ripens, softens, transfigures, like the sunlight, the most improbable things which come within its sphere. A single gifted heart like this is the apostle of its neighbourhood. Every one acknowledges its divine right,

which it never thinks of claiming. There is no need to
claim it; for none resists its unconquerable gentleness.
Joy is like a missioner who speaks of God; sorrow is a
preacher who frightens men out of the deadliness of sin
into the arms of their Heavenly Father, or who weans
them by the pathos of his reasoning from the dangerous
pleasures of the world. These bright hearts are more
like the first than the second. They have a great work
to do for God, and they do it often when they realise it
least. It is the breath they breathe, and the star they
were born under, and the law which encircles them.
They have a light within them which was not delusive
when they were young, and which age will only make
more golden without diminishing its heat. To live with
them is to dwell in a perpetual sunset of unboisterous
mirth and placid gaiety. Who has not known such souls?
Who has not owed all that is best in him, after grace, to
such as those? Happy is he who had such for the
atmosphere of his parental home. Its glory may have
sunk below the horizon, but he himself will be illuminated
by its glow until the hour comes for his own pensive
setting. Of a truth he is the happiest, the greatest, and
the most god-like of men, as well as the sole poet among
men, who has added one true joy to the world's stock of
happiness."*

* FABER'S *Bethlehem*, p. 424.

XXIII.

Order and Quiet in Daily Life

ST. THOMAS says that God moves all things, because He is Himself immovable. All our ideas of perfect work imply stability and order; yet how many of us act as though hurry and bustle, restlessness of mind and body, anxiety and over-eagerness, were the atmosphere of prosperous work! People undertake six times as much as they can perform, and then do less than they really could accomplish, because they waste so much time and force in talk, unnecessary excitement, and want of deliberate method. The old maxim, that "whatever is worth doing at all is worth doing well," has a mine of wisdom in it; and the resolution which saints have made, "to do everything in the most perfect way," will apply to all the common daily duties of an ordinary life as well as to the most exalted spiritual career.

Without wishing to adopt Talleyrand's celebrated precept, "Surtout, point de zèle!" we can most of us look

back into our own lives and see how many failures we have
made, not so much through lack of good-will or energy
as through hurry and want of consideration. Plans for
our own improvement, or the benefit of others, have
dwindled to nothing, because we hurried them on with
a hot haste; good resolutions died away or came to
nothing, thanks to the impetuous eagerness with which
we began, not considering how we should go on; and
then we grew cold through disappointment both with
ourselves and others, and losing zest, slackened our
efforts and fell back, or changed to some fresh object
of pursuit, doomed to a like failure. On the other hand,
sometimes we have succeeded beyond our hopes, and
when we examine, half astonished, into the success which
seems to us scarcely warranted by our efforts, we find
that it is mainly due to the quiet, unobtrusive exertions
of some one else, who we perhaps despised for his
seeming passivity, or we discover that we are indebted
for a favourable result more to what we did not than to
what we did do. Vigorous, energetic natures need so
continually to remind themselves that, let them sow and
water as they will, God alone can give the increase, and
that we are safest when leaving Him to steer the vessel,
content ourselves to ply our own oar steadily. Once out
of breath, we can make but little way running.

It is curious to trace, all through St. Francis de Sales'

life and writings, his continued warfare against "empresse-
ment;" *i.e.* over-eagerness and impetuous haste.* Yet
certainly no one would accuse him of torpor or inactivity, mental or bodily. The *Devout Life* is full of
teaching of this kind. "The care and diligence which
we are bound to give to business are very different from
anxious, fretting eagerness. Care and anxious solicitude
are widely different. The angels are careful for our
salvation, and seek it diligently; but assuredly they are
altogether free from anxiety and restlessness in its pursuit. All over-eagerness perplexes reason and judgment,
and hinders us in the very matters which excite it."

* The very last time that St. Francis ever saw Mdme. de Chantal
in this life, he observed that they had two or three hours to spend
together, and as there were many subjects both desired to discuss,
asked her which should speak first. Mdme. de Chantal, longing
for the guidance she prized above all earthly blessings, exclaimed
eagerly that she must begin, as there were many things concerning
her soul which greatly needed the Bishop's consideration. "What,
still so eager?" was the reply she met with. "No, we will not
begin to talk of you yet; we will talk about our congregation."
And for four hours they did talk business, and poor Mdme. de
Chantal never again enjoyed the privilege she so craved for, of
laying all her troubles and perplexities before the beloved guide of
her soul; for a few days later, and he had passed from this life!
But who can believe that she was the loser for her obedience, or
that her saintly director hindered her perfection by what must have
cost any human, sensitive woman's heart so dear?

In one of his letters, St. Francis describes a person soured and embittered by constant failure, irritable, depressed with an intellectual and moral miasma. "Dear soul" (he represents himself saying), "what ails you?" And the other replies, "'Just look at my past life; I have exhausted myself, and succeeded in nothing; everything has failed, and thwarted me.' To which I lovingly make answer, 'Suffer a friend to offer a timely warning. It is because you have so exhausted yourself that nothing has succeeded. You marvel that, having done so much, you should have accomplished nothing. But the doing so much is the reason of your failure. If you had done less, acted more deliberately, with less noisy effort, perhaps the work would have grown up almost spontaneously around you. As it is, you have lived in a continuous whirlwind, which has blasted your work and your heart alike.'"

Preaching to a congregation of ladies on the example of Mary and Martha, Mgr. Landriot says: "Pious listener, I fancy I see in you a Martha. You are in perpetual motion; you are for ever moving everything around you—furniture, people, affairs; and if by chance your hands and feet are quiet for an hour, then your tongue takes up the charge, and upsets one, worries another, fidgets every one near you, from garret to cellar. 'It is all well meant!' I hear you exclaim, with scarce

repressed impatience. Very likely. Nevertheless I must
repeat it, You are so many Marthas, and you are
damaging both yourselves and your work. If you were
merely careful, I should have nothing to say. In that
case you would not excite yourself so much, and things
would go on better. Try to be in your own household
what God is in the midst of His creation, the moving
Spirit, Himself immovable. If you can preserve your
own heart and mind in stability, you will soon see everything altered—all around will be still, orderly, regular, if
you are—and just when you seem to be doing nothing,.
everything will prosper. . . . What is done in a hurry is
rarely well done. . . . For instance, if you try to make your
self-examination in restless anxiety, the more you hurry
on the more confused you will grow. Set to work quietly;
handle your conscience as a book which you would take
up calmly, and a few minutes will suffice to read all you
want to know. Again, when preparing for your meditation, if instead of recollecting yourself with a loving
tranquillity, you grow excited about how you shall set
to work, you will disperse your thoughts, and make such
a turmoil and mist within, that your soul is stifled and
knows not what to do. Or supposing that some important, some troublesome matter arises in your household. If you know how to maintain your self-possession,
how to go carefully, but without being excited, into the

matter, probably the whole thing may be quietly settled in a short time. But if you belong to the company of Marthas, and begin to talk, and fidget, and fume, things soon grow worse and worse—yourself first, and then the matter in hand."

We are all ready to grant that those people who are most profuse in their expressions of sympathy, and most lavish in their endearments, are not generally the most really affectionate or truest of friends. St. Francis (who is for ever employing similes taken from his favourite bees) says that the drones, who make no honey, are far more noisy and restless than the working bee ; and certainly most people's experience tends to prove that those who say most do least. Doubtless it is not easy, when pressed on all sides with duties and responsibilities—sometimes, it may be, conflicting duties —to fulfil them all quietly and without excitement ; but, at all events, it is harder to fulfil them amid bustle and confusion of mind and body ; and the person who can take one thing at a time, and quietly do his best, will have a better chance of disentangling the ravelled mass than one who tears wildly through the confusion, adding at every plunge to the existing difficulties.

It is so hard—who does not know it ?—to be quiet and gentle, composed and restful, when everything seems in a whirl around us ; when perplexity, and annoyance, and

discomposure seem to lurk in every corner. Well, but
then life *is* hard; and the path by which we have to
pass through it to a blessed eternity of joy and rest is
both a narrow and a steep one, beset with many prickles
and sharp, jagged rocks. The question is, Cannot we
better travel along it if we go slowly and carefully,
avoiding the prickles and the rocks, than if we rush
headlong, catching at every instant on some unforeseen
obstacle, and drawing hastily back with a wound or
rent? Those who have never tried it will hardly imagine
how much influence a calm exterior has upon all this
mental whirl and worry. I remember hearing a Bishop,
who had toiled more than most men through a long and
incessantly busy life, say, "*I learnt long ago to sit still.*"
One who can sit still calmly and without impatience
through vexatious delays; through wearisome inconse-
quential talk which yet it were unkind to cut hastily
short; through tedious narratives and details which must
be sifted to get at some really weighty matter—such an
one has surely gone several steps towards the victory
which King Solomon says is greater than taking a city;
viz., ruling his spirit. It is told of the mother of a great
statesman, that in her early training she used to teach
the little son for whom her ambition craved a mighty
future to sit still daily for a time, doing nothing and
controlling all restless, fidgety movements. Well, perhaps

in these busy days some will quarrel with the suggestion of learning to do nothing; but even they will grant that in spiritual things we have to learn to "be still" in God's Hands.   And those who have the body in such control that it *can* be still are more likely than others to have the soul likewise in hand.   How many hasty speeches, and breaches of love, and rash conclusions would have been avoided, if the perpetrators could have "sat still" until the first eager impulse to say or do the word or deed that bursts forth was checked?

Once more to quote St. Francis: "Ah, well! we shall soon have entered upon eternity, and then we shall see how trifling all these worldly matters are, and how little it mattered whether they succeeded or not.   Yet now we fret and fume over them as very weighty matters. When we were little, how eagerly we used to collect bits of wood, and clay, and brick, and make our baby-houses and sheds; and if any one overthrew them we wept and lamented sore.   Now we know that they were little worth.   It will be even so one day in Heaven, when we shall perceive that what we clung to so much in this world were mere baby-houses.   I do not want to deny due attention to these trifling concerns; for God has given them to us as duties in this life; but I do want to deny them an eager, restless attention.   Let us attend to our childish matters, since we are children; but do not

let us be childishly absorbed in them, or be too much
perturbed when our baby-houses are overthrown. When
eventide comes, we must go home, and leave our play;
we elder children must go to our Father's house. Be
'patient, then—patient with others, patient with yourself."

XXIV.

Inward Difficulties

IT is not very uncommon to hear persons who are anxious to advance in a really spiritual life say, " I could bear with all these outer trials, if only I had not such an endless succession within, which I know I make for myself!" We feel irritable and unamiable, we weary of prayer, we are tempted to turn away, half-loathing our rules and the salutary discipline with which we have surrounded ourselves.

But there is comfort to be found under these trying and—let us say it fairly—these humiliating conditions. In the first place it is perhaps some comfort to know that very few who are really training in the spiritual life altogether escape such trials; and that because, sharp as they are to bear, they are most powerful in moulding the character and leading it in the ways of self-renunciation and humility. It is so easy to become self-satisfied when all is smooth and well within us, so tempting to turn our rightful thanksgivings into " I thank Thee that I am not

as other men are;" and then comes the spiritual pride
which is such a fatal bar to all spiritual progress. But
interior troubles keep the soul "low," and if, instead of.
fretting against them, irritated because we are irritable,
cross because we feel unamiable, distracted because our
thoughts wander, we would humble ourselves before God,
and accept the trial as a corrective; it would turn to
blessing most assuredly, and we should go on, it might
be in twilight, but certainly not in utter darkness.

One of the most painful of these trials is when we are
so beset that we lose, or fancy that we lose, the power
of answering them in faith; and when our belief seems
to die down, or be coldly thrown back upon us; when our
footing appears all uncertain, clouds hide the mountain
tops to which we were fain to look for our strength,
books, offices, devotions, thoughts which once seemed
to inspire us with fortitude and happiness untold, fall
tame and lifeless before us. "Where is the blessedness
which once we spake of?" is the only utterance which
fits our need. The very recollection of what has been
only seems to make the present state of things worse;
for surely, we say, we cannot have rightly corresponded
to God's grace or it would not be thus with us. Surely
He, finding us altogether unprofitable servants, has for-
saken us, and those warm sungleams of His favour will
never return!

N

Of a truth, these are trying hours; yet it may be some faint consolation to know that nearly all who have set their faces steadily Heavenwards have met with such in one shape or another. And saints have recorded their sorrows, and the course God set before them, either directly or through His ministering servants, to help us on our toilsome way. The substance of their experience seems to be:

First, seek physical calm and quiet. "Wait on the Lord." When you feel utterly cold, chilled to the marrow, lie still at the dear Master's Feet; look up, though you cannot see His Face; hearken, though no sound meets your ear. That same gracious countenance which beamed on the thirty-five-year sufferer at the pool of Bethesda is turned on you, though you have not waited thirty-five years; and the same voice which asked of him, "Wilt thou be made whole?" is asking the like of you. "It is I, be not afraid." "Blessed are they that mourn, for they shall be comforted."

Next, try to avoid an excessive introspection. Rather dwell upon the thought of God than of yourself. Take it for granted that you are all-weak, and He all-powerful; that you will fall, and He lift you up. Accept the shame and pain as your natural lot; remember that most of what troubles you is your own doing, all that uplifts and comforts you, God's doing; think of yourself as a block of marble being hewn and chiselled by Him, and say to yourself, that even this cloud, icy and dark as it now is, will pass away, and the sunshine of His conscious Love will again gladden you.

It is to be noted how, when Jesus appeared with His Resurrection Body to His disciples, giving them His blessing of peace, He showed them the wounds in His Hands and Feet,* as though to impress on them how it was through suffering that He had entered into His glory, and to strengthen them to pass by the like road.

But, some will say, It is the uncertainty which is so hard to bear. I could bear any clouds, any darkness, if I only knew for certain that it was God's discipline, and that He was behind the cloud, shining in His Love, and ready to beam anew upon me.

Surely such may paraphrase for themselves Thomas à Kempis's words, and say, "What should I do if I did know all this for certain?" together with the answer, "Do now what thou wouldest do then, and thou shalt be secure."† Uncertainty, or more correctly speaking a sense of uncertainty, may be the penance laid on us now for self-complacency, or for carelessness and recklessness. All masters of the spiritual life agree in saying that it is not well to be perpetually investigating our own standpoint, or seeking to know precisely where we are;

* St. Luke xxiv. 40. † *De Imitatione Christi*, bk. i. c. xxv.

simplicity, meekness, and trust, all suffer from such over-anxious research, and the trusting soul knows that it is *never* left alone. "Where wert Thou, Lord," St. Catherine of Sienna asked, "when I was so sorely tempted?" And her loving Master replied, "I was close beside thee, my child, beholding thy struggles for the love of Me."

There is probably more of self, and of a craving for ease and satisfaction in all this class of troubles, than we always like to admit to ourselves, otherwise we should readily grant that a journey through a disturbed country must be full of accidents and vexations; we should not be astonished, as it has been said, to find the sky dark at midnight, and we should spend our energies more on trying to get right than on bemoaning ourselves because we have got wrong. Sometimes it is very hard to come even to Holy Communion, feeling so dead, and cold, and dark, that we cannot, or think we cannot, make an act of faith, love, or contrition, or a resolution, save as a purely mechanical act, so lifeless that it appears almost an insult to the All-seeing One. But even so, let us go on calmly. He sees it all, and He knows and understands us better than we do. At such a time it is a help to ask oneself, What does God really require of me in all these acts? To go to Him, to try and do all for Him, and because He wills it. Very well, then I will go on, and do all I ought simply and patiently, whether I find any pleasure in it or not, and leave the rest to Him. He knows what I mean.

There is no true humility without trust and confidence. Nothing so promotes the devil's work as when he can make the soul anxious and untrustful; it is his surest way of hindering it from God.

Sometimes, when inward difficulties and hindrances beset one, it is a help to take each duty as it comes, no matter how trifling, with a definite resolution to do it for God's sake, and not look any further. Thus, I will say this office as reverently and attentively as I can; I will write this letter as carefully as I am able; I will fulfil these uninteresting little household duties, or these dull social claims to the very best of my power, because God gives them me to do; and what am I that I should expect Him to give me greater or more acceptable work?

Mental fatigue sometimes puts an iron lock upon all warm and (as we think) profitable thought. We read, or listen, or follow our usual devotions, knowing that the treasure is there, but unable to make it in any sense our own. Well, it is surely a great thing to know so much as that; and however formal and lifeless the prayer may seem, do not neglect to pray that you may have eyes to see as soon as such sight will help you. An office said, or a meditation made thus, will not be lost.

And it is well to remember, that unless we exercise
some discipline over thoughts and imagination at ordinary times, we shall hardly be able to bring them into
thorough control at seasons of special prayer. The
mind which is suffered to wander habitually from all its
daily work will assuredly wander in prayer; and so we
work round again to the need of an always re-collected
spirit.

XXV.

Fretfulness

WHO has not felt that it is much harder not to be vexed and irritable about trifles than about greater things? A great trouble can be met; but the endless succession of petty worries which beset many lives are the real cause of pettishness, loss of temper, hasty speeches, fretfulness, and so sometimes to a general declension of the spiritual life, till we are tempted to think that God's grace is no longer with us, and we become disheartened. . Perhaps if we look in we shall find that there is something of pride in all this. It is trying, when we have built up a showy though unsubstantial fabric of our own to perceive so many weak points in it; trying to find the beauty of our picture of self marred by a number of what we are pleased to call insignificant trifles. The point is to try and—not escape, but—use these rightly, and so lose nothing thereby.

One rule, which has been found a great help in conquering irritability, is to make a resolution, constantly.

renewed, not to dwell on little vexations; to pass through them, so to say; to go on letting them drop on or off us, as the case may be, like a traveller amid an incommodious hailstorm, without counting, or thinking about, or complaining of each hailstone. How often one has found oneself brooding over and going back again and again to some disagreeable event, some little annoyance, or disrespect, or unkindness inflicted by others, till what really was of small weight at first has become a heavy load, and our first sense of discomposure has attained real wrath, perhaps taking shape in angry word or deed. Now a resolute putting away of such vexations in the first stage would save a great deal of pain—it may be, of sin; a determination not to dwell on the irritating matter, a firm, though not fussy, putting it away; if need be, forcing oneself to turn one's mind to something else, laying aside the occupation which suggests the cause of annoyance. Sometimes even such homely remedies as a brisk walk, an amusing book, or the like—any such measures will help in conquering the evil. Of course all these must only be used as subordinate means to the most effectual,—prayer and throwing oneself upon God. If the provoking cause of irritable feelings is to be found in those around us, in the petty jealousies and follies which will beset us as long as we are all poor earthly men and women, few remedies will be found so effectual as prayer for those who annoy us. One can hardly long feel bitter and sharp towards people for whom we pray, realising, as we must do in such prayer, that we are all children of One Father.

Another way of conquering one class of provocations to irritability and peevishness is to resist forecasting and undue dwelling on results and consequences. All these must and will depend on God's Will solely; be it ours to do what we honestly believe to be right, and then make a firm resolution not to give way to a calculating, self-tormenting spirit, but leave all to Him. It is well, especially for those whose natural temperament is down-cast and easily depressed, not to neglect little pleasures and enjoyments; to turn the eye from a vexatious quarter to the beautiful landscape or glowing flower-bed; the ear that is disposed to listen to the suggestions of evil, to the birds' sweet song, or even to the music we can make for ourselves;—above all, the heart that tends to brood over lowering earthly matters, to the boundless Love and Goodness of God, Which will supply all our need, and make up ten thousand-fold and more for all the deficiencies or disappointments caused by man. Disagreeable impressions are easily made on some sensitive, plastic minds. If you refuse all deliberate consent to them, you should not trouble any more about them. Your discomfort may be very much owing to physical causes for which you are in no wise to blame; only do not give way to it, or nurse it. Offer it to God, even if you feel as though you did so with your lips only; and avoid talking about what annoys you in others, or complaining of them. Tell God as much about it as you will, but let your annoyances be a secret to all besides, except your spiritual guide. It may be that an extra Communion made with special intention will be a great help in overcoming the painful or irritable feeling aroused. It is well to bear in mind that resolutions made with respect to any such troubles (whether before the Blessed Sacrament or in meditation) should always be for a very short time, and then renewed, if they are to be a real help. If I resolve never to give way again to my vexation or irritability concerning such and such a thing, or towards such and such persons, I am almost sure to break my resolutions at the first provocation, and then, after a few failures, I shall probably either think it useless to make resolutions only to break them, or feel so ashamed of my inconsistency, that I shall cease to make resolutions at all. But if the resolution be, *e.g.* "For this day, or for the next six hours, I will, God helping me, avoid, or do," &c., I am at once more likely to keep it, or if I fail, to take practical measures for better success another time. Sensitiveness (we all need to beware lest we confound it with touchiness) is rather a trial than a fault. Its first movements are not guilty; if offered at once to God, they become rather means of advancing in grace. But then the haunting memory which disturbs or distracts, the self-colloquy which feeds pride, the dwelling on faults or offences of others which fosters anger, all these must be resolutely put away the moment we are conscious that they are taking possession of us. Ejaculatory prayer is a very stronghold in all such troubles.

All thoughts verging on evil, whether of the class of doubting, speculative thoughts, thoughts tending to impurity or sensuality, to harsh-judgments and uncharitable opinions; whatever, in short, we feel we could not willingly lay bare to the saintly living friend, or the Guardian Angel ever watching by us, need to be resolutely and at once put away; as also many which, though not positively bad in themselves, may lead us on, as we very well know, to what will for us be evil. Those accustomed to deal with souls say, that men and women innumerable are led into sin by giving way to unchecked thoughts, castle-building, and the like.

Silence is always a virtue doubtless, but specially with respect to grievances and annoyances. We rub a gnat-bite till it swells into a lump; and we talk about an affront or a suspicion till it is inflamed and magnified beyond measure. It is often a pleasure to feel that some secret of our heart is only shared by some very

dear friend; it all lies between his soul and mine. Even
so let us try to keep our vexations and grievances a
secret between God and ourselves. As mere worldly
policy, the less we weary others with our complaints and
bemoanings, the more sympathy we are likely to get;
but silence acquires a double value when it is kept out
of a spirit of self-restraint and intention to please God.
Mortification of self by retrenching unprofitable, uncharitable, useless words, is a great matter, and would
make a most helpful discipline for many who cannot do
much in the way of Lenten abstinence. And when we
have attained (if by God's grace we may attain) to a
habit of external restraint in speech, let us go on to
restrain our imagination, and suppress those interior
dialogues and monologues in which self is generally
glorified or flattered, and charity and humility seldom
gainers. Then fewer shadows would come between our
souls and God; fewer distractions in prayer and at celebration would have to be confessed; meditation would
become easier and clearer; and we should be more
habitually able to realise and dwell in the Presence of
God.

XXVI

Faith

A FAITHFUL spirit does not necessarily imply a clear or deep insight into God's eternal truths, but rather the possession of a light bright enough to steer by through all the troubles and shadows of life, holding stedfastly to God's word. Theologians tell us that faith is really more an act of the will than an exercise of the intelligence. "My God, I believe all taught me by Thy Church, because it is through her that Thou revealest Thy truth. I submit heart and mind to Thy word." This is a real act of faith. We have light sufficient to believe what we cannot see. If we could see all that we believe, there were no call upon our faith.

A faithful spirit implies a thorough sense of dependence upon God, and a habit of seeing all things pertaining to time and to eternity in His light. Such a spirit moulds the whole life; he who possesses it will always seek first the Will of God; he will take up his cross whenever he meets it; he will mortify self-love, and close his heart to mere worldly affections, and his mind to its hollow maxims.

This spirit of faith, if acted upon throughout, will cause a rapid growth in the spiritual life. There is not a detail in our daily course which it does not touch, restraining, shaping, enlarging, stimulating, and in all things setting before us as our example Christ crucified. "God has appointed that Heaven should be reached by no other way than that of the Cross. All Christians must travel on it; only some go in carriages and some afoot. The carriage-folk break down not unfrequently, and the foot-travellers ofttimes meet with a sprain; for there is no key which will open Heaven's gates, save the Cross."

People sometimes think they have no faith, because they are not conscious of feeling it. In the beginnings of the spiritual life the soul is generally quiet and responsive to the mysteries of the faith. It seems to see and appreciate them; and doubtless this is a season of great blessing and encouragement. But in most cases it is succeeded by a mental condition, in which the appreciative glow seems gone for ever; when a dry, bare faith in dogmatic verities is all the Christian can grasp. This is the time for calm, patient abiding; not yielding to discouragement, not dwelling upon the varying shades of feeling, but stedfastly obeying the word of the Lord in the spirit of the words, "I KNOW in whom I have believed." You know that your love and confidence are given to your Master; do not be continually trying to manipulate yourself, in order to know how much you feel. Rest upon His Mercy. Every morning make an act disavowing intentional coldness or whatever can militate against your love for Him, and then do not fidget about your more or less lively feelings and emotions.

If a season comes when you appear to be unable to grasp even the very elements of the faith with any satisfying tenacity, accept the trial humbly and trustfully, wait without fretting, and it will pass in God's own time.

It is incalculable what mischief is done by a restless anxiety to be always sensible of a conscious impression of faith, grace, &c. If you try to read by firelight, and every minute poke up the fire to try to make a blaze, before long you will put it all out; and so it is with the heart. Even when we feel as if we had no solid standing ground, when clouds hide or obscure our faith, the only safe course is to go on stedfastly, holding on to the clue given us by the Church, and making acts of belief, trust, and faith, as we are able from time to time. God does not require of us an intellectual or intelligent faith, though such may be a great gift and help; but He does require an absolute, faithful submission of our will and our judgment.

It may sometimes be a help to remind ourselves that

we should not feel any distress on the subject if our
faith were really cold and dead; the very trouble itself
is a proof that our faith is sincere, although we can feel
so little. The great thing is, to give up no religious act
or duty because at that moment we have not such an
amount of feeling respecting it as we judge needful, in
other words, as makes the duty pleasant to us. Principles,
not feelings, however warm and attractive, will make
confessors of the faith.

Sometimes it is a help, amid the mists which surround
the soul, and make a clear, well-planned meditation, or
what we call a contrite confession or a devout communion, impossible, to dwell upon the veil with which
it has pleased our dear Lord to hide His own Presence
in the holy Eucharist. When a sense of flatness,
insipidity, or tastelessness comes over us, it is often well
to use some different devotions—a short litany, a fervent
hymn; some prayer used perhaps in childhood and since
laid aside, or some other connected with any special
season of past life, some holy death-bed, or great
sorrow; one of these will help us to gather up the
strings which are hanging loosely—

> " Faith for all defects supplying
> When the feeble senses fail."

St. Chrysostom somewhere says, that when God pours
His sweetness in upon our souls we are of course His

humble debtors; but when we bear dryness and weariness in full submission to His Will He becomes our
debtor, and we need never fear but that He will pay us
abundantly and above measure.

There is often more love of self than of God, it has
been said, in the constant desire some persons have to
be taking stock, so to say, of their spiritual condition,
feelings, and emotions. All such pre-occupation fixes the
soul's gaze on something lower than its rightful aim, and
dries up the source of living faith and trust. After all,
how everything works back to the old story—LESS OF SELF,
AND MORE OF GOD. More dwelling on His trustworthi-
ness than on our own mistrust, more energy in giving
our will into His keeping than in cultivating beautiful
thoughts, soft tears, or ecstatic feelings. Great saints
have told us, that even when we fall it is safer to look to
God's Mercy, which will raise us up, even than to dwell
excessively on our own penitence. We talk about our
foes,—but oh what a treacherous foe self is! and yet how
insufficiently we are on our guard against it! How apt
we are to forget that there is such a thing as spiritual
egotism!

€be Profitable Use of Faults

THE first object of a Christian must be the sanctification of his soul. To this end often remind
yourself that God has placed you where you are to know,
love, and serve Him, and to dwell with Him for ever;
not to achieve this or that, however good or desirable it
may seem to you. If we could keep this as a constant
reality before us, it would colour most of our lives
differently to what they actually are. We should hearken
to no voice save His; we should act with a clear, definite
object; thoughts and words would be subject to a controlling law. Our very faults would be used as stepping-
stones. One stepping-stone would be a clearer knowledge
of self, another the humiliation to which our faults and that
clearer knowledge both tend, and a third the stimulus to
go on and do better which such awakened perceptions
produce. Probably whenever we find ourselves feeling
surprised and discomposed at our faults, there is more
wounded pride than penitence in question. Why should

I be surprised that such an one as I should fall?
Simultaneously with the act of contrition following on
wakening to the consciousness of a fault, should come
one of thanks to God for opening our eyes to see it.
But for His grace we should be blind, and the very
sense of His Presence in this revelation ought to draw
us with greater love and confidence to Him. Who does
not know what it is to rise up from a fault—perceived,
confessed, and forgiven—with an almost joyous sense of
new energy, strength, and will to persevere? Our faults,
steadily faced and dealt with, go a long way to root out
that tendency to seek holiness because "it is so graceful
to be a saint," which besets some of us. Too happy we
may think ourselves then, if by long and patient striving
with God's grace the faults may be rooted out: there will
be no time to look at ourselves from the graceful point
of view! "It cannot be too earnestly urged on those
who seek the spiritual life, not to try to be holy in order
to feel holy,"* has been well said. And again: "Dismiss
all solicitude because you do not feel an urgent desire
after perfection. Desire presupposes passion, or at least
a strong attraction; and God does not always give us a
sensible attraction for mortification and self-renunciation,
which are the very groundworks of perfection. From
time to time He leaves us to our own strength, that is,

* "Etre saints pour le savoir."

to our own weakness, the more to quicken us to a sense
of our need of His help in any progress we hope to
make in the spiritual life. It is a very difficult passage
between what is natural and supernatural, and one not
to be made without convulsing our shrinking nature.
When we experience this inward moral agony, or an
interior rebellion against the inspirations of grace or the
guidance God has given us, we need to redouble our
stedfastness in all spiritual exercises. Self-renunciation
is only possible through prayer, above all, that earnest
prayer which seeks the help of grace to overcome our
natural resistance to God's Will. To this end continually
renew the offering of yourself to God; such offering com-
prises all you need—submission, self-denial, a generous
spirit. A free gift of self to God includes everything.
Our Lord gave us His example when He was pleased to
be offered in the Temple as an infant, that we might
offer up ourselves continually within the sanctuary of
our hearts. To give definite aim and purpose to this
offering, combine with it a resolution to conquer yourself
on some special point for the space of a week. The
weakest will, if really in earnest, find courage to give
up or accept, as the case may be, for so short a
time. And thus nature is beguiled, and renewing your
resolution from week to week you will obtain a decisive
victory—not a complete one, inasmuch as our combat

with evil tendencies must be lifelong. But grace flows
on in proportion to our efforts, and the difficulty of those
efforts diminishes as we persevere."

Do not let your growth in holiness depend upon surrounding circumstances, but rather constrain those circumstances to minister to your growth. Beware of looking
onward, or out of the present in any way, for the sanctification of your life. The only thing you can really control
is the present—the actual moment that is passing by.
Sanctify *that* from hour to hour, and you sanctify your
whole life; but brood over the past, or project yourself
into the future, and you will lose all. Restlessness and
fidgetiness will hinder this sanctification of the present
moment as it passes. The little act of obedience, love,
self-restraint, meekness, patience, devotion, offered to
you actually, is all you can do now, and if you neglect
that to fret about something else at a distance, you lose
your real opportunity of serving God. A moment's
silence, when some irritating words are said by another,
may seem a very small thing; yet at that moment it is
your one duty, your one way of serving and pleasing
God, and if you break it, you have lost your opportunity.
If you want to walk up a mountain, you know it must
be done by separate and several steps; and these will
carry you thither if you simply intend to go on till you
reach the top, and so persevere. Just so you are sure to

attain your spiritual end—perfection, if you go on step by step, with no object in view save to give yourself to God, and to be His only.

Do not despise short steps; God watches over little things no less than over great ones. What, in truth, of ours can be great in His sight? He Who controls the world, and watches over the very hairs of our head!

XXVIII.

Single-mindedness

THOMAS À KEMPIS says that "it is easier not to speak a word at all than not to speak more words than we should." And again, "No man speaks securely but he that holds his peace willingly."* And in truth, when we begin to reckon up all the careless, hasty, insincere, uncharitable, flippant, unprofitable words which pass our lips, it is a very terrible investigation. Yet if we think of the gift of speech as what it really is—one of God's choicest endowments bestowed on His creature man, the faculty from which He has named His own Son the WORD, surely we must marvel that we do not handle it more warily.

How can we sully our lips with untrue, insincere, or exaggerated words, when we remember that within those lips we so often receive Him Who is the very Truth? Yet how frequently such words, in one way or another, are spoken! St. Francis de Sales continually presses upon

* Book I. c. xx.

those he addresses that they study to be absolutely sincere within and without, treating all dissimulation and untruthfulness as characteristics of a mere worldly spirit, unworthy of true Christians. Mgr. Landriot says that an hour's conversation with one who is perfectly true and sincere is like a refreshing bath to one spent and stifled with heat. Not that such sincerity implies a lack of discretion or reserve, which speedily becomes uncharitable through want of consideration for the feelings of others. But simple sincerity is a very divine grace, inasmuch as God is altogether True and single. And Fénélon says that sincere goodness is perfectly simple and single-minded, without mystery or excitement—neither exalting nor unduly depressing itself, courting neither reputation nor success, doing no harm to any, silent under false judgments, content with little, free from manœuvring, pretension, and affectation.

Sincerity of character keeps a person from attempting to convey any false impression, by dress, manners, &c., as well as in conversation. It checks the tendency to bring forward his own merits or capabilities in indirect ways; it makes him shun all show, whether of piety, learning, or anything else, especially where such are merely a pretence; it gives tact and a sense of proportion, unconsciously often, to those who use them. Probably nothing would tend more to purify the soul, and make it

meet to approach the Altar fitly, than a firm resolution,
renewed from Communion to Communion—to aim at
absolute sincerity in every detail of life, making this the
subject of special examination, and carefully noting down
our failures. This we should soon find was at the root
of most sins of the tongue; for surely our uncharitable
words, our words of detraction, our boastful words, and
many more which sully the soul and hinder our spiritual
progress, are all more or less untrue, wanting in a spirit
of simple sincerity. Half the things we say, and regret
that we have said, would never be uttered if we were
perfectly single-minded, content to be and to seem
what we really are. But we want to appear something
else—better, cleverer, more esteemed, and forthwith the
double-mindedness or duplicity tries to convey a false
impression to the minds of others. This clearly is a
point on which we need to turn the fullest light inwards
upon our consciences, hunting out and carefully banish-
ing every species of falsity and insincerity. Any one
who will do this heartily, and with a little perseverance,
will be amazed to find how many and various are the
small dishonesties and shams in his own life and words;
and as he discovers this, the thought of how it all must
look to the All-seeing Eye, Which cannot abide "false
ways," will assuredly lead him to cry from the bottom
of his heart, "Deliver me, O Lord, from unclean lips!"

XXIX

The Presence of God

NO one path can lead us so directly towards perfection as a constant abiding in the Presence of God. When we realise that we are safe, neither devil nor man can harm us. God has set His temple within our hearts, and if we banish Him thence, what good thing can we hope or look for? All the minor troubles and contradictions of life lose their sting when brought into that Presence. God has promised to fill up whatever is wanting to us with Himself. Is not this a thought which will stay us up under any trouble, and lead us on with rapid steps towards perfection? If friends fail us, or hopes are withered, or toil frustrated, what does it matter if He will fill up the blank?

Spiritual writers often caution us against imagining that in order to live in the continual Presence of God we must be always framing deliberate acts thereof, dwelling exclusively upon it. The wife whose whole earthly affections are centred on her husband, is not always telling him or affirming how much she loves him; but her love is her life, the very atmosphere she breathes; it influences her every act. And so with the Christian; an habitual recollection of His Presence hinders nothing. Work, business, devotion to the needs of others—everything is penetrated by it; and the soul may live in Him through a day of such active employment that there has been no time to go aside and make a formal act of His Presence. But those who seek to live such a life will almost inevitably form a habit of turning to Him perpetually, offering all they do or say to Him in ejaculatory mental prayer, and so gradually prayer will really become their life: they will fulfil St. Paul's injunction, to "pray without ceasing."

All spiritual counsels might be reduced to one, it has been said—"Strive to live more with God than with men." But we are so engrossed with earthly things that we grow slack concerning the things of God.

We are often so engrossed with the things of this world that we become slothful in the things which are of God. We are slack and unloving; we haggle over how much is actually necessary to be given to Him; and self—that never quite subdued foe to the spiritual life—bargains and chaffers, trying to get all it can on the one side, without giving up more than can be helped on the other. Yet if once we allow ourselves to dwell on all God is and has been to us, we can scarce be so ungenerous as to grudge Him whatever He asks—which, after all, is only our heart's love—for our own great and endless profit.

Again we come back to the point. We must dwell more on God, and less on self; we must commune with Him; tell Him freely of our joys and sorrows, our needs and longings. Practically, when so doing, we are making acts of faith, hope, and charity; and as we refer all that concerns us to Him, we go more and more out of ourselves. His Will becomes a more prominent feature in our mental horizon; our own troubles and desires sink before it. Thus when harassed or distressed, if instead of dwelling upon our own suffering, or the unkindness or injustice which causes it, we throw ourselves out upon God, letting the outpour of an over-full heart flow into His Bosom, there will assuredly be a sense of relief, of *stayedness*, such as nothing else can give. A habit of mind which turns all things to Him is practically dwelling in His continual Presence. Thus in disappointments caused by others, instead of fretting, if we call to mind how often we disappoint God;—when friendship or affection fails to give all we need, if we bethink us how we fail towards our dearest Friend and Lover, and so on;— we shall find the practice (as it is called) of His Presence becoming a greater reality, and more easy day by day. Some people find it a help in their self-examination to take some such point as, "How far has my day been dedicated to my dear Lord in word and thought? and how far have my religious duties been done in a spirit of living love to Him?"

There are times when we all feel our souls reaching out to God, craving for Him, consciously or it may be unconsciously expressing the truth that the being He has created for Himself can know no rest, save in Him. The more we crave, the more abundant the satisfaction He will pour into our souls; but we shall never be completely satisfied in this life; "the fulness of joy" is to be the portion of His redeemed ones in the life to come. The nearest approach to it here is in that oneness of will with the Will of God which makes a Christian ready to accept all things that can possibly arrive, certain that all is guided and directed by Him, and therefore that all must be well. Those who by God's grace have attained, through much prayer and many sacraments, to this most blessed "indifference" (as it is technically called by spiritual writers), could tell us much of the calm, the peace, the expansion and evenness which fill their hearts. Calm; for the Lord's voice is heard across the tossing sea of life, saying, "It is I; be not afraid." Peace; for His words are ever echoing, "My peace I give unto you." Expansion; for where He is there is perfect liberty. Evenness; for He makes the rough way smooth to His faithful ones. The world and its tone becomes less and less to them daily; their joy is of a kind which it knows little of, and with which it cannot intermeddle. Ties and treasures, pure and blameless, fondly cherished, may drop off; but the joy and peace of the soul, which cleaves only closer to God, will not diminish. "Some souls strip themselves of this or that," a holy man once said; "I have been stripped of all."

Two rules have been given to guide souls seeking thus to dwell in the continual Presence of God: 1. Daily to offer the will to God, with a firm resolution to depend solely upon Him in all things. 2. A resolution, let it cost us what it may, never to act in the smallest degree contrary to His Will, wheresoever it is made plain to us.

Then we must take things as they come, thankful alike for what He gives and what He refuses; remembering that we cannot expect always to have sunshine and ease if we are the servants of a suffering Master. If we would tread in His Footsteps, we must reckon on many a thorn, many a nail, jagged and piercing; many a spear-point, pricking, piercing our hearts; many a season of loneliness, desolation, parching thirst, and weary waiting. But as we learn to see all our own trials in the light of His Presence, as the chord of self melts into the harmony of His heavenly choir, we shall take all these things gladly, and the "not I" of St. Paul will become an increasing reality to us.

XXX

Resolutions

PROBABLY every soul which has made even some small advance in self-knowledge and discipline is often disturbed at the feebleness of its own resolutions. We resolve, oh how earnestly! on our knees in meditation, at confession, at the Altar, in Retreat; and then so soon we have to acknowledge to broken resolutions, scattered to the winds. Wise spiritual guides generally counsel us (1) to be cautious and quiet in making our resolutions; (2) not to make a great many, but rather to be content with few and simple, but such as we can fulfil, and deliberately with our whole heart intend to fulfil. I have repeatedly heard experienced conductors of Retreats say, that they would much rather those under them would make one most commonplace little resolution; e.g. to get up a quarter of an hour earlier than before, or to be exact to the hour appointed for getting up, or to be strictly punctual in the day's duties, or to give ten minutes at some fixed time to spiritual reading, or to say one short

collect for self-control, patience, or the like;—any such
ordinary, plain resolution, rather than high-flown, impetuous, manifold resolutions, which in the very nature
of things cannot, or at least certainly will not, be kept.
Then having selected the resolution which will for the
present most help our progress in the spiritual life, it
should be made thoughtfully and prayerfully, not hastily:
if made in confession or at Retreat, told to our spiritual
father; if apart in meditation or at Holy Communion,
solemnly and deliberately offered to God; and this done,
it should be looked upon as a pledge given to God—a
hedge inclosing us in for Him from the outer distractions
which beset us—an engagement which, in our frailty it is
true, we may break, but for which we must give account,
if we do so, to Him Who vouchsafed to receive our
pledge.

In order to keep the sacredness of our resolutions
before us, it is well further:

I. To make them for a very brief time; *i.e.* not to
resolve to abstain from uncharitable, impetuous, or exaggerated words, or self-indulgence in some treacherous
luxury, &c., for a month, or even a week, but for a day,
if the resolution be made in meditation, or from one
confession or Communion to the next.

II. To make the resolution, whatever it be, a subject
of self-examination each night; perhaps, if it be concern-

ing some besetting fault or pressing hindrance, at midday
also.

III. To tell our confessor, in our next confession, how
far we have failed, either in keeping the resolution,
or in duly renewing it; seeking his counsel as to the
best course to adopt, whether to persevere steadily in
that particular form of resolution, or to give it some fresh
and more telling shape.

IV. In the next Retreat, carefully to go over past
resolutions, especially that made on the last similar
occasion; diligently looking into the causes of failure,
and studying how best to meet them, and, probably,
taking counsel with the Conductor of the Retreat as to
the subject.

V. Some reference to the standing resolution should
be made daily in prayer, less that we may be successful
in keeping it, than that we may have the will to please
God in it as in all else, and that He would give such
fruition to our labour as seems best to Him.

Some people have been perplexed by the number of
resolutions given in books of meditation. These are
probably intended more as suggestive than as rule; and
if any one find it conduce more to his own spiritual
good to go on renewing the same resolution, however
homely, for a length of time, he will do well to persevere,
only giving heed not to drop into a conventional habit,

P

and lose meaning. Where any one has the acquisition
of some grace, or the victory over some besetting sin,
really at heart, it is wonderful how all subjects will be
brought to bear upon that point, and the same resolution
may be renewed for a length of time, without in any way
forcing the topics of meditation.

One of Satan's favourite devices for the hindrance of
souls is to distract us from the actual present moment,
either by leading our minds to dwell on and dread the
past or future, or by some passing delusion or pre-occupation. A definite resolution is a great help against this. It
is like the stake firmly fixed here and there on a slippery
bank, which we can grasp, and lift ourselves up by, till
we have passed that immediate spot of danger. Then
again we must beware of another of the devil's snares :
for when we have failed, it may be many times, and
broken our resolution over and over again, and are
smarting under the consciousness of our own weakness
and inconsistency, he takes advantage of the moment,
and tells us that it is no use, we shall never succeed; he
mocks our feebleness, he bids us be ashamed of telling
again and again in confession the same broken resolutions;
he hints that our confessor will despise us, or be weary of
us ; he suggests that it is profane to make such frequent
resolutions before God's Altar, and break them so soon;
he throws out some bait to make our meditations cold

and slovenly, ended by a careless conventional resolution. And, alas! it is so easy to listen to such whispers. But then indeed is the time to gather oneself together, and renew our desires, our prayers, our promises and resolutions more fervently than ever, despite of all difficulties, all hindrances, all shame at failure, all penalty for defeat. The only real danger at such a time is just what Satan will carefully hide from us; viz., discouragement, settling down into a hopeless feeling which shuts us up from God and His ministering priest, to brood over our own shame and discomfort, not to ponder upon our weakness and need of the Holy Spirit's help and guidance. Never let us sit down with folded hands to bemoan ourselves. We have fallen, broken our resolution—which seemed so easy, so light, as we knelt to make it in church—and that not seven times, but seventy times seven. Well, Who was it that had promised forgiveness even to that, and without limit, if we go to Him in loving penitence, and say, "Father, I have sinned"? Let us arise up cheerfully, because He is our own dear Lord, in calm sorrow, because we have not served Him as He deserved; let us reject, and cast away, and abhor the thing that displeases Him, reaching out a feeble hand to Him, certain that His strong right Hand will be stretched out to lift us up, and the broken resolution, broken ninety-nine times, shall, by His grace, be kept the hundredth.

To some there is danger in dwelling too searchingly on the causes of failure. We may need to search out some hidden weakness which has led to it; but more often it is better to begin again, rather looking on to see how we can keep upright now, than to find out why we fell before. But this is a point which it is usually wiser to refer to our own spiritual guide, who will be the best judge where to fix our searching attention.

Sometimes resolutions rise unbidden to our hearts. A sermon which touches some special place within the soul, some lovely strain of chant or hymn, some bright ray of God's own light sent streaming into the conscience from His Altar when the great Sacrifice is offered up, some word spoken by a saintly friend in conversation, or the pages of some book, taken up, so to say, by chance; any or all of these will rouse a lively sense of some sin, or need, or longing, and a resolution forms itself, we know not how, and takes shape. All such inspirations (for is not every good and holy thought an inspiration from the Comforter, a revelation of light upon the conscience from Himself?) must be watchfully and reverently handled, and diligently used. Some persons have found it helpful to write down their dispositions or resolutions, and ponder them afterwards, whether in meditation or under advice. The first movement to some act of vigorous self-denial, severance from a danger, or adoption of some higher,

more devoted course, has not unfrequently been first felt
thus; and the conscience once awakened to perceive
God's Will, it is ours to use the light given, and follow
on. Of course we must beware of giving way to mere
emotional, unreal excitement, misleading us to look upon
our own heated fancies as God's call; but the more we
habitually live in His Presence, the less danger there is
of this. Mistrust ourselves we well may, but if "the
Lord is my Rock and my salvation," we need not greatly
fear. We shall abide calm, though the storm burst
around; and day by day His love, and a right use of
His means of grace, will develop our good, which is
His, and come to wither the evil which is our own.
Probably it is always wise to submit any such new or
unexpected drawings, or the impetus given in any
particular direction to our spiritual life, to the guidance
of our confessor, and to follow his advice in acting upon
such.

XXXI.

Common Things

HIGH spiritual gifts are not given to us all, and that only will be required of us which is given. But no one who will honestly let the light of God's word in upon his conscience will deny that grace is given to all, which requires a stedfast return in the details of daily life. Let us see in that light whether we are doing all we can; whether we are offering a regular, careful habit of life to God; whether we are punctual, diligent, exact, treating our time as a trust from Him, for which we must give account. To some He gives an active mind which delights in work, which is methodical, well-arranged, vigorous, practical. Such an one needs watchfulness, lest he glory in his gifts as though they were his own; lest the satisfaction he finds in his work, his regularity, his diligence, fill up his heart, and take the place of God, and he cease to work for Him; lest he become self-complacent and self-reliant, intolerant of the slowness, or disorder, or inactivity of others, unkind and uncharitable in his firmness, which

easily becomes rigidity. Surely he should thank God for
the power of taking delight in work, as for good health,
or any other temporal blessing, and then keep a very
close watch on the sanctification of his vigour and energy.
If we find ourselves keen and energetic in secular matters,
business, literature, art, society, or what not, while we are
disposed to flag and be less vigorous in spiritual things, it
is certainly time to seek for a very clear light to be thrown
within our conscience; for there is something wrong.

Then again, the slack, indolent temperament, disposed
to self-indulgence and delay, will find a very practical
and helpful discipline in strict punctuality, a fixed habit
of rising to the minute, when once a time is settled on;
in being always ready for meals, services, or the various
daily matters in which our unpunctuality makes others
uncomfortable. Persons have found their whole spiritual
life helped and strengthened by stedfastly conquering a
habit of dawdling, or of reading newspapers and desultory
bits of books, when they ought to be setting about some
duty, or of denying themselves in some trifling matter
wholly unconnected with health; *e.g.* sitting lazily over the
fire, picking out the easiest chair in the room, indulging
in little luxuries of food, &c., for mere indulgence' sake.
We are sometimes half ashamed of admitting to ourselves,
still more to others, that we care about such things, and
yet, trifles as they may be, they shape and influence the

character very considerably; and if a cup of cold water given for Christ's sake can have its own weight and importance in His sight, why need we doubt that the little luxury given up to another, or altogether set aside, is also a fact known to and weighed by Him? Perhaps the victory over our own pride in accepting such things is in itself not unimportant, and those in positions of superiority can help others beneath them not a little, by not shrinking from letting it be seen and known that they care for and attend to little things. One of the speakers on Personal Holiness in family life, at the late Congress (Stoke, 1875), referred to this; viz., the help it would often be to those below to know that the heads of the family habitually retired for their seasons of prayer, meditation, spiritual reading, and the like. Young persons have been encouraged to observe the Church's appointed abstinences by seeing elders obey them diligently; others, wishing but shrinking from going to confession, have been helped to go by seeing a parent, a master or a mistress, regular in their duties: stedfast, consistent, God-fearing ways tell on all around, whether family or neighbours.

Again, little habits of courtesy and consideration are by no means a thing apart from the spiritual life. I remember many years ago hearing Mr. Keble say that he always supposed St. Paul must have been the most

perfectly courteous Christian gentleman, in the true sense
of the word, that ever was. And who can for a moment
doubt but that "Our Lady" was the embodiment of all
that saintly sweetness, and gracefulness, and loveliness
of person and manner could combine? It might be an
interesting occupation to trace out the courtesy and consideration ("in honour preferring one another,") of the
saints recorded in Holy Scripture:—Abraham offering Lot
the choice of country, and ministering to the angels at
Mamre; Rebekah and Rachel drawing water for the way-
farer; Moses helping the priest of Midian's daughters;
Solomon's "soft answer" and "pleasant words, which
are as an honeycomb;" and innumerable other like
illustrations.

A thirst for praise and admiration is a stumbling-block
to many souls, inasmuch as vanity is the besetting sin of
so many of us. A resolution to avoid speaking of oneself
so as to attract notice or praise—better still perhaps, to
avoid all unnecessary speaking of oneself of any kind—
will help this difficulty; or again, to avoid leading up to
topics which will lead to the gratification of such vanity;
to restrain ourselves from saying all we know and could
say on a given subject, but which will bring neither glory
to God nor good to man. Such self-discipline will tell in
time. A clever, satirical, or sharp saying kept back; a
little display of superior knowledge or social advantage

checked; an unnecessary revelation of some good work withheld (to say nothing of the repression of boasting, ill-natured wit, amusing detraction, flippant brilliancy, and the like)—each of these will be like one of the footsteps our Alpine climbers cut in the glacier with their ice-hatchet; a step upwards in the perilous and slippery ascent. So, too, the voluntary ceding to another of the preferred place or position, of the unappropriated credit of some good or kindly act, the ready dropping back from being first in notice, esteem, honour, and the like— matters concerning which we are, most of us, let us say what we please, extremely sensitive—or the strict truthfulness which bravely embarrasses itself with a troublesome explanation rather than leave a false impression; which will not flatter recklessly when conscious that praise is expected; which spoils a good story rather than add what is not true to it; which has courage to profess ignorance of things it sees itself expected to know; which can freely tell out the good or graceful deed of some one personally unattractive and antipathetic—all these and many more like things, which will occur to every mind, may be passed over as common trifles, but they leave a great influence, we may be sure, on our spiritual growth; and those who really wish to advance will not shrink from turning the searching light of self-examination on such corners of their conscience.

XXXII.

Humility

WHILE humility is the foundation-stone of all graces and holiness, it is so delicate and sensitive a virtue that even while we speak of it, or seek to discover whether we possess it, we cast a mist, a blight upon it. Probably no really humble person ever thought himself to be humble. And while earnestly and prayerfully studying to grow in humility, we must beware of self-consciousness and a dwelling upon our own personalities, lest thereby we crush out the rising growth. One great point in attaining humility, we are told by all spiritual writers, is not to be surprised at our own faults and failures. What am I, that I should expect to stand upright? Is it not likely and natural that one so weak, so frail, as I should fall, and that frequently? If instead of being mortified, disappointed, disheartened, because of my faults and falls, I can get up again cheerfully, and go on afresh, trying to do better, though not surprised that I have done badly, there is evidence at least that I am learning to trust less in myself and more in God.

Some means for seeking humility suggested have been:

I. Of course, a continual remembrance of the great example of our Lord, the very Perfect Pattern of true humility, not only in the lowly external position which He took in this world, but in His permitting Himself to be despised, held as a madman, ignorant, a malefactor, even " His own" not perceiving what He was.

II. "Make frequent acts of humility, both inward and outward. Nature may revolt; so much the better; it will be another victory gained. No matter if you are forced to trample certain conventionalities under foot with discretion. The more active worldly impressions are in you, the more vigorously you must strive to eradicate them. Doubtless it will cost you somewhat; but there is no good in trying to separate yourself from the world, if you persist in retaining a worldly mind. There must be no contradiction between your words and deeds; it must be God or the world."

III. "Accept all humiliations meekly; but there is something beyond that, which is to accept them lovingly. Say to our dear Lord, 'Thou sendest me the means of stamping Thine image more clearly on my heart, of making the outline more incisive, and I thank Thee therefore.' Humble yourself in your own inner mind, realising how your faults and imperfections lower you, and make you undeserving of the esteem of your fellow-men, if they knew you as you know yourself. Dwell upon the thought that one drop of the gall of Calvary, falling upon and burning out self-love, is far more precious to your soul's health than all the glories of Mount Tabor. So when the first involuntary emotion of repugnance at some humiliation has subsided, accept it cheerfully, thanking God, and offering it to Him, small though it be, asking that it may be a means of growth, and praying for those who have been the cause of trial to you."

IV. "You will learn to silence all resentful feelings excited by the humiliations inflicted on you by dwelling on the example of our Lord. With that before you, you will become more and more kind and considerate towards those who cause you annoyance, in order to gain a victory over yourself. You will not shun them, but rather accept what is humbling, reminding yourself that it is God's dealing with you, though He uses intermediate instruments. In this way you may gain a very supernatural grace amid most ordinary acts and trials."

V. "It is not well always to avoid the persons and occasions which bring humiliation. Pray continually for the former, and once in the month communicate with

their intention, until you learn entirely to control all
your interior sense of resentment towards them, as well
as all exterior irritation when brought in contact with
them."

vi. "As to the world, pray often that God would
show you what outward acts of humility He requires of
you. When in society, remind yourself that you are not
of the world, our Lord having called you out of it, even
while duty obliges you to mix with it. Avoid any display
in conversation; learn to restrain a clever, caustic, witty
saying, which would do no good to others, but would
foster your own vanity. Try (but without overmuch
effort and self-consciousness) to set aside all the little
gratifications to personal vanity which arise from circumstances of birth, position, fortune, natural gifts, &c.
Never seek to attract admiration or homage; try to put
yourself forward as little as may be, only do so without
affectation. Do not dwell beforehand on the sacrifices
and humiliations which may come upon you day by day;
think of them only in a general way, with a resolution
to meet them humbly and calmly, and renew this resolution daily in your particular examination. It is often
well rather to shut your eyes to the difficulties which
self-love raises with a view to discourage and hinder
you.

"Never postpone reparation for a fault, especially a

fault against charity; try to acknowledge that you have been wrong with a good grace. All self-excusing and pretexts for avoiding censure, or escaping what is disagreeable and humiliating, are unworthy of those who seek to win a heavenly mind. It is a great grace when any one has learnt to feel, 'I have done nothing for God; the little I have tried to do is all blurred and marred with faults, with bad or worthless motives.' Thank God as He gives you more and more of such insight; it is His way of teaching you humility.

"Humility is most assuredly the source of peace; but it is true too to say, that peace is the source of humility, provided it be the true peace which comes of God. For instance, you feel annoyed, humiliated by some rough words or harsh act; how can you accept such with a really humble heart, if you give way to excitement and disturbance? All such come of pride, and tend to foster it; and it is only as you grow calm and quiet that you can be in any sense humble. Humility in peace, and peace in humility; take this as your watchword, but do not let it be a mere vague form of speech; put it into practice. When the moment of trial comes, whether from within or from without, bow yourself down, and say, 'I am thought useless, good for nothing. Well, it is humbling to be made to see it; but it is God's way of teaching me detachment.' Sometimes in the same manner

you must accept the consciousness of your own helpless-
ness, or of your want of spiritual life and ardour.   You
long to feel warm and devout, and you are cold and
formal.   Then hold on the closer to God alone; trust
Him 'through evil report and good report,' and remember what St. Paul says—'It is a very small thing
that I be judged of any man's judgment: yea, I judge
not mine own self.'

. "The way in which you are called on specially to
practise humility is in bearing patiently with all these
blasts and counterblasts, these contradictions and vexations which, in your case, are essentially providential.
Say honestly to yourself, 'God does not will that I
should meet with the cordiality or sympathy which I
long for in those among whom I live.' But my dear
Lord met with endless contradictions and uncongeniali-
ties among men; He knows exactly what I suffer, and
how I feel the trial; and it is fitting that His servant
should tread in His steps. This is the true way to grow
strong."   But remember that humility is not a grace to
be acquired in a few months, it is the work of a lifetime.
And if you would commend the religious principles you
love to the world without, it must be by such forbearance,
and cheerfulness, and humility. Worldly people like that
in act on the part of others, at which they jeer as a matter
of principle, and you will win more souls to God by a

bright, patient, loving endurance of the petty disagreeables of daily life, than by the stiffest pretensions to
devotion, unaccompanied by such a practical illustration
of it. Remember that every good thought, every kindly
impulse, is a direct gift from God, and never refuse to
accept it, or harden your heart against His gifts.

XXXIII

Self-Renunciation

IT has been said that this is the hardest of all Christian graces, and that therefore our Lord did not set it before every one indiscriminately, but only before those who, loving Him already, and loved by Him, sought to advance in that love, and whom He therefore called to cast aside self-love for His sake.

All the ways of the world and of our ordinary worldly education and life tend to surround us with an atmosphere altogether opposed to the Spirit of Jesus Christ; and if we would come close to Him, it can only be by stripping ourselves of our worldly entanglements, cutting loose our worldly cords, and repressing the subtle tendencies of self-love which worldly habits have fostered, in order to attain to the simplicity, the mortification, and the humility of our Master. A true evangelical spirit, ready to take up the cross and follow Him, consists chiefly in the practical realization of these three virtues. As a Christian realizes, *i.e.* brings them to bear upon and in his own daily life, so he grows in likeness to his Lord, to her who is "blessed among women," and to the saints, whom God has

> "Set before us in our way,
> Lest we should faint or stray;"

and as this likeness grows, his likeness to the world, its notions and ways must diminish, and so the severance gradually becomes complete.

Saints have found matter for meditation during many months on our Saviour's words, "If any man will come after Me, let him take up his cross daily and follow Me." "IF!" as though our dear Master would sadly say how few are entire and hearty in their will to follow Him. We talk and feel; but unless we act this avails little, and to act we need a firm will, prepared to give up and overcome everything. Happy they in whom by God's grace this firm will is established; for they will "run and leap" in His ways. But still their path will be a rugged one; for there is no progress in the road marked by the Master's Footsteps save by self-abnegation, self-renunciation, forgetfulness of ease and comfort, and pleasing of the earthly longings. True self-renunciation implies a simple, unconstrained putting aside of self, by means of which we throw off all the promptings of self-love, the suggestions of vanity and conceit, the cravings for praise and admiration, the excessive desire for sympathy; in short, all that lies at the root of perpetual self-seeking. Then the soul, stripped of such cumbering weights, carries its cross lightly, or at least patiently, and takes everything, great and small, which is laid upon it as coming from God's Hand, and therefore as right, even as acceptable; and the one desire to do all, and bear all for Him, and to please Him, becomes so entirely the mainspring of life that self shrivels up, and withers out for want of being ministered to and fed. It is often humiliating to see how steadily and unremittingly men of the world pursue their worldly objects; how doggedly and unflinchingly they set themselves to overcome all difficulties, and bear all hardships to attain the point they have in view, sacrificing ease, rest, health, and too often all moral good also. And yet what is any such point in comparison with ours, although we shrink from a little hardness, a little effort and self-sacrifice to win it?

Do not imagine that self-renunciation is a single great act, a thing to be done once and for ever. Of course some are called to great acts of self-sacrifice, in which a whole life turns upon some one decision or renunciation; but these are exceptions. To most Christians it comes in the form of a daily work, a calm, deliberately sustained will to let nothing come between us and the Master's

call to rise up and follow Him. It means perseverance in
duties, however small and irksome, in the steady repressing
of natural defects and tendencies to evil, in choosing the
right rather than the pleasant line of action in a hundred
trifling details for which we get no credit, and no thanks.
And yet it is not an altogether dry, hard, unloving virtue;
for no one ever yet gave up the veriest trifle for God's
sake who did not receive a reward within his heart
priceless in its richness. But much prayer and much
watchfulness are needed for the acquisition of such a
habit. As it has been observed, if Jacob wrestled long
with an angel, how can we expect to conquer the devil,
the world, and the flesh easily, and without much vigorous
effort?

Self-conquest is indeed a life's work, and we must not
be disheartened if very often we feel as though we had
made but little way—nay, as if we were slipping back
again. It is only by degrees that we can advance, by
patiently, and it may be wearily, attaining the habit of
mind which makes self-renunciation become our way of
life.

Next to constant prayer, perhaps the most helpful
practical rule, is every morning to forecast briefly the
probable events of the day, the trials, temptations, and
snares likely to beset us, and to prepare, as far as in us
lies, to meet them. To this add a resolution to fulfil

little duties as well as possible, and to keep a check over our thoughts; for it is possible to deny oneself strictly in outward things, and all the while to counteract the good to be gained thereby, by unrestrained indulgence of the thoughts and imagination. Frequently to offer our natural shrinkings, our petty weaknesses, our morti-fied vanity or self-conceits to God, will also be a great help in acquiring a habit of self-renunciation. As we lose sight of ourselves, we grow in conscious intelligence of God. It was David who, after saying, "So foolish was I, and ignorant: I was as a beast before Thee," went on to say, "Nevertheless I am continually with Thee: Thou hast holden me by my right hand." (Ps. lxxiii. 22, 23.)

In practical detail, we have to practise self-renunciation as regards others; and with respect to those to whom we owe deference, we must be firm in adhering to whatever is a real duty, while readily giving up whatever is a matter of mere personal feeling, individual judgment or taste. So with respect to those over whom we are placed, self-renunciation does not consist in abdicating the authority committed to us by God, but by exercising it calmly, gently, and evenly, without allowing the in-trusion of self.

Where important decisions have to be made, and our inclination, or it may be our real deliberate judgment is against the advice of those set over us, a person who has attained a true spirit of self-renunciation will be able to state his own opinion quietly and reasonably, and then, if unable to act upon it, he will accept the adverse position as God's Will, and do the best he can under the circumstances. In smaller matters, where our own wills and wishes clash with those of others, it is generally best to give up where no principle is involved, at least for the time, even when convinced that more good is to be done our way. The time may come for re-asserting our convictions, when they will be better received in consequence of previous gentleness and self-abnegation.

As far as possible our aim must be to have no will save God's; and some holy people have found great help in making some one definite act of giving up their own will daily. Yet how entirely Faber speaks for us all, when he says—

> " I wish to have no wishes left,
> But to leave all to Thee;
> And yet I wish that Thou shouldst will
> Things that I wish should be."

One great step towards self-renunciation is learning to sit lightly to all our favourite or most prized occupations, and even duties—work, study, prayer, &c. Those who have not tried can hardly believe how hard it sometimes is to leave some such duty, or to submit without a murmur to interruption. So again our daily intercourse with those among whom we live is fertile in occasions for self-renunciation. People do not listen to our grievances or our hopes with the interest we demand; our little kindnesses or attentions are unappreciated or coldly received; the performance of another, which we think vastly inferior to our own, is praised, while ours is unnoticed; our little sacrifices are ignored; all these troubles, of which we should be half ashamed to speak even to a dear friend, are so many steps in the path of self-renunciation if we accept them from that point of view, and let self be quietly put out by them. All writers on the inner details of the spiritual life strongly advise us never to complain of the slights or other wounds inflicted on our self-love. Complaints are like an irritating ointment which keeps a sore open.

Even in the matter of our own faults we may practise self-renunciation by not allowing ourselves to dwell in a spirit of vexation upon them. Realising our own many imperfections may well take away self-confidence, but not peace; and, as it has been well said, he who seeks to build up peace on a knowledge of his own progress or virtues, is building on self, not on God, and his house must fall.

"You want to die a slow death to self by means of moral pin-pricks," a spiritual guide writes. "You live a

great deal too much in yourself—in an atmosphere of
self-love. One time you are hurt because you are not
praised; another time because you do not get enough
sympathy. Try to bear these troubles patiently, not
stoically. Let yourself suffer, and unite all that tries you
to our Lord. So alone will you find any real rest. There
is no peace or enjoyment, save in accepting whatever
He sends or allows. You should aim at *rejoicing* in the
fulfilment of God's Will, even when it involves a sacrifice
of yours; and supposing that you had the power to alter
circumstances, and fit them to your own mind, and you
should be able to prefer accepting what He has chosen.
Pour out all your vexations and disappointments freely
into God's Bosom, but do not talk about them to others,
or dwell upon them in your own mind; all such nursing
up troubles weakens the spirit of self-sacrifice in us. You
should try less to get rid of what causes you pain than to
use it profitably for your soul's good and to God's glory.
That is how saints are made. Life is made up of continual trials, and the only way to meet them is to be
ready to die at last of pin-pricks. When you feel jarred,
sore, desolate, whisper, 'Even so, Father; Thy Will be
done;' and though you may feel as if you scarcely could
mean what you say, He will hear you, and He will fill
up the void in your heart. If you do not try to become
more indifferent to all these troubles, to let the many

little vexations which harass you drop before they rankle, your life will be very hard, but not profitable; whereas the constant effort to use your many worries well will be acceptable in God's sight, and a powerful means of progress in your spiritual life."

XXXIV

The Interior Life

THE interior life is opposed in everything to the sensual life. It is a perpetual warfare with the senses, a continual effort to follow the leadings of God's Holy Spirit, in contrast with the drawings and tendencies of the world and of self. It is a constant seeking after union with our dear Lord, a yielding of heart and mind to His guidance, a study of His example, and a diligent attempt to frame our own life upon it—a perpetual meditation upon His acts, His words, until we are moulded upon them. What would He have said or done were He now upon earth in His Sacred Humanity? That is the ever-prevailing thought and rule of the interior life.

The interior life is one of confidence; not even spiritual dryness and desolation will greatly affect that trustful spirit which grows out of constant communing with God. It tells upon the whole character and bearing of those who seek after it. We know a man of the world by his tone, speech, and manner; and the interior Christian will be known in like manner by his tone, speech, and manner, as God's child. Not that he will be always "talking good," but the whole stamp of his life will show the source which feeds it, and men will feel of him, as of those we read of in the gospel, that "they had been with Jesus."

The whole secret of the interior life is the Love of God. All else is only a means to that. Many prayers, much asceticism, will only promote the interior life in so far as they kindle the Love of God more and more in our hearts. We are not born wicked, some one has said, but we are born idolators of self, or of other earthly treasures which minister to self; and God, in His Love for our souls, strips us of our idols. We know it must be done; we know it is right; but nature shrinks, and nothing but Love can make the process bearable. Love alone gilds all suffering, and gives grace and virtue to outward means. External mortification is merely the door to an interior life—stop short on the threshold and it is worthless.

"Your heart is too full of self, and God wants to empty it; let Him do so. You are too much disposed to rest in the affection of others, and in your influence over them. Try to offer more to Him, all the pleasure or satisfaction you derive from this, as also the pain you sometimes feel when it fails you, or when you are conscious of having lost influence by some foolish act or word."

Spiritual writers dwell much on the danger of indolence in the interior life; *i.e.* a sort of passivity and loss of energy in keeping up the constant effort to do what is right, and avoid what is wrong in trifles. Sometimes natural temperament has a great deal to do with this; but it must not be yielded to, and we must rouse ourselves at all cost, and strive to keep up an earnest, steady pursuit after holiness. Spiritual indolence has been compared to a worm hidden beneath the stalk of a choice fruit, so that within all is worthless. So a life may have a fair outward seeming, adorned it may be possibly with many good works, and the frequentation of sacraments, and yet, when at the last it is laid bare before God's Judgment-seat, the interior life may prove empty or decayed. Indolence revolts against the continual warfare needed against small faults, which keep cropping out afresh perhaps, in spite of perseverance. St. Francis de Sales says that the Christian's life is a perpetual series of mendings. Ah well! the day will come when the dear Master will make all whole and perfect, and the white garment of the saints will be given to His faithful servants, instead of the patched, worn robe they have left here!

If you want to test wherein your danger of spiritual indolence lies (it was suggested in a Retreat), try to find out what you don't want to fight, what you don't want to be blamed for, and what others are most apt to blame in you, and thereby to annoy you. This will probably be the point on which to fix your industrious labour. Of course lukewarmness is merely one form of indolence; and a lack of sufficient dread of venial sin another. Spiritual exercises performed out of mere routine; inattentive prayers mechanically said; confessions of what we call small faults, without any firm purpose of amendment; communions without real, hearty efforts to obtain grace; daily life drifting on without any definite intention, order, or method, contentment with a lower state of holiness than one might attain to; all these are symptoms of spiritual indolence, needing careful attention. If we despise or neglect such tokens, the soul will be soiled with perpetual little stains, and the spirit of indolence will cast its mists thicker and thicker around us, until we are so blinded by them that we cannot discover our own danger, and it becomes hard, well-nigh impossible, to rouse us.

So we shall go on, struggling, striving to the end, seeking for the light of God's Holy Spirit on our conscience to cleanse and purge every corner of it, till it be meet for the dear Master's sight, and "then cometh the end," when the day's labour is ended, and the weary servants are bidden to rest; when the sounds of the world are stilled, and we shall hear His Voice, the Voice of the Beloved, calling more clearly, more sweetly than it has ever yet done, "Arise, my love, my fair one, and come away. For, lo, the winter is past, the rain is over and gone; the flowers appear upon the earth. . . . Arise, my love, my fair one, and come away."

THE END.

August, 1875.

A CLASSIFIED CATALOGUE
· OF BOOKS

Selected from the Publications of

Messrs. RIVINGTON

WATERLOO PLACE, LONDON

HIGH STREET, OXFORD; TRINITY STREET, CAMBRIDGE

Contents.

1. The Holy Scriptures.

The Holy Bible; with Notes and Introductions. By Chr. Wordsworth, D.D., Bishop of Lincoln. New Edition. 6 Vols. Imperial 8vo. 120s.

    Vol.   I.—The Pentateuch. 25s.

    Vol. II.—Joshua to Samuel. 15s.

    Vol. III.—Kings to Esther. 15s.

    Vol. IV.—Job to Song of Solomon. 25s.

    Vol. V.—Isaiah to Ezekiel. 25s.

    Vol. VI.—Daniel, Minor Prophets, and Index. 15s.

The New Testament of our Lord and

Saviour JESUS CHRIST, in the original Greek; with Notes, Introductions, and Indices. By CHR. WORDSWORTH, D.D., Bishop
of Lincoln. New Edition. 2 Vols. Imperial 8vo. 60s.

> Vol. I.—Gospels and Acts. 23s.
> Vol. II.—Epistles, Apocalypse, and Index. 37s.

The Greek Testament. With a Critically

Revised Text; a Digest of Various Readings; Marginal
References to Verbal and Idiomatic Usage; Prolegomena;
and a Critical and Exegetical Commentary. For the use of
Theological Students and Ministers. By HENRY ALFORD,
D.D., late Dean f Canterbury. New Edition. 4 Volumes.
8vo. 102s.

> The Volumes are sold separately as follows :—
> Vol. I.—The Four Gospels. 28s.
> Vol. II.—Acts to 2 Corinthians. 24s.
> Vol. III.—Galatians to Philemon. 18s.
> Vol. IV.—Hebrews to Revelation. 32s.

The New Testament for English

Readers: containing the Authorized Version, with a revised
English Text; Marginal References; and a Critical and Explanatory Commentary. By HENRY ALFORD, D.D., late
Dean of Canterbury. New Edition. 2 Volumes, or 4 Parts.
8vo. 54s. 6d.

> The Volumes are sold separately, as follows :—
> Vol. 1, Part I.—The Three first Gospels. 12s.
> Vol. 1, Part II.—St. John and the Acts. 10s. 6d.
> Vol. 2, Part I.—The Epistles of St. Paul. 16s.
> Vol. 2, Part II.—Hebrews to Revelation. 16s.

The Psalms. Translated from the Hebrew.

With Notes, chiefly Exegetical. By WILLIAM KAY, D.D., Rector of Great Leghs, late Principal of Bishop's College, Calcutta. Second Edition. 8vo. 12s. 6d.

"Like a sound Churchman, he reverences Scripture, upholding its authority against sceptics; and he does not denounce such as differ from him in opinion with a dogmatism unhappily too common at the present day. Hence, readers will be disposed to consider his conclusions worthy of attention; or perhaps to adopt them without inquiry. It is superfluous to say that the translation is better and more accurate on the whole than our received one, or that it often reproduces the sense of the original happily."—ATHENÆUM.

"Dr. Kay has profound reverence for Divine truth; and exhibits considerable reading, with the power to make use of it."—BRITISH QUARTERLY REVIEW.

"The execution of the work is careful and scholarly."—UNION REVIEW.

"To mention the name of Dr. Kay is enough to secure respectful attention to his new translation of the Psalms. It is enriched with exegetical notes containing a wealth of sound learning, closely occasionally, perhaps too closely condensed. Good care is taken of the student not learned in Hebrew; we hope the Doctor's example will prevent any abuse of this consideration, and stimulate those who profit by it to follow him into the very text of the ancient Revelation."—JOHN BULL.

Ecclesiastes: the Authorized Version, with

a running Commentary and Paraphrase. By the Rev. THOS. PELHAM DALE, M.A., Rector of St. Vedast with St. Michael City of London, and late Fellow of Sidney Sussex College, Cambridge. 8vo. 7s. 6d.

Daniel the Prophet: Nine Lectures

delivered in the Divinity School of the University of Oxford. With copious Notes. By the Rev. E. B. PUSEY, D.D., Regius Professor of Hebrew, Canon of Christ Church, Oxford. Third Edition. 8vo. 10s. 6d.

Commentary on the Minor Prophets;

with Introductions to the several Books. By the Rev. E. B. PUSEY, D.D., Regius Professor of Hebrew, Canon of Christ Church, Oxford. 4to.

Parts I., II., III., IV., V., 5s. each.

A Companion to the Old Testament;

being a Plain Commentary on Scripture History, down to the Birth of our Lord. Small 8vo. 3s. 6d.

Also in 2 Parts :

Part I.—The Creation of the World to the Reign of Saul.
Part II.—The Reign of Saul to the Birth of Our Lord.

Small 8vo. 2s. each.

[Especially adapted for use in Training Colleges and Schools.]

"*A very compact summary of the Old Testament narrative, put together so as to explain the connection and bearing of its contents, and written in a very good tone ; with a final chapter on the history of the Jews between the Old and New Testaments. It will be found very useful for its purpose. It does not confine itself to merely chronological difficulties, but comments briefly upon the religious bearing of the text also.*"—GUARDIAN.

"*A most admirable Companion to the Old Testament, being far the most concise yet complete commentary on Old Testament history with which we have met. Here are combined orthodoxy and learning, an intelligent and at the same time interesting summary of the leading facts of the sacred story. It should be a text-book in every school, and its value is immensely enhanced by the copious and complete index.*"—JOHN BULL.

"*This will be found a very valuable*

aid to the right understanding of the Bible. It throws the whole Scripture narrative into one from the creation downwards, the author thus condensing Prideaux, Shuckford, and Russell, and in the most reverential manner bringing to his aid the writings of all modern annotators and chronologists. The book is one that should have a wide circulation amongst teachers and students of all denominations.*"—BOOKSELLER.

"*The handbook before us is so full and satisfactory, considering its compass, and sets forth the history of the old covenant with such conscientious minuteness, that it cannot fail to prove a godsend to candidates for examination in the Rudimenta Religionis as well as in the corresponding school at Cambridge. . . . Enough has been said to express our value of this useful work, which cannot fail to win its way into our schools, colleges, and universities.*"—ENGLISH CHURCHMAN.

A Companion to the New Testament.

Uniform with "A Companion to the Old Testament." Small 8vo.

Commentary on the Book of Isaiah,

Critical, Historical, and Prophetical : including a Revised English Translation. With Introduction and Appendices on the Nature of Scripture Prophecy, the Life and Times of Isaiah, the Genuineness of the later Prophecies, the Structure and History of the whole Book, the Assyrian History in Isaiah's days, and various difficult passages. By the Rev. T. R. BIRKS, M.A., Vicar of Holy Trinity, Cambridge. 8vo. 12s.

A Key to the Narrative of the Four

Gospels. By the Rev. JOHN PILKINGTON NORRIS, M.A., Canon of Bristol, and formerly one of H.M. Inspectors of Schools. New Edition. Small 8vo. 2s. 6d.

Forming a Volume of " Keys to Christian Knowledge."

" *This is very much the best book of its kind we have seen. The only fault is its shortness, which prevents its going into the details which would support and illustrate its statements, and which, in the process of illustrating them, would fix them upon the minds and memories of its readers. It is, however, a great improvement upon any book of its kind we know. It bears all the marks of being the condensed work of a real scholar, and of a divine too. The bulk of the book is taken up with a ' Life of Christ,' compiled from the Four Gospels, so as to exhibit its steps and stages and salient points. The rest of the book consists of independent chapters on special points.*"— LITERARY CHURCHMAN.

" *This book is no ordinary compendium, no mere ' cram-book;' still less is it an ordinary reading-book for schools; but the schoolmaster, the Sunday-school teacher, and the seeker after a comprehensive knowledge of Divine truth will find it worthy of its name. Canon Norris writes simply, reverently, without great display of* learning, giving the result of much careful study in a short compass, and adorning the subject by the tenderness and honesty with which he treats it. We hope that this little book will have a very wide circulation, and that it will be studied; and we can promise that those who take it up will not readily put it down again.*"—RECORD.

" *This is a golden little volume. . . . Its design is exceedingly modest. Canon Norris writes primarily to help ' younger students' in studying the Gospels. But this unpretending volume is one which all students may study with advantage. It is an admirable manual for those who take Bible Classes through the Gospels. Closely sifted in style, so that all is clear and weighty; full of unostentatious learning, and pregnant with suggestion; deeply reverent in spirit, and altogether Evangelical in spirit; Canon Norris's book supplies a real want, and ought to be welcomed by all earnest and devout students of the Holy Gospels.*"—LONDON QUARTERLY REVIEW.

A Key to the Narrative of the Acts of

the Apostles. By the Rev. JOHN PILKINGTON NORRIS, M.A., Canon of Bristol, and formerly one of H.M. Inspectors of Schools. New Edition. Small 8vo. 2s. 6d.

Forming a Volume of " Keys to Christian Knowledge."

" *The book is one which we can heartily recommend.*"—SPECTATOR.

" *Few books have ever given us more unmixed pleasure than this.*"— LITERARY CHURCHMAN.

" *This is a sequel to Canon Norris's ' Key to the Gospels,' which was published two years ago, and which has become a general favourite with those* who wish to grasp the leading features of the life and work of Christ. The sketch of the Acts of the Apostles is done in the same style; there is the same reverent spirit and quiet enthusiasm running through it, and the same instinct for seizing the leading points in the narrative.*"—RECORD.

A Devotional Commentary on the

Gospel Narrative.   By the Rev. ISAAC WILLIAMS, B.D.,
formerly Fellow of Trinity College, Oxford.   New Edition.
8 Vols.   Crown 8vo.   5s. each.   Sold separately.

THOUGHTS ON THE STUDY OF THE HOLY GOSPELS.

Characteristic Differences in the Four Gospels—Our Lord's Manifestations of
Himself—The Rule of Scriptural Interpretation furnished by our Lord—
Analogies of the Gospel—Mention of Angels in the Gospels—Places of our
Lord's Abode and Ministry—Our Lord's mode of dealing with His
Apostles—Conclusion.

A HARMONY OF THE FOUR EVANGELISTS.

Our Lord's Nativity—Our Lord's Ministry (second year)—Our Lord's Ministry
(third year)—The Holy Week—Our Lord's Passion—Our Lord's Resurrection.

OUR LORD'S NATIVITY.

The Birth at Bethlehem—The Baptism in Jordan—The First Passover.

OUR LORD'S MINISTRY (Second Year).

The Second Passover—Christ with the Twelve—The Twelve sent forth.

OUR LORD'S MINISTRY (Third Year).

Teaching in Galilee—Teaching at Jerusalem—Last Journey from Galilee to
Jerusalem.

THE HOLY WEEK.

The Approach to Jerusalem—The Teaching in the Temple—The Discourse on
the Mount of Olives—The Last Supper.

OUR LORD'S PASSION.

The Hour of Darkness—The Agony—The Apprehension—The Condemnation—
The Day of Sorrows—The Hall of Judgment—The Crucifixion—The
Sepulture.

OUR LORD'S RESURRECTION.

The Day of Days—The Grave Visited—Christ appearing—The going to
Emmaus—The Forty Days—The Apostles assembled—The Lake in
Galilee—The Mountain in Galilee—The Return from Galilee.

*" There is not a better companion to
be found for the season than the beautiful ' Devotional Commentary on the
Gospel Narrative,' by the Rev. Isaac
Williams. A rich mine for devotional
and theological study."*—GUARDIAN.

*" So infinite are the depths and so
innumerable the beauties of Scripture,
and more particularly of the Gospels,
that there is some difficulty in describing the manifold excellences of
Williams' exquisite Commentary. Deriving its profound appreciation of*
*Scripture from the writings of the
early Fathers, it is only what every
student knows must be true to say, that
it extracts a whole wealth of meaning
from each sentence, each apparently
faint allusion, each word in the text."*
—CHURCH REVIEW.

*" Stands absolutely alone in our
English literature ; there is, we should
say, no chance of its being superseded
by any better book of its kind ; and its
merits are of the very highest order."*
—LITERARY CHURCHMAN.

Waterloo Place, London

WILLIAMS' DEVOTIONAL COMMENTARY—*Continued.*

" This is, in the truest sense of the word, a ' Devotional Commentary' on the Gospel narrative, opening out everywhere, as it does, the spiritual beauties and blessedness of the Divine message; but it is something more than this, it meets difficulties almost by anticipation, and throws the light of learning over some of the very darkest passages in the New Testament."—ROCK.

"It would be difficult to select a more useful present, at a small cost, than this series would be to a young man on his first entering into Holy Orders, and many, no doubt, will avail themselves of the republication of these useful volumes for this purpose. There is an abundance of sermon material to be drawn from any one of them."— CHURCH TIMES.

Female Characters of Holy Scripture.

A Series of Sermons. By the Rev. ISAAC WILLIAMS, B.D., formerly Fellow of Trinity College, Oxford. New Edition. Crown 8vo. 5*s.*

CONTENTS.

Eve—Sarah—Lot's Wife--Rebekah—Leah and Rachel—Miriam—Rahab—Deborah—Ruth —Hannah—The Witch of Endor—Bathsheba—Rizpah—The Queen of Sheba—The Widow of Zarephath—Jezebel—The Shunammite —Esther— Elizabeth —Anna — The Woman of Samaria —Joanna — The Woman with the Issue of Blood,—The Woman of Canaan—Martha—Mary —Salome—The Wife of Pilate—Dorcas—The Blessed Virgin.

The Characters of the Old Testament.

A Series of Sermons. By the Rev. ISAAC WILLIAMS, B.D., formerly Fellow of Trinity College, Oxford. New Edition. Crown 8vo. 5*s.*

CONTENTS.

Adam —Abel and Cain — Noah —Abraham — Lot—Jacob and Esau—Joseph--Moses—Aaron— Pharaoh—Korah, Dathan, and Abiram—Balaam—Joshua— Samson — Samuel —Saul—David — Solomon — Elijah —Ahab—Elisha — Hezekiah —Josiah —Jeremiah — Ezekiel —Daniel —Joel—Job—Isaiah—The Antichrist.

" This is one of the few volumes of published sermons that we have been able to read with real pleasure. They are written with a chastened elegance of language, and pervaded by a spirit of earnest and simple piety. Mr. Williams is evidently what would be called a very High Churchman. Occasionally his peculiar Church views are apparent; but bating a few passages

here and there, these sermons will be read with profit by all ' who profess and call themselves Christians.'"—CONTEMPORARY REVIEW.

"A more masterly analysis of Scriptural characters we never read, nor any which is more calculated to impress the mind of the reader with feelings of love for what is good, and abhorrence for what is evil."—ROCK.

The Apocalypse. With Notes and Reflections.

By the Rev. ISAAC WILLIAMS, B.D., formerly Fellow of Trinity College, Oxford. New Edition. Crown 8vo. 5*s.*

Beginning of the Book of Genesis,

with Notes and Reflections. By the Rev. ISAAC WILLIAMS, B.D., formerly Fellow of Trinity College, Oxford. Small 8vo. 7s. 6d.

Ecclesiastes for English Readers. The

Book called by the Jews Koheleth. Newly translated, with Introduction, Analysis, and Notes. By the Rev. W. H. B. PROBY, M.A., formerly Tyrwhitt Hebrew Scholar in the University of Cambridge. 8vo. 4s. 6d.

The Ten Canticles of the Old Testa-

ment Canon, namely, the Songs of Moses (First and Second), Deborah, Hannah, Isaiah (First, Second, and Third), Hezekiah, Jonah, and Habakkuk. Newly translated, with Notes and Remarks on their Drift and Use. By the Rev. W. H. B. PROBY, M.A., formerly Tyrwhitt Hebrew Scholar in the University of Cambridge. 8vo. 5s.

Notes on the Greek Testament. The

Gospel according to S. Luke. By the Rev. ARTHUR CARR, M.A., Assistant-Master at Wellington College, late Fellow of Oriel College, Oxford. Crown 8vo.

Devotional Commentary on the Gospel

according to St. Matthew. Translated from the French of QUESNEL. Crown 8vo. 7s. 6d.

The Acts of the Deacons; being a

Commentary, Critical and Practical, upon the Notices of St. Stephen and St. Philip the Evangelist, contained in the Acts of the Apostles. By EDWARD MEYRICK GOULBURN, D.D., Dean of Norwich. Second Edition. Small 8vo. 6s.

The Life of our Blessed Saviour: an

Epitome of the Gospel Narrative, arranged in order of time from the latest Harmonies. With Introduction and Notes. By the Rev. I. GREGORY SMITH, M.A., Prebendary of Hereford, and Vicar of Great Malvern, Worcestershire. Second Edition. Royal 16mo. 2s.

A Key to the Knowledge and Use of

the Holy Bible. By the Rev. JOHN HENRY BLUNT, M.A., F.S.A., Editor of the "Dictionary of Theology," &c. &c. New Edition. Small 8vo. 2s. 6d.

Forming a Volume of "Keys to Christian Knowledge."

"*Another of Mr. Blunt's useful and workmanlike compilations, which will be most acceptable as a household book, or in schools and colleges. It is a capital book too for schoolmasters and pupil teachers. Its subject is arranged under the heads of—I. The Literary History of the Bible. II. Old Testament Writers and Writings. III. New Testament ditto. IV. Revelation and Inspiration. V. Objects of the Bible. VI. Interpretation of ditto. VII. The Bible a guide to Faith. VIII. The Apocrypha. IX. The Apocryphal Books associated with the* New Testament. Lastly, there is a serviceable appendix of peculiar Bible words and their meanings."—LITERARY CHURCHMAN.

"*We have much pleasure in recommending a capital handbook by the learned Editor of 'The Annotated Book of Common Prayer.'*"—CHURCH TIMES.

"*Merits commendation, for the lucid and orderly arrangment in which it presents a considerable amount of valuable and interesting matter.*"—RECORD.

The Inspiration of Holy Scripture, its

Nature and Proof. Eight Discourses preached before the University of Dublin. By WILLIAM LEE, D.D., Archdeacon of Dublin. Fourth Edition. 8vo. 15s.

On the Inspiration of the Bible. Five

Lectures delivered at Westminster Abbey. By CHR. WORDSWORTH, D.D., Bishop of Lincoln. Small 8vo. 1s. 6d.

Syntax and Synonyms of the Greek

Testament. By the Rev. WILLIAM WEBSTER, M.A., late Fellow of Queen's College, Cambridge. 8vo. 9s.

Bible Readings for Family Prayer.

By the Rev. W. H. RIDLEY, M.A., Rector of Hambleden.
Crown 8vo.

Old Testament—Genesis and Exodus. 2*s.*

The Four Gospels, 3*s.* 6*d.*

St. Matthew and St. Mark. 2*s.*

St. Luke and St. John. 2*s.*

The Acts of the Apostles, 2*s.*

A Complete Concordance to the Old

and the New Testament; or, a Dictionary, and Alphabetical
Index to the Bible, in two Parts.   To which is added, a Con-
cordance to the Apocrypha.   By ALEXANDER CRUDEN,
M.A. With a Life of the Author, by ALEXANDER CHALMERS,
F.S.A., and a Portrait. Fourteenth Edition. Demy 4to. 21*s.*

2. The Prayer Book and the Church Service.

The Annotated Book of Common

Prayer; being an Historical, Ritual, and Theological Commentary on the Devotional System of the Church of England. Edited by the Rev. JOHN HENRY BLUNT, M.A., F.S.A., Editor of the "Dictionary of Sects and Heresies," &c., &c. Sixth Edition. Imperial 8vo. 36s., or half-bound in morocco 48s.

"*The most complete and compendious Commentary on the English Prayer Book ever yet published. Almost everything that has been written by all the best liturgical and historical authorities ancient and modern (of which a 'formidable list is prefixed to the work) is quoted, or referred to, or compressed into the notes illustrative of the several subjects.*"—JOHN BULL.

"*The book is a mine of information and research—able to give an answer almost on anything we wish to know about our present Prayer Book, its antecedents and originals—and ought to be in the library of every intelligent Churchman. Nothing at all like it has as yet been seen.*"—CHURCH REVIEW.

The Annotated Book of Common

Prayer, forming a concise Commentary on the Devotional System of the Church of England. By the Rev. JOHN HENRY BLUNT, M.A., F.S.A., Editor of the "Dictionary of Sects and Heresies," &c., &c. Compendious Edition. Crown 8vo.

Liber Precum Publicarum Ecclesiæ

Anglicanæ. A GULIELMO BRIGHT, D.D., et PETRO GOLDSMITH MEDD, A.M., Presbyteris, Collegii Universitatis in Acad. Oxon. Sociis, Latine redditus. New Edition. With Rubrics in Red. Small 8vo. 6s.

The Prayer Book Interleaved; with

Historical Illustrations and Explanatory Notes arranged parallel to the Text. By W. M. CAMPION, B.A., and W. J. BEAMONT, M.A. With a Preface by the LORD BISHOP OF ELY. Eighth Edition. Small 8vo. 7s. 6d.

"An excellent publication, combining a portable Prayer Book with the history of the text and explanatory notes."—SPECTATOR.

"This book is of the greatest use for spreading an intelligent knowledge of the English Prayer Book, and we heartily wish it a large and continuous circulation."—CHURCH REVIEW.

"The work may be commended as a very convenient manual for all who are interested to some extent in liturgical studies, but who have not time or the means for original research. It would also be most useful to examining chaplains, as a text-book for holy orders."—CHURCH TIMES.

The Book of Common Prayer, and

Administration of the Sacraments and other Rites and Ceremonies of the Church, according to the use of THE PROTESTANT EPISCOPAL CHURCH in the UNITED STATES of AMERICA, together with the Psalter, or Psalms of David. Royal 32mo. French Roan limp. 2s. 6d.

The First Book of Common Prayer of

Edward VI. and the Ordinal of 1549. Together with the Order of the Communion, 1548. Reprinted entire. Edited by the Rev. HENRY BASKERVILLE WALTON, M.A., late Fellow and Tutor of Merton College; with Introduction by the Rev. PETER GOLDSMITH MEDD, M.A., Rector of Barnes, late Senior Fellow of University College, Oxford. Small 8vo. 6s.

An Illuminated Edition of the Book

of Common Prayer, printed in Red and Black, on fine toned paper; with Borders and Titles designed after the manner of the 14th Century. By R. R. HOLMES, F.S.A., and engraved by O. JEWITT. Crown 8vo. White cloth, illuminated. 16s. Morocco elegant. 21s.

The Book of Lessons, Containing the Pro-

per Psalms and Lessons for Sundays and Holy Days, together with the Daily Lessons from the Calendar, and the New Testament. Crown 8vo. 9s.

A Key to the Knowledge and Use of
the Book of Common Prayer. By the Rev. JOHN HENRY
BLUNT, M.A., F.S.A., Editor of the "Annotated Book of
Common Prayer," &c. New Edition. Small 8vo. 2s. 6d.
Forming a Volume of "Keys to Christian Knowledge."

*"Impossible to praise too highly. It
is the best short explanation of our
offices that we know of, and would be
invaluable for the use of candidates for
confirmation in the higher classes."*—
JOHN BULL.
*"A very valuable and practical
manual, full of information, which is
admirably calculated to instruct and
interest those for whom it was evidently*

*specially intended—the laity of the
Church of England. It deserves high
commendation."*—CHURCHMAN.
*"A thoroughly sound and valuable
manual."*—CHURCH TIMES.
*"To us it appears that Mr. Blunt
has succeeded very well. All necessary
information seems to be included, and
the arrangement is excellent."*—LITER-
ARY CHURCHMAN.

Sacraments and Sacramental Ordi-
nances of the Church; being a Plain Exposition of their
History, Meaning, and Effects. By the Rev. JOHN HENRY
BLUNT, M.A., F.S.A., Editor of the "Annotated Book of
Common Prayer," &c. Small 8vo. 4s. 6d.

A Commentary, Expository and De-
votional, on the Order of the Administration of the Lord's
Supper, according to the Use of the Church of England; to
which is added, an Appendix on Fasting Communion, Non-
communicating Attendance, Auricular Confession, the Doctrine
of Sacrifice, and the Eucharistic Sacrifice. By EDWARD
MEYRICK GOULBURN, D.D., Dean of Norwich. Sixth
Edition. Small 8vo. 6s.

Also a Cheap Edition, uniform with "Thoughts on Personal
Religion," and "The Pursuit of Holiness." 3s. 6d.

Notitia Eucharistica; a Commentary,
Explanatory, Doctrinal, and Historical, on the Order of the
Administration of the Lord's Supper, or Holy Communion,
according to the use of the Church of England. By the Rev.
W. E. SCUDAMORE, M.A., Rector of Ditchingham, and
formerly Fellow of St. John's College, Cambridge. 8vo.

The Athanasian Creed: an Examination of Recent Theories respecting its Date and Origin. With a Postscript referring to Professor Swainson's Account of its Growth and Reception, which is contained in his Work entitled "The Nicene and Apostles' Creeds, their Literary History." By G. D. W. OMMANNEY, M.A., Curate of Whitchurch, Somerset. Crown 8vo. 8s. 6d.

The Athanasian Origin of the Athanasian Creed. By J. S. BREWER, M.A., Preacher at the Rolls, and Honorary Fellow of Queen's College, Oxford. Crown 8vo. 3s. 6d.

The "Damnatory Clauses" of the Athanasian Creed rationally explained in a Letter to the Right Hon. W. E. GLADSTONE, M.P. By the Rev. MALCOLM MACCOLL, M.A., Rector of St. George, Botolph Lane. Crown 8vo. 6s.

Comment upon the Collects appointed to be used in the Church of England on Sundays and Holy Days throughout the Year. By JOHN JAMES, D.D., sometime Canon of Peterborough. Fifteenth Edition. 12mo. 3s. 6d.

A Commentary, Practical and Exegetical, on the Lord's Prayer. By the Rev. W. DENTON, M.A. Small 8vo. 5s.

The Psalter, or Psalms of David, pointed as they are to be said or sung in Churches. Printed in red and black. Small 8vo. 2s. 6d.

The New Mitre Hymnal, containing New

Music by Sir JOHN GOSS, Sir GEORGE ELVEY, Dr. STAINER, HENRY GADSBY, Esq., J. BAPTISTE CALKIN, Esq., BERTHOLD TOURS, Esq., JAMES LANGRAN, Esq., and other eminent Composers; together with Scandinavian Tunes now first introduced into this Country. Imperial 8vo. 5s.

An Edition of the Words without the Music may also be had. Imperial 32mo., cloth limp, 1s.; or in cloth boards, extra gilt, 1s. 6d.

A large reduction to purchasers of quantities.

" One of the best, if not the best, book of Christian Psalmody now before the public."—MORNING POST.
" This Hymnal has been compiled with evident care and judgment. The musical part of the book deserves high praise."—SATURDAY REVIEW.

" Admirably adapted to the services of the Church of England."—STANDARD.
" The production of the New Mitre Hymnal is most creditable. It is a volume which does the editor and his publishers honour."—CHURCH TIMES.

Psalms and Hymns adapted to the

Services of the Church of England; with a Supplement of additional Hymns, and Indices. By the Rev. W. J. HALL, M.A. 8vo, 5s. 6d.; 18mo, 3s.; 24mo, 1s. 6d.; limp cloth, 1s. 3d.; 32mo, 1s.; limp cloth, 8d.

Selection of Psalms and Hymns; with

Accompanying Tunes selected and arranged by JOHN FOSTER, of Her Majesty's Chapels Royal. By the Rev. W. J. HALL, M.A. Crown 8vo. 2s. 6d. The Tunes only, 1s. Also an Edition of the Tunes for the Organ. 7s. 6d.

A Book of Litanies, Metrical and Prose.

With an Evening Service. Edited by the Compiler of "The Treasury of Devotion." And accompanying Music arranged under the Musical Editorship of W. S. HOYTE, Organist and Director of the Choir at All Saints', Margaret Street, London. Crown 4to, cloth extra, 7s. 6d.

Also may be had, an Edition of the Words, 32mo, 6d.; or in paper cover, 4d. Or, the Metrical Litanies separately, 32mo, 5d.; or in paper cover, 3d.

3. Devotional Works.

Library of Spiritual Works for English

Catholics. Elegantly printed with red borders, on extra superfine toned paper. Small 8vo. 5s. each.

OF THE IMITATION OF CHRIST. In 4 Books. By THOMAS À KEMPIS. A New Translation.

THE CHRISTIAN YEAR.

THE SPIRITUAL COMBAT; together with the Supplement and the Path of Paradise. By L. SCUPOLI. A New Translation.

THE DEVOUT LIFE. By S. FRANCIS DE SALES. A New Translation.

Other Volumes are in Preparation.

It is hoped that the "Library of Spiritual Works for English Catholics," which will comprise translations, compilations, and other works, will meet a need which has long been felt. As the devotional life of the Church of England has increased, so the demand for spiritual treatises has become more and more urgent, and has arisen from all classes of society. This series of books, some well-known, some already oftentimes translated, and others, it may be, yet to be presented for the first time in an English dress, is intended to meet this want.

The aim of the translators is twofold. First, to provide the reader with a fair rendering of the original as far as possible unmutilated. It has been a common complaint of late, that translations have been marred by the absence of parts of the original, the exclusion of which a more intelligent view of Catholic devotion in the present day has rendered unnecessary. In these editions these omissions have been to a great extent supplied; yet at the same time any term or expression which may come under the imputation of being "un-English" has been reduced, as far as may be without destroying the thought, to its equivalent in Anglican phraseology and belief. Secondly, to translate the original into ordinary English, and thus to avoid the antiquated and stilted style of writing, which often makes books of this kind distasteful, or even sometimes unintelligible.

The Star of Childhood : a First Book of

Prayers and Instruction for Children. Compiled by a Priest. Edited by the Rev. T. T. CARTER, M.A., Rector of Clewer, Berks. With Illustrations reduced from Engravings by FRA ANGELICO. Second Edition. Royal 16mo. 2s. 6d.

"*All the instructions, all of the Hymns, and most of the Prayers here are excellent. And when we use the cautionary expression 'most of the,' &c., we do not mean to imply that all the prayers are not excellent in themselves, but only to express a doubt whether in some cases they may not be a little too elaborate for children. Of course it by no means follows that when you use a book you are to use equally every portion of it; what does not suit one may suit a score of others, and this book is clearly compiled on the comprehensive principle. But to give a veracious verdict on the book it is needful to mention this. We need hardly say that it is well worth buying, and of very high order of merit.*"—LITERARY CHURCHMAN.

"*Messrs. Rivington have sent us a manual of prayers for children, called 'The Star of Childhood,' edited by the Rev. T. T. Carter, a very full collection, including instruction as well as devotion, and a judicious selection of hymns.*"—CHURCH REVIEW.

"*The Rev. T. T. Carter, of Clewer, has put forth a much-needed and excellent book of devotions for little children, called 'The Star of Childhood.'*"—MONTHLY PACKET.

"*One amongst the books before us deserves especial notice, entitled 'The Star of Childhood,' and edited by the Rev. T. T. Carter; it is eminently adapted for a New Year's Gift. It is a manual of prayer for children, with hymns, litanies, and instructions. Some of the hymns are illustrative of our Lord's life; and to these are added reduced copies from engravings of Fra Angelico.*"—PENNY POST.

"*Supposing a child to be capable of using a devotional manual, the book before us is, in its general structure, as good an attempt to meet the want*

as could have been put forth. In the first place it succeeds, where so many like efforts fail, in the matter of simplicity. The language is quite within the compass of a young child; that is to say, it is such as a young child can be made to understand; for we do not suppose that the book is intended to be put directly into his hands, but through the hands of an instructor."—CHURCH BELLS.

"*To the same hand which gave us the 'Treasury of Devotion' we are indebted for this beautiful little manual for children. Beginning with prayers suited to the comprehension of the youngest, it contains devotions, litanies, hymns, and instructions, carefully proportioned to the gradually increasing powers of a child's mind from the earliest years, until Confirmation. This little book cannot fail to influence for good the impressible hearts of children, and we hope that ere long it will be in the hands of all those who are blessed with Catholic-minded parents. It is beautifully got up, and is rendered more attractive by the capital engravings of Fra Angelico's pictures of scenes of our Lord's childhood. God-parents could scarcely find a more appropriate gift for their God-children than this, or one that is more likely to lead them to a knowledge of the truth.*"—CHURCH UNION GAZETTE.

"*A first book of Prayers and instruction for children, compiled by a priest, and edited by the Rev. T. T. Carter, Rector of Clewer. It is a very careful compilation, and the name o its editor is a warrant for its devotional tone.*"—GUARDIAN.

"*A handsomely got up and attractive volume, with several good illustrations from Fra Angelico's mos famous paintings.*"—UNION REVIEW.

and at **Oxford and Cambridge**

Short Devotional Forms, for Morn-

ing, Night, and Midnight, and for the Third, Sixth, Ninth Hours and Eventide of each Day of the Week. Arranged to meet the Exigencies of a Busy Life. By EDWARD MEYRICK GOULBURN, D.D., Dean of Norwich. Third Edition. 18mo. 1s. 6d.

Prayers and Meditations for the Holy

Communion. By JOSEPHINE FLETCHER. With a Preface by C. J. ELLICOTT, D.D., Lord Bishop of Gloucester and Bristol. With rubrics and borders in red. Royal 32mo. 2s. 6d.
An Edition without the red rubrics. 32mo. 1s.

" Devout beauty is the special character of this new manual, and it ought to be a favourite. Rarely has it happened to us to meet with so remarkable a combination of thorough practicalness with that almost poetic warmth which is the highest flower of genuine devotion. It deserves to be placed along with the manual edited by Mr. Keble so shortly before his decease, not as superseding it, for the scope of the two is different, but to be taken along with it. Nothing can exceed the beauty and fulness of the devotions before communion in Mr. Keble's book, but we think that in some points the devotions here given after Holy Communion are even superior to it."— LITERARY CHURCHMAN.

" Bishop Ellicott has edited a book of 'Prayers and Meditations for the Holy Communion,' which, among Eucharistic manuals, has its own special characteristic. The Bishop recommends it to the newly confirmed, to the tender-hearted and the devout, as having been compiled by a youthful person, and as being marked by a peculiar 'freshness.' Having looked through the volume, we have pleasure in seconding the recommendations of the good Bishop. We know of no more suitable manual for the newly con-

*firmed, and nothing more likely to engage the sympathies of youthful hearts. There is a union of the deepest spirit of devotion, a rich expression of experimental life, with a due recognition of the objects of faith, such as is not always to be found, but which characterises this manual in an eminent degree."—*CHURCH REVIEW.

*" The Bishop of Gloucester's imprimatur is attached to 'Prayers and Meditations for the Holy Communion,' intended as a manual for the recently confirmed, nicely printed, and theologically sound."—*CHURCH TIMES.

*" Among the supply of Eucharistic Manuals, one deserves special attention and commendation. 'Prayers and Meditations' merits the Bishop of Gloucester's epithets of 'warm, devout, and fresh.' And it is thoroughly English Church besides."—*GUARDIAN.

*" We are by no means surprised that Bishop Ellicott should have been so much struck with this little work, on accidentally seeing it in manuscript, as to urge its publication, and to preface it with his commendation. The devotion which it breathes is truly fervent, and the language attractive, and as proceeding from a young person the work is altogether not a little striking."—*RECORD.

A Plain Guide to the Holy Communion.

By the Rev. PLUMPTON WILSON, LL.B., Rector of Knaptoft, Leicestershire. Third Edition. 18mo. 2s. 6d.

Meditations on the Life and Mysteries

of Our Lord and Saviour Jesus Christ. From the French. By the Compiler of "The Treasury of Devotion." Edited by the Rev. T. T. CARTER, M.A., Rector of Clewer, Berks; Honorary Canon of Christ Church, Oxford. Crown 8vo.

Vol. I.—The Hidden Life of Our Lord. 3s. 6d.

Vol. II.—The Public Life of Our Lord. 2 Parts. 5s. each.

Vol. III.—The Suffering Life and the Glorified Life of Our Lord. 3s. 6d.

The Treasury of Devotion: a Manual of

Prayers for General and Daily Use. Compiled by a Priest. Edited by the Rev. T. T. CARTER, M.A., Rector of Clewer, Berks. Eighth Edition. 16mo, 2s. 6d.; cloth limp, 2s. Bound with the Book of Common Prayer, 3s. 6d.

The Path of Holiness: a First Book of

Prayers, with the Service of the Holy Communion, for the Young. Compiled by a Priest. Edited by the Rev. T. T. CARTER, M.A., Rector of Clewer, Berks. With Illustrations. Crown 16mo, 1s. 6d.; or cloth limp, 1s.

The Guide to Heaven: a Book of Prayers

for every want. (For the Working Classes.) Compiled by a Priest. Edited by the Rev. T. T. CARTER, M.A., Rector of Clewer, Berks. New Edition. 16mo, 1s. 6d.; cloth limp, 1s. An Edition in Large Type. Crown 8vo. 1s. 6d.; cloth limp, 1s.

The Way of Life: a Book of Prayers and

Instruction for the Young at School, with a Preparation for Confirmation. Compiled by a Priest. Edited by the Rev. T. T. CARTER, M.A., Rector of Clewer, Berks. Imperial 32mo. 1s. 6d.

Aids to Prayer; or, Thoughts on the

Practice of Devotion.   With Forms of Prayer for Private Use.
By DANIEL MOORE, M.A., Chaplain in Ordinary to the Queen,
and Vicar of Holy Trinity, Paddington.   Second Edition.
Square 32mo.   *2s. 6d.*

Words to Take with Us.   A Manual of

Daily and Occasional Prayers, for Private and Common Use.
With Plain Instructions and Counsels on Prayer.   By W. E.
SCUDAMORE, M.A., Rector of Ditchingham, and formerly
Fellow of S. John's College, Cambridge.   New Edition,
revised.   Small 8vo.   *2s. 6d.*

"'*Words to Take with Us,*' *by W. E. Scudamore, is one of the best manuals of daily and occasional prayer we have seen. At once orthodox and practical, sufficiently personal, and yet not perplexingly minute in its details, it is calculated to be of inestimable value in many a household.*"—JOHN BULL.

"*We are again pleased to see an old friend on the editorial table, in a third edition of Mr. Scudamore's well-known Manual of Prayers. The special pro-per collects for each day of the week, as well as those for the several seasons of the Christian year, have been most judiciously selected. The compiler moreover, while recognising the full benefits to be derived from the Book of Common Prayer, has not feared to draw largely from the equally invaluable writings of ancient Catholicity. The preface is a systematic arrangement of instructions in prayer and meditation.*"—CHURCH REVIEW.

Faith and Life : Readings for the greater

Holy Days, and the Sundays from Advent to Trinity.   Compiled from Ancient Writers.   By WILLIAM BRIGHT, D.D.,
Canon of Christ Church, and Regius Professor of Ecclesiastical
History in the University of Oxford.   Second Edition.   Small
8vo.   *5s.*

Sacra Privata : The Private Meditations

and Prayers of the Right Rev. THOMAS WILSON, D.D., late
Lord Bishop of Sodor and Man, accommodated to general use.
New Edition, with a Memoir of the Author.   32mo.   *1s.*
Also an Edition in large type.   Small 8vo.   *2s.*

The Hour of Prayer; being a Manual of

Devotion for the Use of Families and Schools. With a Preface by the Rev. W. E. SCUDAMORE, M.A., Rector of Ditchingham, and formerly Fellow of S. John's College, Cambridge. Crown 8vo. 3s. 6d.

Family Prayers. Compiled from various

Sources (chiefly from Bishop Hamilton's Manual), and arranged on the Liturgical Principle. By EDWARD MEYRICK GOUL-BURN, D.D., Dean of Norwich. New Edition. Large type. Crown 8vo. 3s. 6d. Cheap Edition. 16mo. 1s.

Manual of Family Devotions, arranged

from the Book of Common Prayer. By the Hon. AUGUSTUS DUNCOMBE, D.D., Dean of York. Printed in red and black. Small 8vo. 3s. 6d.

Household Prayer, from Ancient and

Authorized Sources : with Morning and Evening Readings for a Month. By the Rev. P. G. MEDD, M.A., Rector of Barnes, and Examining Chaplain to the Bishop of Rochester. Small 8vo. 4s. 6d.

A Book of Family Prayer. Compiled

by WALTER FARQUHAR HOOK, D.D., F.R.S., Dean of Chichester. Eighth Edition, with red rubrics. 18mo. 2s.

Daily Devotions; or, Short Morning

and Evening Services for the use of a Churchman's Household. By CHARLES C. CLERKE, D.D., Archdeacon of Oxford. 18mo. 1s.

From Morning to Evening: a Book for

Invalids. From the French of M. l'Abbé Henri Perreyve. Translated and adapted by an Associate of the Sisterhood of S. John Baptist, Clewer. Crown 8vo. 5s.

Self-Renunciation. From the French.

With Introduction by the Rev. T. T. CARTER, M.A., Rector of Clewer, Berks. Crown 8vo. 6s.

"*It is excessively difficult to review or criticise, in detail, a book of this kind, and yet its abounding merits, its practicalness, its searching good sense and thoroughness, and its frequent beauty, too, make us wish to do something more than announce its publication. . . . . The style is eminently clear, free from redundance and prolixity.*"—LITERARY CHURCHMAN.

"*Few save Religious and those brought into immediate contact with them are, in all probability, acquainted with the French treatise of Guilloré, a*

portion of which is now, for the first time we believe, done into English. . . . . Hence the suitableness of such a book as this for those who, in the midst of their families, are endeavouring to advance in the spiritual life. Hundreds of devout souls living in the world have been encouraged and helped by such books as Dr. Neale's 'Sermons preached in a Religious House.' For such the present work will be found appropriate, while for Religious themselves it will be invaluable."—CHURCH TIMES.

Spiritual Guidance. With an Introduc-

tion by the Rev. T. T. CARTER, M.A., Rector of Clewer, Berks. Crown 8vo. 6s.

"*It is as good for the clergy as for the laity, and we set much store by many of the 'Maxims for Beginners' as the subject of Direction which meet the reader at the outset of the volume. They are full of plain common sense, which is generally the same thing as the highest wisdom, and if they were read, pondered, and acted on, would do incalculable good to both priests and people.*"—UNION REVIEW.

"*As a work intended for general use, it will be found to contain much valuable help, and may be profitably studied by any one who is desiring to make progress in spiritual life. Much of the contents of this little book will be found more or less applicable to all persons amid the ordinary difficulties and trials of life, and a help to the training of the mind in habits of self-discipline.*"—CHURCH TIMES.

Vita et Doctrina Jesu Christi; or,

Meditations on the Life of our Lord. By AVANCINI. In the Original Latin. Adapted to the use of the Church of England by a CLERGYMAN. Imperial 32mo. 2s. 6d.

The Virgin's Lamp: Prayers and Devout

Exercises for English Sisters. By the Rev. J. M. NEALE, D.D., late Warden of Sackville College, East Grinsted. Small 8vo. 3s. 6d.

Waterloo Place, London

Voices of Comfort. Edited by the Rev.

THOMAS VINCENT FOSBERY, M.A., sometime Vicar of St. Giles's, Reading. Second Edition. Small 8vo. 7s. 6d.

[This Volume, of prose and poetry, original and selected, aims at revealing the fountains of hope and joy which underlie the griefs and sorrows of life.

It is so divided as to afford readings for a month. The key-note of each day is given by the title prefixed to it, such as : 'The Power of the Cross of Christ, Day 6. Conflicts of the Soul, Day 17. The Communion of Saints, Day 20. The Comforter, Day 22. The Light of Hope, Day 25. The Coming of Christ, Day 28.' Each day begins with passages of Holy Scripture. These are followed by articles in prose, which are succeeded by one or more short prayers. After these are Poems or passages of poetry, and then very brief extracts in prose or verse close the section. The book is meant to meet, not merely cases of bereavement or physical suffering, but 'to minister specially to the hidden troubles of the heart, as they are silently weaving their dark threads into the web of the seemingly brightest life.']

Hymns and Poems for the Sick and

Suffering. In connexion with the Service for the Visitation of the Sick. Selected from various Authors. Edited by the Rev. THOMAS VINCENT FOSBERY, M.A., sometime Vicar of St. Giles's, Reading. New Edition. Small 8vo. 3s. 6d.

[This Volume contains 233 separate pieces ; of which about 90 are by writers who lived prior to the eighteenth century ; the rest are modern, and some of these original. Amongst the names of the writers (between 70 and 80 in number) occur those of Sir J. Beaumont ; Sir T. Brown ; F. Davison ; Elizabeth of Bohemia ; P. Fletcher ; G. Herbert ; Dean Hickes ; Bishop Ken ; Norris ; Quarles ; Sandys ; Bishop J. Taylor ; Henry Vaughan ; and Sir H. Wotton. And of modern writers :—Mrs. Barrett Browning ; Bishop Wilberforce ; S. T. Coleridge ; Sir R. Grant ; Miss E. Taylor ; W. Wordsworth ; Archbishop Trench ; Rev. Messrs. Chandler, Keble, Lyte, Monsell, and Moultrie.]

The Christian Year : Thoughts in Verse

for the Sundays and Holy Days throughout the Year. Elegantly printed with red borders. 16mo. 2s. 6d. Cheap edition, without the red borders, limp cloth, 1s., or in paper cover, 6d.

Forming a Volume of "Rivington's Devotional Series."

Also a New Edition, forming a Volume of the "Library of Spiritual Works for English Catholics." Small 8vo. 5s. [See page 16.]

Spiritual Life. By JOHN JAMES, D.D.,

sometime Canon of Peterborough. 12mo. 5s.

---

and at Oxford and Cambridge

Consoling Thoughts in Sickness.

Edited by HENRY BAILEY, B.D. Small 8vo. 1s. 6d.; or in Paper Cover, 1s.

A Manual for the Sick; with other

Devotions. By LANCELOT ANDREWES, D.D., sometime Lord Bishop of Winchester. Edited with a Preface by H. P. LIDDON, D.D., Canon of St. Paul's. With Portrait. Third Edition. Large type. 24mo. 2s. 6d.

Sickness; its Trials and Blessings.

Fine Edition. Small 8vo. 3s. 6d. Cheap Edition, 1s. 6d.; or in Paper Cover, 1s.

Help and Comfort for the Sick Poor.

By the same Author. New Edition. Small 8vo. 1s.

Prayers for the Sick and Dying. By

the same Author. Fourth Edition. Small 8vo. 2s. 6a.

Consolatio; or, Comfort for the

Afflicted. Edited by the Rev. C. E. KENNAWAY. With a Preface by SAMUEL WILBERFORCE, D.D., late Lord Bishop of Winchester. New Edition. Small 8vo. 3s. 6d.

Twenty-one Prayers, composed from the

Psalms, for the Sick and Afflicted. With Hints on the Visita- tion of the Sick. By the Rev. JAMES SLADE, M.A., Vicar of Bolton. Seventh Edition. 12mo. 3s. 6d.

Christian Watchfulness, in the Pros-

pect of Sickness, Mourning, and Death. By JOHN JAMES, D.D., sometime Canon of Peterborough. New Edition. 12mo. 3s.

Thomas à Kempis, Of the Imitation

of Christ. With Red borders. 16mo. 2s. 6d.

Also a Cheap Edition, without the red borders, 1s., or in
Paper Cover, 6d.

· Forming a Volume of " Rivington's Devotional Series."

" A very beautiful edition. We commend it to the Clergy as an excellent gift-book for teachers and other workers."—CHURCH TIMES.

" This work is a precious relic of mediæval times, and will continue to be valued by every section of the Christian Church."—WEEKLY REVIEW.

" A beautifully printed pocket edition of this marvellous production of a man, who, out of the dark mists of *popery, saw so much of experimental religion. Those who are well grounded in evangelical truth may use it with profit."*—RECORD.

" A very cheap and handsome edition."—ROCK.

" This new edition is a marvel of cheapness."—CHURCH REVIEW.

" Beautifully printed, and very cheap editions of this long-used handbook of devotion."—LITERARY WORLD.

Also a New Translation, forming a Volume of the " Library
of Spiritual Works for English Catholics." Small 8vo. 5s.
[See page 16.]

Introduction to the Devout Life.

From the French of S. Francis de Sales, Bishop and Prince
of Geneva. A New Translation. With red borders. 16mo.
2s. 6d.

Forming a Volume of " Rivington's Devotional Series."

" A very beautiful edition of S. Francis de Sales' 'Devout Life:' a prettier little edition for binding, type, and paper, of a very great book is not often seen."—CHURCH REVIEW.

" The translation is a good one, and the volume is beautifully got up. It would serve admirably as a gift book to those who are able to appreciate so spiritual a writer as St. Francis."—CHURCH TIMES.

" It has been the food and hope of countless souls ever since its first appearance two centuries and a half ago, and it still ranks with Scupoli's 'Combattimento Spirituale,' and Arvisenet's 'Memoriale Vitæ Sacerdotalis,' as *among the very best works of ascetic theology.*—UNION REVIEW.

" We should be curious to know by how many different hands 'The Devout Life' of S. Francis de Sales had been translated into English. At any rate, its popularity is so great that Messrs. Rivington have just issued another translation of it. The style is good, and the volume is of a most convenient size."—JOHN BULL.

" This volume will be highly valued. The 'Introduction to the Devout Life' is preceded by a sketch of the life of the author, and a dedicatory prayer of the author is also given."—PUBLIC OPINION.

Also a New Translation, forming a Volume of the " Library
of Spiritual Works for English Catholics." Small 8vo. 5s.
[See page 16.]

The English Poems of George Herbert,

together with his Collection of Proverbs, entitled JACULA
PRUDENTUM.   With red borders.   16mo.   2s. 6d.

Forming a Volume of "Rivington's Devotional Series."

" *This beautiful little volume will be found specially convenient as a pocket manual. The 'Jacula Prudentum,' or proverbs, deserve to be more widely known than they are at present. In many copies of George Herbert's writings these quaint sayings have been unfortunately omitted.*"—ROCK.

" *George Herbert is too much a household name to require any introduction. It will be sufficient to say that Messrs. Rivington have published a most compact and convenient edition of the poems and proverbs of this illustrious English divine.*"—ENGLISH CHURCHMAN.

" *An exceedingly pretty edition, the most attractive form we have yet seen from this delightful author, as a gift-book.*"—UNION REVIEW.

" *A very beautiful edition of the quaint old English bard. All lovers of the 'Holy' Herbert will be grateful to Messrs. Rivington for the care and pains they have bestowed in supplying them with this and withal convenient copy of poems so well known and so deservedly prized.*"—LONDON QUARTERLY REVIEW.

" *A very tasteful little book, and will doubtless be acceptable to many.*"—RECORD.

" *We commend this little book heartily to our readers. It contains Herbert's English poems and the 'Jacula Prudentum,' in a very neat volume, which does much credit to the publishers; it will, we hope, meet with extensive circulation as a choice gift-book at a moderate price.*"—CHRISTIAN OBSERVER.

A Short and Plain Instruction for the

better Understanding of the Lord's Supper ; to which is annexed
the Office of the Holy Communion, with proper Helps and
Directions.   By the Right Rev. THOMAS WILSON, D.D.,
sometime Lord Bishop of Sodor and Man.   Complete Edition,
in large type, with rubrics and borders in red.   16mo.   2s. 6d.

Also a Cheap Edition, without the red borders, 1s., or in
Paper Cover, 6d.

Forming a Volume of " Rivington's Devotional Series."

" *The Messrs. Rivington have published a new and unabridged edition of that deservedly popular work, Bishop Wilson on the Lord's Supper. The edition is here presented in three forms, suited to the various members of the household.*"—PUBLIC OPINION.

" *We cannot withhold the expression of our admiration of the style and* elegance in which this work is got up.—PRESS AND ST. JAMES' CHRONICLE.

" *A departed Author being dead yet speaketh in a way which will never be out of date; Bishop Wilson on the Lord's Supper, published by Messrs. Rivington, in bindings to suit all tastes and pockets.*" — CHURCH REVIEW.

The Rule and Exercises of Holy Living.

By the Right Rev. JEREMY TAYLOR, D.D., sometime Bishop of Down and Connor, and Dromore. With red borders. 16mo. 2s. 6d.

Also a Cheap Edition, without the red borders, 1s.

Forming a Volume of " Rivington's Devotional Series."

The Rule and Exercises of Holy Dying.

By the Right Rev. JEREMY TAYLOR, D.D., sometime Bishop of Down and Connor, and Dromore. With red borders. 16mo. 2s. 6d.

Also a Cheap Edition, without the red borders, 1s.

The 'HOLY LIVING' and the 'HOLY DYING' may be had bound together in one Volume, 5s. ; or without the red borders, 2s. 6d.

Forming a Volume of " Rivington's Devotional Series."

*" The publishers have done good service by the production of these beautiful editions of works, which will never lose their preciousness to devout Christian spirits. We have only to testify to the good taste, judgment, and care shown in these editions. They are extremely beautiful in typography and in the general getting up."—*ENGLISH INDEPENDENT.

*" We ought not to conclude our notice of recent devotional books, without mentioning to our readers the above new, elegant, and cheap reprint, which we trust will never be out of date or out of favour in the English branch of the Catholic Church."—*LITERARY CHURCHMAN.

*" These manuals of piety, written by the pen of the most beautiful writer and the most impressive divine of the English Church, need no commendation from us. They are known to the world, read in all lands, and translated, we have heard, into fifty different languages. For two centuries they have fed the faith of thousands upon thousands of souls, now we trust happy with their God, and perhaps meditating in Heaven with gratitude on their celestial truths, kindled in their souls by a writer who was little short of being inspired."—*ROCK.

*" These little volumes will be appreciated as presents of inestimable value."—*PUBLIC OPINION.

A Practical Treatise concerning Evil

Thoughts: wherein their Nature, Origin, and Effect are distinctly considered and explained, with many Useful Rules for restraining and suppressing such Thoughts ; suited to the various conditions of Life, and the several tempers of Mankind, more especially of melancholy Persons. By WILLIAM CHILCOT, M.A. New Edition. With red borders. 16mo. 2s. 6d.

Forming a Volume of " Rivington's Devotional Series."

The Spirit of S. Francis de Sales, Bishop

and Prince of Geneva. Translated from the French by the Author of "The Life of S. Francis de Sales," "A Dominican Artist," &c., &c. Crown 8vo. 6s.

"*S. Francis de Sales, as shown to us by the Bishop of Belley, was clearly as bright and lively a companion as many a sinner of witty reputation. He was a student of human nature on the highest grounds, but he used his knowledge for amusement as well as edification. Naturally we learn this from one of his male friends rather than from his female adorers. This friend is Jean-Pierre Camus, Bishop of Belley, author, we are told, of two hundred books—one only however still known to fame, the Spirit of S. Francis de Sales, which has fairly earned him the title of the ecclesiastical Boswell.*"
—SATURDAY REVIEW.

"*An admirable translation of Bishop Camus' well-known collection of that good man's sayings and opinions. . . . . Among the best passages in the book are those on charity, on controversy (at p. 404), on true devotion as exemplified in a right fulfilling of our own vocation, and upon hearing the Word of God; the condemnation at page 41 of those who are always finding fault with preachers is almost identical with George Herbert's stanzas on the same subject. As a whole, we can imagine no more delightful companion than 'The Spirit of S. Francis de Sales,' nor, we may add, a more useful one.*"—PEOPLE'S MAGAZINE.

The Hidden Life of the Soul. From

the French. By the Author of "A Dominican Artist," "Life of Bossuet," &c., &c. New Edition. Small 8vo. 2s. 6d.

"'*The Hidden Life of the Soul,' by the author of 'A Dominican Artist,' is from the writings of Father Grou, a French refugee priest of 1792, who died at Lulworth. It well deserves the character given it of being 'earnest and sober,' and not 'sensational.*'"
—GUARDIAN.

"*From the French of Jean Nicolas Grou, a pious Priest, whose works teach resignation to the Divine will. He loved, we are told, to inculcate simplicity, freedom from all affectation and unreality, the patience and humility which are too surely grounded in self-knowledge to be surprised at a fall, but withal so allied to confidence*

in God as to make recovery easy and sure. This is the spirit of the volume which is intended to furnish advice to those who would cultivate a quiet, meek, and childlike spirit."—PUBLIC OPINION.

"*There is a wonderful charm about these readings—so calm, so true, so thoroughly Christian. We do not know where they would come amiss. As materials for a consecutive series of meditations for the faithful at a series of early celebrations they would be excellent, or for private reading during Advent or Lent.*"—LITERARY CHURCHMAN.

The Office of the Most Holy Name;

a Devotional Help for Young Persons. New Edition. 18mo. 1s.

Ancient Hymns. From the Roman

Breviary. For Domestic Use every Morning and Evening of the Week, and on the Holy Days of the Church. To which are added, Original Hymns, principally of Commemoration and Thanksgiving for Christ's Holy Ordinances. By RICHARD MANT, D.D., sometime Lord Bishop of Down and Connor. New Edition. Small 8vo. 5s.

"*Real poetry wedded to words that breathe the purest and the sweetest spirit of Christian devotion. The translations from the old Latin Hymnal are close and faithful renderings.*" —STANDARD.

"*As a Hymn writer Bishop Mant deservedly occupies a prominent place in the esteem of Churchmen, and we doubt not that many will be the readers who will welcome this new edition of his translations and original compositions.*"—ENGLISH CHURCHMAN.

"*A new edition of Bishop Mant's 'Ancient Hymns from the Roman Breviary' forms a handsome little volume, and it is interesting to compare some of these translations with the more modern ones of our own day.*

While we have no hesitation in awarding the palm to the latter, the former are an evidence of the earliest germs of that yearning of the devout mind for something better than Tate and Brady, and which is now so richly supplied."—CHURCH TIMES.

"*This valuable manual will be of great assistance to all compilers of Hymn Books. The translations are graceful, clear, and forcible, and the original hymns deserve the highest praise. Bishop Mant has caught the very spirit of true psalmody, his metre flows musically, and there is a tuneful ring in his verses which especially adapts them for congregational singing.*"—ROCK.

The Mysteries of Mount Calvary.

Translated from the Latin of Antonio de Guevara. Edited by the Rev. ORBY SHIPLEY, M.A. Square crown 8vo. 3s. 6d.

Counsels on Holiness of Life. Trans-

lated from the Spanish of "The Sinner's Guide" by Luis de Granada. Edited by the Rev. ORBY SHIPLEY, M.A. Square crown 8vo. 5s.

Preparation for Death. Translated from

the Italian of Alfonso, Bishop of S. Agatha. Edited by the Rev. ORBY SHIPLEY, M.A. Square crown 8vo. 5s.

Examination of Conscience upon Special

Subjects. Translated and abridged from the French of Tronson. Edited by the Rev. ORBY SHIPLEY, M.A. Square crown 8vo. 5s.

Thoughts on Personal Religion; being

a Treatise on the Christian Life in its Two Chief Elements, Devotion and Practice. By EDWARD MEYRICK GOULBURN, D.D., Dean of Norwich. New Edition. Small 8vo. 6s. 6d. Also a Cheap Edition, 3s. 6d.

Presentation Edition, elegantly printed on Toned Paper. Two vols. Small 8vo. 10s. 6d.

The Pursuit of Holiness: a Sequel to

"Thoughts on Personal Religion," intended to carry the Reader somewhat farther onward in the Spiritual Life. By EDWARD MEYRICK GOULBURN, D.D., Dean of Norwich. Fourth Edition. Small 8vo. 5s. Also a Cheap Edition, 3s. 6d.

The Gospel of the Childhood: a Practi-

cal and Devotional Commentary on the Single Incident of our Blessed Lord's Childhood (St. Luke ii. 41 to the end) ; designed as a Help to Meditation on the Holy Scriptures, for Children and Young Persons. By EDWARD MEYRICK GOULBURN, D.D., Dean of Norwich. Second Edition. Square 16mo. 5s.

An Introduction to the Devotional

Study of the Holy Scriptures. By EDWARD MEYRICK GOULBURN, D.D., Dean of Norwich. Ninth Edition. Small 8vo. 3s. 6d.

Evangelical Life, as seen in the Ex-

ample of our Lord Jesus Christ. By JOHN JAMES, D.D. sometime Canon of Peterborough. Second Edition. 12mo. 7s. 6d.

Private Devotions for School-boys;

with Rules of Conduct. By WILLIAM HENRY, Third Lord Lyttleton. New Edition. 32mo. 6d.

A Companion to the Lord's Supper.
By the Plain Man's Friend.   Fifth Edition.   18mo.   8*d.*

Strena Christiana; a Christian New
Year's Gift; or, Brief Exhortations to the Chief Outward Acts
of Virtue. Translated from the Latin of Sir Harbottle
Grimston, Bart., Member of Parliament, 1640.   32mo.   1*s.* 6*d.*
Or the Latin and English together.   32mo.   2*s.* 6*d.*

4. Parish Work.

The Book of Church Law. Being an

Exposition of the Legal Rights and Duties of the Clergy and Laity of the Church of England. By the Rev. JOHN HENRY BLUNT, M.A., F.S.A. Revised by WALTER G. F. PHILLIMORE, B.C.L., Barrister-at-Law, and Chancellor of the Diocese of Lincoln. Crown 8vo. 7s. 6d.

CONTENTS.

BOOK I.—THE CHURCH AND ITS LAWS.—The Constitutional Status of the Church of England—The Law of the Church of England—The Administration of Church Law.

BOOK II.—THE MINISTRATIONS OF THE CHURCH.—Holy Baptism—Confirmation—The Holy Communion—Divine Service in General—Holy Matrimony—The Churching of Women—The Visitation of the Sick—The Practice of Confession—The Burial of the Dead.

BOOK III.—THE PAROCHIAL CLERGY.—Holy Orders—Licensed Curates—The Cure of Souls.

BOOK IV.—PAROCHIAL LAY OFFICERS.—Churchwardens—Church Trustees—Parish Clerks, Sextons and Beadles—Vestries.

BOOK V.—CHURCHES AND CHURCHYARDS.—The Acquisition of Churches and Churchyards as Ecclesiastical Property—Churches and Ecclesiastical Persons—Churches and Secular Persons.

BOOK VI.—THE ENDOWMENTS OF THE PAROCHIAL CLERGY.—Incomes—Parsonage Houses—The Sequestration of Benefices.

APPENDIX.—The Canons of 1603 and 1865—The Church Discipline Act of 1840—The Benefices Resignation Act of 1871—The Ecclesiastical Dilapidations Act of 1871—The Sequestration Act of 1871—Index.

" *We have tested this work on various points of a crucial character, and have found it very accurate and full in its information. It embodies the results of the most recent Acts of the Legislature on the clerical profession and the rights of the laity.*"—STANDARD.

" *Already in our leading columns we have directed attention to Messrs. Blunt and Phillimore's 'Book of Church Law,' as an excellent manual for ordinary use. It is a book which should stand on every clergyman's shelves ready for use when any legal matter arises about which its possessor is in doubt. . . . It is to be hoped that the authorities at our Theological Colleges sufficiently recognize the value of a little legal knowledge on the part* of the clergy to recommend this book to their students. It would serve admirably as the text-book for a set of lectures, and we trust we shall hear that its publication has done something to encourage the younger clergy to make themselves masters of at least the general outlines of Ecclesiastical Law, as it relates to the Church of England.*"—CHURCH TIMES.

" *There is a copious index, and the whole volume forms a Handy-book of Church Law down to the present time, which, if found on the library shelves of most of the clergy, would often save them from much unnecessary trouble, vexation, and expense.*"—NATIONAL CHURCH.

Waterloo Place, London

Directorium Pastorale. The Principles

and Practice of Pastoral Work in the Church of England. By the Rev. JOHN HENRY BLUNT, M.A., F.S.A., Editor of "The Annotated Book of Common Prayer," &c., &c. Third Edition, revised. Crown 8vo. 7s. 6d.

"This is the third edition of a work which has become deservedly popular as the best extant exposition of the principles and practice of the pastoral work in the Church of England. Its hints and suggestions are based on practical experience, and it is further recommended by the majority of our Bishops at the ordination of priests and deacons."—STANDARD.

"Its practical usefulness to the paro-chial clergy is proved by the acceptance it has already received at their hands, and no faithful parish priest, who is working in real earnest for the extension of spiritual instruction amongst all classes of his flock, will rise from the perusal of its pages without having obtained some valuable hints as to the best mode of bringing home our Church's system to the hearts of his people."—NATIONAL CHURCH.

Priest and Parish. By the Rev. HARRY

JONES, M.A., Rector of St. George's-in-the-East, London. Square crown 8vo. 6s. 6d.

Ars Pastoria. By FRANK PARNELL, M.A.,

Rector of Oxtead, near Godstone. Small 8vo. 2s.

Instructions for the Use of Candidates

for Holy Orders, and of the Parochial Clergy; with Acts of Parliament relating to the same, and Forms proposed to be used. By CHRISTOPHER HODGSON, M.A., Secretary to the Governors of Queen Anne's Bounty. Ninth Edition. 8vo. 16s.

Post-Mediæval Preachers: Some Ac-

count of the most Celebrated Preachers of the 15th, 16th, and 17th Centuries; with Outlines of their Sermons, and Specimens of their style. By the Rev. S. BARING-GOULD, M.A. Post 8vo. 7s.

Flowers and Festivals; or, Directions

for the Floral Decoration of Churches. By W. A. BARRETT, Mus. Bac., Oxon., of St. Paul's Cathedral. With Coloured Illustrations. Second Edition. Square 16mo. 5s.

The Chorister's Guide. By W. A. BAR-

RETT, Mus. Bac., Oxon, of St. Paul's Cathedral. Second Edition. Square 16mo. 2s. 6d.

" . . . One of the most useful books of instructions for choristers—and, we may add, choral singers generally—that has ever emanated from the musical press. . . . Mr. Barrett's teaching is not only conveyed to his readers with the consciousness of being master of his subject, but he employs words terse and clear, so that his meaning may be promptly caught by the neophyte. . . ."—ATHENÆUM.

" A nicely graduated, clear, and excellent introduction to the duties of a chorister."—STANDARD.

" It seems clear and precise enough to serve its end."—EXAMINER.

" A useful manual for giving boys such a practical and technical knowledge of music as shall enable them to sing both with confidence and precision."—CHURCH HERALD.

"In this little volume we have a manual long called for by the requirements of church music. In a series of thirty-two lessons it gives, with an

admirable conciseness, and an equally observable completeness, all that is necessary a chorister should be taught out of a book, and a great deal calculated to have a value as bearing indirectly upon his actual practice in singing."—MUSICAL STANDARD.

" We can highly recommend the present able manual."—EDUCATIONAL TIMES.

" A very useful manual, not only for choristers, or rather those who may aim at becoming choristers, but for others, who wish to enter upon the study of music."—ROCK.

" The work will be found of singular utility by those who have to instruct choirs."—CHURCH TIMES.

" A most grateful contribution to the agencies for improving our Services. It is characterised by all that clearness in combination with conciseness of style which has made 'Flowers and Festivals' so universally admired."—TORONTO HERALD.

Church Organs: their Position and Con-

struction. With an Appendix containing some Account of the Mediæval Organ Case still existing at Old Radnor, South Wales. By FREDERICK HEATHCOTE SUTTON, M.A., Vicar of Theddingworth. With Illustrations. Imperial folio. 6s. 6d.

Notes on Church Organs: their Position

and the Materials used in their Construction. By C. K. K. BISHOP. With Illustrations. Small 4to. 6s.

Stones of the Temple; or, Lessons
from the Fabric and Furniture of the Church. By WALTER
FIELD, M.A., F.S.A., Vicar of Godmersham. With numerous
Illustrations. Second Edition. Crown 8vo. 7s. 6d.

" *Any one who wishes for simple information on the subjects of Church-
architecture and furniture, cannot do
better than consult ' Stones of the
Temple.' Mr. Field modestly dis-
claims any intention of supplanting
the existing regular treatises, but his
book shows an amount of research, and
a knowledge of what he is talking
about, which make it practically useful as well as pleasant. The woodcuts
are numerous, and some of them very
pretty.*"—GRAPHIC.

"*A very charming book, by the Rev.
Walter Field, who was for years
Secretary of one of the leading Church
Societies. Mr. Field has a loving reverence for the beauty of the* domus
mansionalis Dei, *as the old law books
called the Parish Church. . . . .
Thoroughly sound in Church feeling,
Mr. Field has chosen the medium of a
tale to embody real incidents illustrative of the various portions of his subject. There is no attempt at elaboration of the narrative, which, indeed,
is rather a string of anecdotes than a
story, but each chapter brings home to
the mind its own lesson, and each is
illustrated with some very interesting
engravings. . . . The work will
properly command a hearty reception
from Churchmen. The footnotes are
occasionally most valuable, and are
always pertinent, and the text is sure
to be popular with young folks for
Sunday reading.*"—STANDARD.

"*Mr. Field's chapters on brasses,
chancel screens, crosses, encaustic tiles,
mural paintings, porches and pave-
ments, are agreeably written, and
people with a turn for Ritualism will
no doubt find them edifying. The*

*volume, as we have said, is not without
significance for readers who are unable
to sympathise with the object of the
writer. The illustrations of Church-
architecture and Church ornaments
are very attractive.*"—PALL MALL
GAZETTE.

" '*Stones of the Temple' is a grave
book, the result of antiquarian, or
rather ecclesiological, tastes and of
devotional feelings. We can recommend it to young people of both sexes,
and it will not disappoint the most
learned among them. . . . Mr.
Field has brought together, from well
known authorities, a considerable mass
of archæological information, which
will interest the readers he especially
addresses.*"—ATHENÆUM.

"*Very appropriate as a Christmas
present, is an elegant and instructive
book, which is in great measure a republication of some papers with which
many of our readers are familiar.
The first sixteen chapters of 'Stones
of the Temple,' by Walter Field, appeared in the 'Church Builder.' They
are now completed by fourteen more,
and both together furnish a full and
clear account of the meaning and history of the several parts of the fabric
and of the furniture of the Church.
It is illustrated with a number of carefully drawn pictures, sometimes of
entire churches, sometimes of remarkable monuments, windows, or wall
paintings. We may add that the style
of the commentary, which is cast in the
form of a dialogue between a parson
and some of his parishioners, and hangs
together by a slight thread of story, is
quiet and sensible, and free from exaggeration or intolerance.*"—GUARDIAN.

A Handy Book on the Ecclesiastical
Dilapidations Act, 1871. With the Amendment Act, 1872.
By EDWARD G. BRUTON, F.R.I.B.A., Diocesan Surveyor,
Oxford. With Analytical Index and Precedent Forms. Second
Edition. Crown 8vo. 5s.

and at Oxford and Cambridge

The Church Builder : a Quarterly Journal

of Church Extension in England and Wales. Published in
connexion with "The Incorporated Church Building Society."
13 Volumes. With Illustrations. Crown 8vo. 1s. 6d. each.
[Sold separately.

List of Charities, General and Diocesan,

for the Relief of the Clergy, their Widows and Families. New
Edition. Small 8vo. 3s.

5. The Church and Doctrine.

The Holy Catholic Church; its Divine
Ideal, Ministry, and Institutions. A short Treatise. With a Catechism on each Chapter, forming a Course of Methodical Instruction on the subject. By EDWARD MEYRICK GOULBURN, D.D., Dean of Norwich. Second Edition. Crown 8vo. 6s. 6d.

CONTENTS.

"*Dr. Goulburn has conferred a great boon on the Church of England by the treatise before us, which vindicates her claim as a branch of the Catholic Church on the allegiance of her children, setting forth as he does, with singular precision and power, the grounds of her title-deeds, and the Christian character of her doctrine and discipline.*"—STANDARD.

"*His present book would have been used for an educational book even if he had not invited men to make that use of it by appending a catechism to each particular chapter, and thus founding a course of methodical instruction upon his text. We have not yet come across any better book for giving to Dissenters or to such inquirers as hold fast to Holy Scripture. It is, we need scarcely say, steeped in Scripturalness, and full of bright and suggestive interpretations of particular texts.*"—ENGLISH CHURCHMAN.

". . . . *Must prove highly useful, not only to young persons, but to the very large class, both Churchmen and Dissenters, who are painfully ignorant of what the Catholic Church really is, and of the peculiar and fixed character of her institutions.*"—ROCK.

"*The catechetical questions and answers at the end of each chapter will be useful both for teachers and learners, and the side-notes at the head of the paragraphs are very handy.*"—CHURCH TIMES.

"*It contains a great deal of instructive matter, especially in the catechisms—or, as they might be called, dialogues—and is instinct with a spirit at once temperate and uncompromising. It is a good book for all who wish to understand, neither blindly asserting it nor being half ashamed of it, the position of a loyal member of the English Church.*"—GUARDIAN.

---

and at Oxford and Cambridge

Dictionary of Doctrinal and Historical

Theology.   By Various Writers.   Edited by the Rev. JOHN HENRY BLUNT, M.A., F.S.A., Editor of the "Annotated Book of Common Prayer," &c., &c.   Second Edition.   Imperial 8vo, 42s., or half-bound in morocco, 52s. 6d.

"*Taken as a whole the articles are the work of practised writers, and well-informed and solid theologians. . . . . We know no book of its size and bulk which supplies the information here given at all; far less which supplies it in an arrangement so accessible, with a completeness of information so thorough, and with an ability in the treatment of profound subjects so great.   Dr. Hook's most useful volume is a work of high calibre, but it is the work of a single mind.   We have here a wider range of thought from a greater variety of sides.   We have here also the work of men who evidently know what they write about, and are somewhat more profound (to say the least) than the writers of the current Dictionaries of Sects and Heresies.*"— GUARDIAN.

"*Thus it will be obvious that it takes a very much wider range than any undertaking of the same kind in our language; and that to those of our clergy who have not the fortune to spend in books, and would not have the leisure to use them if they possessed them, it will be the most serviceable and reliable substitute for a large library we can think of.   And in many cases, while keeping strictly within its province as a Dictionary, it contrives to be marvellously suggestive of thought and reflections, which a serious-minded man will take with him and ponder over for his own elaboration and future use.   We trust most sincerely that the book may be largely used.   For a present to a Clergyman on his ordination, or from a parishioner to his pastor, it would be most appropriate.   It may indeed be called 'a box of tools for a working clergyman.*'"—LITERARY CHURCHMAN.

"*Seldom has an English work of equal magnitude been so permeated with Catholic instincts, and at the same time seldom has a work on theology been kept so free from the drift*

of rhetorical incrustation.   Of course, it is not meant that all these remarks apply in their full extent to every article.   In a great Dictionary there are compositions, as in a great house there are vessels, of various kinds.   Some of these at a future day may be replaced by others more substantial in their build, more proportionate in their outline, and more elaborate in their detail.   But admitting all this, the whole remains a home to which the student will constantly recur, sure to find spacious chambers, substantial furniture, and (which is most important) no stinted light.*"—CHURCH REVIEW.

"*Within the sphere it has marked out for itself, no equally useful book of reference exists in English for the elucidation of theological problems. . . . Entries which display much care, research, and judgment in compilation, and which will make the task of the parish priest who is brought face to face with any of the practical questions which they involve far easier than has been hitherto.   The very fact that the utterances are here and there somewhat more guarded and hesitating than quite accords with our judgment, is a gain in so far as it protects the work from the charge of inculcating extreme views, and will thus secure its admission in many places where moderation is accounted the crowning grace.*"—CHURCH TIMES.

"*It will be found of admirable service to all students of theology, as advancing and maintaining the Church's views on all subjects as fall within the range of fair argument and inquiry.   It is not often that a work of so comprehensive and so profound a nature is marked to the very end by so many signs of wide and careful research, sound criticism, and well-founded and well-expressed belief.*"— STANDARD.

Dictionary of Sects, Heresies, Ecclesias-
tical Parties and Schools of Religious Thought. By Various
Writers. Edited by the Rev. JOHN HENRY BLUNT, M.A.,
F.S.A., Editor of the "Dictionary of Doctrinal and Historical
Theology," the "Annotated Book of Common Prayer," &c.,
&c. Imperial 8vo, 36s., or half-bound in morocco, 48s.

"Taken as a whole, we doubt not that the Dictionary will prove a useful work of reference ; and it may claim to give in reasonable compass a mass of information respecting many religious schools knowledge of which could previously only be acquired from amid a host of literature. The articles are written with great fairness, and in many cases display careful scholarly work."—ATHENÆUM.

"A very comprehensive and bold undertaking, and is certainly executed with a sufficient amount of ability and knowledge to entitle the book to rank very high in point of utility."—GUARDIAN.

*"That this is a work of some learning and research is a fact which soon becomes obvious to the reader.—*SPECTATOR.

"A whole library is condensed into this admirable volume. All authorities are named, and an invaluable index is supplied."—NOTES AND QUERIES.

"We have tested it rigidly, and in almost every instance we have been satisfied with the account given under the name of sects, heresy, or ecclesiastical party."—JOHN BULL.

"After all deductions, it is the fullest and most trustworthy book of the kind that we possess. The quantity of information it presents in a convenient and accessible form is enormous, and having once appeared, it becomes indispensable to the theological student."—CHURCH TIMES.

"It has considerable value as a copious work of reference, more especially since a list of authorities is in most cases supplied."—EXAMINER.

The Doctrine of the Church of England,
as stated in Ecclesiastical Documents set forth by Authority
of Church and State, in the Reformation Period between 1536
and 1662. Edited by the Rev. JOHN HENRY BLUNT, M.A.,
F.S.A., Editor of the "Dictionary of Doctrinal and Historical
Theology," the "Annotated Book of Common Prayer," &c.
&c. 8vo. 7s. 6d.

The Position of the Celebrant at the
Holy Communion, as ruled by the Purchas Judgment, con-
sidered in a Letter to the Lord Bishop of Winchester. By
MORTON SHAW, M.A., Rector of Rougham, Suffolk, Rural
Dean. Third Edition. 8vo. 5s., or in Paper Cover, 3s. 6d.

Prophecies and the Prophetic Spirit

in the Christian Era: an Historical Essay. By JOHN J.
IGN. VON DÖLLINGER, D.D., D.C.L.   Translated, with
Introduction, Notes, and Appendices, by the Rev. ALFRED
PLUMMER, M.A., Master of University College, Durham,
late Fellow of Trinity College, Oxford. 8vo.   10s. 6d.

Lectures   on   the   Reunion   of   the

Churches. By JOHN J. IGN. VON DÖLLINGER, D.D., D.C.L.
Authorized Translation, with Preface by HENRY NUTCOMBE
OXENHAM, M.A., late Scholar of Balliol College, Oxford.
Crown 8vo.   5s.

". . . Marked by all the author's well-known varied learning, breadth of view, and outspoken spirit. The momentous question which the Doctor discusses has long occupied the thoughts of some of the most earnest and enlightened divines in all branches of the Christian communion, though wide apart in other points of belief and practice. On the infinite importance of reunion among Christian Churches in their endeavour to evangelize the yet remaining two-thirds of the human race—strangers to any form of Christianity—the author enlarges with power and eloquence; and this topic is one of unusual and lasting interest, though, of course, only one among a host of others equally important and equally well discussed."—STANDARD.

"In the present state of thought respecting the union of the Churches, these Lectures will be welcomed by very many persons of different schools of religious thought. They are not the hasty words of an enthusiast, but the calm, well-considered, and carefully prepared writings of one whose soul is profoundly moved by his great subject. They form a contribution to the literature of this grave question, valuable alike for its breadth of historical survey, its fairness, the due regard paid to existing obstacles, and the practical character of its suggestions."—LONDON QUARTERLY REVIEW.

Letters from Rome on the Council.

By QUIRINUS.   Reprinted from the "Allgemeine Zeitung."
Authorized Translation.   Crown 8vo.   12s.

The Pope and the Council.   By JANUS.

Authorized Translation from the German.   Fourth Edition.
Crown 8vo.   7s. 6d.

Waterloo Place, London

Apostolical Succession in the Church

of England. By the Rev. ARTHUR W. HADDAN, B.D., late Rector of Barton-on-the-Heath. 8vo. 12s.

"*Thoroughly well written, clear and forcible in style, and fair in tone. It cannot but render valuable service in placing the claims of the Church in their true light before the English public.*"—GUARDIAN.

"*Among the many standard theological works devoted to this important subject Mr. Haddan's will hold a high place.*"—STANDARD.

"*We should be glad to see the volume widely circulated and generally read.*"—JOHN BULL.

"*A weighty and valuable treatise, and we hope that the study of its sound and well-reasoned pages will do much to fix the importance, and the full meaning of the doctrine in question, in the minds of Church people. . . .*

We hope that our extracts will lead our readers to study Mr. Haddan for themselves."—LITERARY CHURCHMAN.

"*This is not only a very able and carefully written treatise upon the doctrine of Apostolical Succession, but it is also a calm yet noble vindication of the validity of the Anglican Orders: it well sustains the brilliant reputation which Mr. Haddan left behind him at Oxford, and it supplements his other profound historical researches in ecclesiastical matters. This book will remain for a long time the classic work upon English Orders.*"—CHURCH REVIEW.

"*A very temperate, but a very well reasoned book.*"—WESTMINSTER REVIEW.

The Civil Power in its Relations to the

Church; considered with Special Reference to the Court of Final Ecclesiastical Appeal in England. By the Rev. JAMES WAYLAND JOYCE, M.A., Prebendary of Hereford, and Examining Chaplain to the Bishop of Hereford. 8vo. 10s. 6d.

Defence of the English Ordinal, with

some Observations upon Spiritual Jurisdiction and the Power of the Keys. By the Rev. W. R. CHURTON, M.A., Fellow of King's College, Cambridge, and Honorary Canon of Rochester Cathedral. 8vo. 3s.

The Religion, Discipline, and Rites of

the Church of England. Written at the Instance of Edward Hyde, Earl of Clarendon. By JOHN COSIN, sometime Bishop of Durham. Now first published in English. By the Rev. FREDERICK MEYRICK, M.A. Small 8vo. 1s.

Eight Lectures on the Miracles; being

the Bampton Lectures for 1865. By J. B. MOZLEY, D.D., Regius Professor of Divinity, and Canon of Christ Church, Oxford. Third Edition, revised. Crown 8vo. 7s. 6d.

"*There is great brightness and beauty in many of the images in which the author condenses the issues of his arguments. And many passages are marked by that peculiar kind of eloquence which comes with the force of close and vigorous thinking; passages which slime-like steal through their very temper, and which are instinct with a controlled energy, that melts away all ruggedness of language. There can be no question that, in the deeper qualities of a scientific theology, the book is thoroughly worthy of the highest reputation which had been gained by Mr. Mozley's previous writings.*"—CONTEMPORARY REVIEW.
"*Mr. Mozley's Bampton Lectures*

are an example, and a very fine one, of a mode of theological writing which is characteristic of the Church of England, and almost peculiar to it. The distinguishing features, a combination of intense seriousness with a self-restrained, severe calmness, and of very vigorous and wide-ranging reasoning on the realities of the case. . . . . Mr. Mozley's book belongs to that class of writings of which Butler may be taken as the type. It is strong, genuine argument about difficult matters, fairly facing what is difficult, fairly trying to grapple, not with what appears the gist and strong point of a question, but with what really and at bottom is the knot of it."—TIMES.

The Happiness of the Blessed con-

sidered as to the Particulars of their State: their Recognition of each other in that State: and its Differences of Degrees. To which are added Musings on the Church and her Services. By RICHARD MANT, D.D., sometime Lord Bishop of Down and Connor. New Edition. Small 8vo. 3s. 6d.

"*A welcome republication of a treatise once highly valued, and which can never lose its value. Many of our readers already know the fulness and discrimination with which the author treats his subject, which must be one of the most delightful topics of meditation to all whose hearts are where the only true treasure is, and particularly to those who are entering upon the evening of life.*"—CHURCH REVIEW.
"*The value of this book needs not to be referred to, its standard character having been for many years past established. The edition in which it reappears has evidently been carefully prepared, and will be the means of making it more generally known.*"— BELL'S MESSENGER.

"*All recognise the authority of the command to set the affections on things above, and such works as the one now before us will be found helpful towards this good end. We are, therefore, sincerely glad that Messrs. Rivington have brought out a new edition of Bishop Mant's valuable treatise.*"—RECORD.
"*This beautiful and devotional treatise, which it is impossible to read without feeling a more deepened interest in the eternal blessedness which awaits the true servants of our God, concludes very appropriately with 'Musings on the Church and her Services,' which we cordially recommend to our readers.*" —ROCK.

Out of the Body. A Scriptural Inquiry.

By the Rev. JAMES S. POLLOCK, M.A., Incumbent of S. Alban's, Birmingham. Crown 8vo. 5s.

CONTENTS.

Introduction—Scope of the Inquiry—The Presentiment—The Anticipation—The Departure—The Life of the Body—The Life of the Spirit—Dream-Life – The Spirit-World—Spirit-Groups—Helping one another—Limits of Communication—Spiritual Manifestations.

" We have read this book with interest. . . We esteem the honesty with which it is evidently written, and we admire the courage which the author has shown in searching the Bible for evidences as to the destination of departed spirits, and in accepting such evidences as he has found, without attempting to explain them away or venturing to ignore them—two modes of proceeding which characterise most Scriptural exigesis."—BIRMINGHAM MORNING NEWS.

" The work is divided into twelve chapters, which we should imagine, from their style, to have originally formed sermons. . . . The writer discusses with considerable ability, and in a devout and reverent frame of mind, bringing whatever he has to say to the test of the Scriptures. The tone which pervades the book is as much to be commended as the interesting matter with which its pages abound."—SPIRITUAL MAGAZINE.

The Origin and Development of Religious Belief. By the Rev. S. BARING-GOULD, M.A., Author of " Curious Myths of the Middle Ages."

Vol. I. MONOTHEISM and POLYTHEISM. Second Edition. 8vo. 15s.

Vol. II. CHRISTIANITY. 8vo. 15s.

" The ability which Mr. Baring-Gould displays in the treatment of a topic which branches out in so many directions, and requires such precise handling, is apparent. His pages abound with the results of large reading and calm reflection. The man of culture, thought, philosophic cast, is mirrored in the entire argument. The book is sound and healthy in tone. It excites the reader's interest, and brightens the path of inquiry opened to his view. The language, too, is appropriate, neat, lucid, often happy, sometimes wonderfully terse and vigorous." —ATHENÆUM.

" Mr. Baring-Gould has undertaken a great and ambitious work. And no one can deny that he possesses some eminent qualifications for this great work. He has a wealth of erudition of the most varied description, especially in those particular regions of mediæval legend and Teutonic mytho-

logy which are certain to make large contributions to the purpose he has in hand. It is a contribution to religious thought of very high value."—GUARDIAN.

" Mr. Baring-Gould's work, from the importance of its subject and the lucid force of its expositions, as well as from the closeness of argument and copiousness of illustration with which its comprehensive views are treated, is entitled to attentive study, and will repay the reader by amusement and instruction."—MORNING POST.

" Our space warns us that we are attempting in vain to compress into a few columns the contents of four hundred pages of a work which has had few equals for brilliancy, learning, and point in this department of literature. We therefore conclude by recommending the volume itself to all students of mind and theology."—CHURCH TIMES.

Our Mother Church: being Simple Talk

on High Topics.   By ANNE MERCIER.   New Edition.
Small 8vo.   3s. 6d.

"We have rarely come across a book dealing with an old subject in a healthier and, as far as may be, more original manner, while yet thoroughly practical. It is intended for and admirably adapted to the use of girls. Thoroughly reverent in its tone, and bearing in every page marks of learned research, it is yet easy of comprehension, and explains ecclesiastical terms with the accuracy of a lexicon without the accompanying dulness. It is to be hoped that the book will attain to the large circulation it justly merits."—JOHN BULL.

"We have never seen a book for girls of its class which commends itself to us more particularly. The author, who is the wife of an earnest parish priest of the Anglican school, near London, calls her work 'simple talk on great subjects,' and calls it by a name that describes it almost as completely as we could do in a longer notice than we can spare the volume. Here are the headings of the chapters:—

'The Primitive Church,' 'Primitive Places and Modes of Worship,' 'The Early English Church,' 'The Monastic Orders,' 'The Friars,' 'A Review of Church History,' 'The Prayer Book,' (four chapters), 'Symbolism,' 'Church Architecture,' 'Windows and Bells,' 'Church Music,' 'Church Work.' No one can fail to comprehend the beautifully simple, devout, and appropriate language in which Mrs. Mercier embodies what she has to say; and for the facts with which she deals she has taken good care to have their accuracy assured."—STANDARD.

"The plan of this pleasant-looking book is excellent. It is a kind of Mrs. Markham on the Church of England, written especially for girls, and we shall not be surprised to find it become a favourite in schools. It is really a conversational hand-book to the English Church's history, doctrine, and ritual, compiled by a very diligent reader from some of the best modern Anglican sources."—ENGLISH CHURCHMAN.

A Selection from the Spiritual Letters

of S. Francis de Sales, Bishop and Prince of Geneva.   Translated by the Author of "Life of S. Francis de Sales," "A Dominican Artist," &c. &c.   Crown 8vo.   6s.

"It is a collection of epistolary correspondence of rare interest and excellence. With those who have read the Life, there cannot but have been a strong desire to know more of so beautiful a character as S. Francis de Sales. He was a model of Christian saintliness and religious virtue for all time, and one everything relating to whom, so great were the accomplishments of his mind as well as the devotion of his heart, has a charm which delights, instructs, and elevates."—CHURCH HERALD.

"A few months back we had the pleasure of welcoming the Life of S. Francis de Sales. Here is the pro-

mised sequel:—the 'Selection from his Spiritual Letters' then announced:—and a great boon it will be to many. The Letters are addressed to people of all sorts:—to men and to women:—to laity and to ecclesiastics, to people living in the world, or at court, and to the inmates of Religious Houses. And what an idea it gives one of the widely ramifying influence of one good man and of the untiring diligence of a man, who in spite of all his external duties, could find or make the time for all these letters. We hope that with our readers it may be totally needless to urge such a volume on their notice."—LITERARY CHURCHMAN.

The Apostolic Fathers. The Epistles of

S. Clement, S. Ignatius, S. Barnabas, S. Polycarp, together
with the Martyrdom of S. Ignàtius and S. Polycarp. Translated into English, with an Introductory Notice, by CHARLES
H. HOOLE, M.A. Small 8vo. 5s. 6d.

The Argument Delivered before the

Judicial Committee of the Privy Council. By ARCHIBALD
JOHN STEPHENS, LL.D., one of Her Majesty's Counsel in the
case of THOMAS BYARD SHEPPARD against WILLIAM EARLY
BENNETT, Clerk. With an Appendix containing their Lord-
ships' Judgment. 8vo. 9s.

St. John Chrysostom's Liturgy. Trans-

lated by H. C. ROMANOFF, Author of "Sketches of the Rites
and Customs of the Greco-Russian Church," &c. With Illustrations. Square crown 8vo. 4s. 6d.

The Intermediate State of the Soul

between Death and the Resurrection. A Sermon preached at
the Church of All Saints, Windsor. By CHR. WORDSWORTH,
D.D., Bishop of Lincoln. 18mo. 1s.

Report of the Proceedings at the Re-

union Conference held at Bonn, September 1874. With a
Preface by HENRY PARRY LIDDON, D.D., D.C.L., Canon
of St. Paul's, and Ireland Professor of Exegesis in the University
of Oxford. Small 8vo. 3s. 6d.

A Vicar's View of Church Patronage.

By the Rev. J. GODSON, M.A., Vicar of Ashby Folville, in
the Diocese of Peterborough. Small 8vo, cloth limp. 2s.

Dogmatic Faith: an Inquiry into the

Relation subsisting between Revelation and Dogma. Being the Bampton Lectures for 1867. By EDWARD GARBETT, M.A., Incumbent of Christ Church, Surbiton. New Edition. Crown 8vo. 5*s.*

6. Sermons.

Some Elements of Religion. Lent
Lectures. By HENRY PARRY LIDDON, D.D., D.C.L., Canon
of St. Paul's, and Ireland Professor of Exegesis in the University of Oxford. Second Edition. Crown 8vo. 5s.

CONTENTS.

The Idea of Religion—God, the Object of Religion—The Subject of Religion,
the Soul—The Obstacle to Religion, Sin—Prayer, the Characteristic
action of Religion—The Mediator, the Guarantee of Religious Life.

The Divinity of our Lord and Saviour
Jesus Christ. Being the Bampton Lectures for 1866.
By HENRY PARRY LIDDON, D.D., D.C.L., Canon of St.
Paul's, and Ireland Professor of Exegesis in the University of
Oxford. Fifth Edition. Crown 8vo. 5s.

Sermons Preached before the Univer-
sity of Oxford. By HENRY PARRY LIDDON, D.D., D.C.L.,
Canon of St. Paul's, and Ireland Professor of Exegesis in
the University of Oxford. Fifth Edition, revised. Crown
8vo. 5s.

CONTENTS.

God and the Soul—The Law of Progress—The Honour of Humanity—The
Freedom of the Spirit—Immortality—Humility and Action—The Conflict
of Faith with undue Exaltation of Intellect—Lessons of the Holy Manger
—The Divine Victim—The Risen Life—Our Lord's Ascension, the
Church's Gain—Faith in a Holy Ghost—The Divine Indwelling a motive
to Holiness.

---

and at Oxford and Cambridge

The Life of Justification. A Series of

Lectures delivered in Substance at All Saints', Margaret Street, in Lent, 1870. By the Rev. GEORGE BODY, B.A., Rector of Kirkby Misperton. Fourth Edition. Crown 8vo. 4s. 6d.

CONTENTS.

Justification the Want of Humility—Christ our Justification—Union with Christ the Condition of Justification—Conversion and Justification—The Life of Justification—The Progress and End of Justification.

"*On the whole we have rarely met with a more clear, intelligible and persuasive statement of the truth as regards the important topics on which the volume treats. Sermon II. in particular, will strike every one by its eloquence and beauty, but we scarcely like to specify it, lest in praising it we should seem to disparage the other portions of this admirable little work.*"— CHURCH TIMES.

"*These discourses show that their author's position is due to something more and higher than mere fluency, gesticulation, and flexibility of voice. He appears as having drunk deeply at the fountain of St. Augustine, and as understanding how to translate the burning words of that mighty genius*

into the current language of to-day." —UNION REVIEW.

"*There is real power in these sermons:—power, real power, and plenty of it. . . . There is such a moral veraciousness about him, such a profound and over-mastering belief that Christ has proved a bonâ-fide cure for unholiness, and such an intensity of eagerness to lead others to seek and profit by that means of attaining the true sanctity which alone can enter Heaven—that we wonder not at the crowds which hang upon his preaching, nor at the success of his fervid appeals to the human conscience. If any one doubts our verdict, let him buy this volume. No one will regret its perusal.*"—LITERARY CHURCHMAN.

The Life of Temptation. A Course of

Lectures delivered in Substance at St. Peter's, Eaton Square, in Lent, 1872; also at All Saints', Margaret Street, in Lent, 1869. By the Rev. GEORGE BODY, B.A., Rector of Kirkby Misperton. Third Edition. Crown 8vo. 4s. 6d.

CONTENTS.

The Leading into Temptation—The Rationale of Temptation—Why we are Tempted—Safety in Temptation—With Jesus in Temptation—The End of Temptation.

"*Regeneration and conversion seem here to occupy their proper places in the Christian economy, and the general subject of temptation is worked out with considerable ability.*"—CHURCH TIMES.

"*This is another volume of simple,*

earnest, soul-stirring words, dealing with the mysteries of Christian experience."—LONDON QUARTERLY REVIEW.

"*A collection of sermons, pious, earnest, and eloquent.*" —ENGLISH CHURCHMAN.

Waterloo Place, London

Sermons on the Epistles and Gospels

for the Sundays and Holy Days throughout the Year. By the
Rev. ISAAC WILLIAMS, B.D., Author of a "Devotional Com-
mentary on the Gospel Narrative." New Edition. 2 Vols.
Crown 8vo. 5s. each. Sold separately.

CONTENTS OF VOL. I.

The King of Salem—The Scriptures bearing Witness—The Church bearing
Witness—The Spirit bearing Witness—The Adoption of Sons—Love
strong as Death—The Love which passeth Knowledge—Of such is the
Kingdom of Heaven—The Spirit of Adoption—The Old and the New
Man—The Day Star in the Heart—Obedience the best Sacrifice—The
Meekness and Gentleness of Christ—The Faith that overcometh the
World—Our Refuge in Public Troubles—Light and Safety in Love—
The Great Manifestation—Perseverance found in Humility—Bringing
forth Fruit with Patience—The most excellent Gift—The Call to Re-
pentance—The accepted Time—Perseverance in Prayer—The Unclean
Spirit returning—The Penitent refreshed—Our Life in the Knowledge
of God—The Mind of Christ—The Triumph of the Cross—The Man of
Sorrows—The Great Sacrifice—The Memorial of the Great Sacrifice—
The Fulfilment—Buried with Christ—The Power of Christ risen—Walking in Newness of Life—Belief in the Resurrection of Christ—The Faith
that overcometh the World—Following the Lamb of God—A little while
—The Giver of all Good—Requisites of effectual Prayer—Ascending
with Christ—The Days of Expectation—They shall walk with Me in
White—The Holy Spirit and Baptism—Let all Things be done in order.

CONTENTS OF VOL. II.

The Door opened in Heaven—Love the mark of God's Children—The Gospel a
Feast of Love—The Lost Sheep—Mercy the best preparation for Judgment—The peaceable ordering of the World—Brotherly Love and the Life
in Christ—The Bread which God giveth—By their Fruits ye shall know
them—Looking forward, or Divine Covetousness—The Day of Visitation—
The Prayer of the Penitent—Weakness of Faith—Love the fulfilling of the
Law—Thankfulness the Life of the Regenerate—My Beloved is Mine and
I am His—The Knowledge which is Life Eternal—The Sabbath of Christ
found in Meekness—Christ is on the Right Hand of God—The Forgive-
ness of Sins—Love and Joy in the Spirit—The Warfare and the Armour of
Saints—The Love of Christians—The Earthly and Heavenly Citizenship—
Mutual Intercessions—Gleanings after Harvest—Bringing unto Christ—
Slowness in believing—Grace not given in Vain—The Refiner's Fire—The
Lost Crown—Faith in the Incarnation—Value of an Inspired Gospel—The
severe and social Virtues—Go and do thou likewise—Joy at hearing the
Bridegroom's Voice—The Strength of God in Man's Weakness—Hidden
with Christ in God—Do good, hoping for nothing again—The good ex-
change—War in Heaven—Healing and Peace—The Sacrament of Union—
They which shall be accounted Worthy.

Parochial and Plain Sermons. By JOHN

HENRY NEWMAN, B.D., formerly Vicar of St. Mary's, Oxford.
Edited by the Rev. W. J. COPELAND, B.D., Rector of
Farnham, Essex. New Edition. 8 Volumes. Crown 8vo.
5s. each. Sold separately.

CONTENTS OF VOL. I.

Holiness necessary for Future Blessedness—The Immortality of the Soul—
Knowledge of God's Will without Obedience—Secret Truths—Self-denial
the Test of Religious Earnestness—The Spiritual Mind—Sins of Ignorance
and Weakness—God's Commandments not grievous—The Religious use
of exalted Feelings—Profession without Practice—Profession without
Hypocrisy—Profession without Ostentation—Promising without Doing—
Religious Emotion—Religious Faith Rational—The Christian Mysteries—
The Self-wise Inquirer—Obedience the Remedy for Religious Perplexity
—Times of Private Prayer—Forms of Private Prayer—The Resurrection
of the Body—Witnesses of the Resurrection—Christian Reverence--The
Religion of the Day—Scripture a Record of Human Sorrow—Christian
Manhood.

CONTENTS OF VOL. II.

The World's Benefactors—Faith without Sight—The Incarnation—Martyrdom
—Love of Relations and Friends—The Mind of Little Children—Cere-
monies of the Church—The Glory of the Christian Church—His Conver-
sion viewed in Reference to His Office—Secrecy and Suddenness of Divine
Visitations—Divine Decrees—The Reverence due to Her—Christ, a
Quickening Spirit—Saving Knowledge—Self-contemplation—Religious
Cowardice—The Gospel Witnesses—Mysteries in Religion—The Indwell-
ing Spirit—The Kingdom of the Saints—The Gospel, a Trust committed
to us—Tolerance of Religious Error—Rebuking Sin—The Christian
Ministry—Human Responsibility—Guilelessness—The Danger of Riches—
The Powers of Nature—The Danger of Accomplishments—Christian Zeal
—Use of Saints' Days.

CONTENTS OF VOL. III.

Abraham and Lot—Wilfulness of Israel in rejecting Samuel—Saul—Early years
of David—Jeroboam—Faith and Obedience—Christian Repentance—
Contracted Views in Religion—A particular Providence as revealed in
the Gospel—Tears of Christ at the Grave of Lazarus—Bodily Suffering—
The Humiliation of the Eternal Son—Jewish Zeal a Pattern to Christians
—Submission to Church Authority—Contest between Truth and False-
hood in the Church—The Church Visible and Invisible—The Visible
Church an Encouragement to Faith—The Gift of the Spirit—Regenerating
Baptism—Infant Baptism—The Daily Service—The Good Part of Mary—
Religious Worship a Remedy for Excitements—Intercession—The Inter-
mediate State.

CONTENTS OF VOL. IV.

The Strictness of the Law of Christ—Obedience without Love, as instanced in
the Character of Balaam—Moral Consequences of Single Sins—Acceptance of Religious Privileges compulsory—Reliance on Religious Observances—The Individuality of the Soul—Chastisement amid Mercy—Peace
and Joy amid Chastisement—The State of Grace—The Visible Church
for the sake of the Elect—The Communion of Saints—The Church a

NEWMAN'S PAROCHIAL AND PLAIN SERMONS—
Continued.

Home for the Lonely—The Invisible World—The Greatness and Little-
ness of Human Life—Moral Effects of Communion with God—Christ
Hidden from the World—Christ Manifested in Remembrance—The Gain-
saying of Korah—The Mysteriousness of our Present Being—The Ventures
of Faith—Faith and Love—Watching—Keeping Fast and Festival.

CONTENTS OF VOL V.

Worship, a Preparation for Christ's Coming—Reverence, a Belief in God's
Presence—Unreal Words—Shrinking from Christ's Coming—Equanimity—
Remembrance of past Mercies—The Mystery of Godliness—The State of
Innocence—Christian Sympathy—Righteousness not of us, but in us—The
Law of the Spirit—The New Works of the Gospel—The State of Salva-
tion—Transgressions and Infirmities—Sins of Infirmity—Sincerity and
Hypocrisy—The Testimony of Conscience—Many called, few chosen—
Present Blessings—Endurance, the Christian's portion—Affliction a School
of Comfort—The thought of God, the stay of the Soul—Love the one thing
needful—The Power of the Will.

CONTENTS OF VOL. VI.

Fasting, a Source of Trial—Life, the Season of Repentance—Apostolic Absti-
nence, a Pattern for Christians—Christ's Privations, a Meditation for
Christians—Christ the Son of God made Man—The Incarnate Son, a
Sufferer and Sacrifice—The Cross of Christ the Measure of the World—
Difficulty of realizing Sacred Privileges—The Gospel Sign addressed to
Faith—The Spiritual Presence of Christ in the Church—The Eucharistic
Presence—Faith the Title for Justification—Judaism of the present day—
The Fellowship of the Apostles—Rising with Christ—Warfare the Condi-
tion of Victory—Waiting for Christ—Subjection of the Reason and Feel-
ings to the Revealed Word—The Gospel Palaces—The Visible Temple—
Offerings for the Sanctuary—The Weapons of Saints—Faith without
Demonstration—The Mystery of the Holy Trinity—Peace in Believing.

CONTENTS OF VOL. VII.

The Lapse of Time—Religion, a Weariness to the Natural Man—The World
our Enemy—The Praise of Men—Temporal Advantages—The Season of
Epiphany—The Duty of Self-denial—The Yoke of Christ—Moses the
Type of Christ—The Crucifixion—Attendance on Holy Communion—
The Gospel Feast—Love of Religion, a new Nature—Religion pleasant
to the Religious—Mental Prayer—Infant Baptism—The Unity of the
Church—Steadfastness in the Old Paths.

CONTENTS OF VOL. VIII.

Reverence in Worship—Divine Calls—The Trial of Saul—The Call of David—
Curiosity a Temptation to Sin—Miracles no remedy for Unbelief—Josiah,
a Pattern for the Ignorant—Inward Witness to the Truth of the Gospel—
Jeremiah, a Lesson for the Disappointed—Endurance of the World's Cen-
sure—Doing Glory to God in Pursuits of the World—Vanity of Human
Glory—Truth hidden when not sought after—Obedience to God the Way
to Faith in Christ—Sudden Conversions—The Shepherd of our Souls—
Religious Joy—Ignorance of Evil.

and at Oxford and Cambridge

NEWMAN'S PAROCHIAL AND PLAIN SERMONS—
Continued.

" *Dr. Newman's sermons stand by themselves in modern English literature; it might be said, in English literature generally. There have been equally great masterpieces of English writing in this form of composition, and there have been preachers whose theological depth, acquaintance with the heart, earnestness, tenderness, and power have not been inferior to his. But the great writers do not touch, pierce, and get hold of minds as he does, and those who are famous for the power and results of their preaching do not write as he does. His sermons have done more perhaps than any one thing to mould and quicken and brace the religious temper of our time ; they have acted with equal force on those who were nearest and those who were furthest from him in theological opinion.*"—SATURDAY REVIEW.

" *They are undeniably models of style in writing of the most faultless kind. As addresses to a miscellaneous multitude they would have been failures ; but as addresses to a cultivated audience of university students and tutors they are without a rival.*" —PALL MALL GAZETTE.

. . . . "We have said nothing of the exquisite manner of these sermons, the manner of a mind at once tender and holy, at once loving and austere, at once real and dramatic, at once full of insight into human nature and full of the humility which springs from a higher source."—SPECTATOR.

" *We anticipate from the reappearance of the series a large measure of good both to the Church and to individuals ; for Dr. Newman's influence as a teacher was, in his Oxford days, almost unrivalled.*"—CHURCH TIMES.

" *We hope, and have no doubt, that as the value of these Sermons becomes more largely known they will become increasingly popular in the English Communion.*"—CHURCH NEWS.

" *They are rich in practical instruction of a kind too seldom heard from the pulpit.*"—LONDON REVIEW.

" *In reading these sermons, it is impossible to withhold one's high admiration for the many fine qualities which they display :—plain, unambiguous statement of Christian doctrine according to the preacher's view of it,—practical application of Church dogmas to individual life, character and conduct,—instructive exposition of Scripture, all conveyed in a faultless style and with well-sustained eloquence.*" — NONCONFORMIST.

. . . . " The noble sincerity of the preacher, and his classical reserve of diction, the poise and justness of the few ornaments with which he decorates his discussions, and above all, their touching and profound faith, must win the admiration and respect of every one who reads them."—LONDON REVIEW.

" *These Sermons may still do much good ; and we thank the publishers and editor for the spirit—for it required some—to do this service to religion.*"—CHRISTIAN REMEMBRANCER.

" *Sermon-writers cannot do better than study the clear, sharp, polished, and yet simple style in which the meaning of the once great Anglican preacher is conveyed.*"—ENGLISH CHURCHMAN.

" *The modest and extensive erudition, the large and exact information, the chaste and finished style, and the deep and serious earnestness which combined to give such freshness and force to his spoken discourses, reappear in many of the noble and edifying sermons now before us.*"—WATCHMAN.

. . . . " There cannot be a handsomer present for Churchmen of the new generation."—CHURCH REVIEW.

" *Few theologians go as deep as Dr. Newman and carry with them the same lucidity of thought and language. In this point, as well as in others, his sermons might well be taken as a model for a pulpit style, even by those who are not always disposed to follow him in his theology.*" — GLASGOW DAILY HERALD.

Lectures on the Doctrine of Justifica-

tion. By JOHN HENRY NEWMAN, B.D., sometime Fellow of Oriel College, Oxford. New Edition. Crown 8vo. 5s.

CONTENTS.

Faith considered as the Instrument of Justification—Love considered as the Formal Cause of Justification—Primary Sense of the term Justification—Secondary Senses of the term Justification—Misuse of the term Just or Righteous—On the Gift of Righteousness—The Characteristics of the Gift of Righteousness—Righteousness viewed as a Gift and as a Quality—Righteousness the Fruit of our Lord's Resurrection—The Office of Justifying Faith—The Nature of Justifying Faith—Faith viewed relatively to Rites and Works—on preaching the Gospel—Appendix.

Sermons Bearing upon Subjects of the

DAY. By JOHN HENRY NEWMAN, B.D., sometime Fellow of Oriel College, Oxford. Edited by the Rev. W. J. COPELAND, B.D., Rector of Farnham, Essex. New Edition. Crown 8vo. 5s.

CONTENTS.

The Work of the Christian—Saintliness not forfeited by the Penitent—Our Lord's Last Supper and His First—Dangers to the Penitent—The Three Offices of Christ—Faith and Experience—Faith and the World—The Church and the World—Indulgence in Religious Privileges—Connection between Personal and Public Improvement—Christian Nobleness—Joshua, a Type of Christ and His Followers—Elisha, a Type of Christ and His Followers—The Christian Church a continuation of the Jewish—The Principle of continuity between the Jewish and Christian Churches—The Christian Church an Imperial Power—Sanctity the Token of the Christian Empire—Condition of the Members of the Christian Empire—The Apostolical Christian—Wisdom and Innocence—Invisible Presence of Christ—Outward and Inward Notes of the Church—Grounds for Steadfastness in our Religious Profession—Elijah the Prophet of the Latter Days—Feasting in Captivity—The Parting of Friends.

" They exhibit all the writer's incisiveness, force of analogy, and wide acquaintance with Scripture." . . . —CHURCH REVIEW.
" Apart from the surpassing literary merits of these discourses, they are memorable as the last words spoken from the pulpit of the English Church *by a divine whom all men of all creeds delight to honour."*—DAILY TELEGRAPH.
. . . . *" The pure coinage of a powerful brain, acting under the impulses of an enthusiastic, earnest, and highly conscientious heart."*—THE ROCK.

and at Oxford and Cambridge

Fifteen Sermons preached before the

University of Oxford, between A.D. 1826 and 1843. By JOHN
HENRY NEWMAN, B.D., sometime Fellow of Oriel College,
Oxford. New Edition. Crown 8vo. 5s.

CONTENTS.

The Philosophical Temper first enjoined by the Gospel—The Influence of Natura l
and Revealed Religion respectively—Evangelical Sanctity the Perfection
of Natural Virtue—The Usurpations of Reason—Personal Influence, the
means of Propagating the Truth—Our Justice, as a Principle of Divine
Governance—Contest between Faith and Light—Human Responsibility,
as Independent of Circumstances—Wilfulness the Sin of Saul—Faith and
Reason, contrasted as Habits of Mind—The Nature of Faith in Relation
to Reason—Love the Safeguard of Faith against Superstition—Implicit
and Explicit Reason—Wisdom, as contrasted with Faith and with Bigotry
—The Theory of Developments in Religious Doctrine.

. . . . *"We think he has con-* *of Father Newman's writings so con-*
ferred a valuable boon on the Church, *cisely written in proportion to the*
by not merely reprinting them in their *largeness of their significance. They*
original shape, but adding a Catholic *are not to be once read and then mere-*
preface and Catholic notes. As to the *ly remembered, but rather to be studied*
earlier sermons, there are none perhaps *again and again."*—DUBLIN REVIEW.

Sermons Preached on Different Occa-

sions. By EDWARD MEYRICK GOULBURN, D.D., Dean of
Norwich. Fourth Edition. Small 8vo. 6s. 6d.

CONTENTS.

Confession, and the Doctrine of the English Church thereupon—The Moral
Instincts which lead Men to the Confessional—Pure Religion and Unde-
filed—God Keeping and Breaking Silence—The Kingdom that comes not
with Observation—Jacob's Dream—The contagious Influence of Faithful
Prophesying—Final Impenitence—Final Impenitence exemplified—The
Goodness and Severity of God as Manifested in the Atonement—Remedy,
the only Form of Doing Good—The Search after Wisdom—The Grounds
of True Patriotism—Christ Wielding the Keys of Death and of the World
unseen—The Revelation of the Triune God and its Diffusion—The
Dispensations—Learning a requisite for the Ministry of the Present Day
—Human Instrumentality employed in Man's Salvation—The Stolen Testi-
mony—The Building up of the Family—On Preaching Christ Crucified—
Have Salt in Yourselves—The Last Sunday of 1861.

Farewell Counsels of a Pastor to his

Flock, on Topics of the Day. By EDWARD MEYRICK GOUL-
BURN, D.D., Dean of Norwich. Third Edition. Small 8vo.
4s.

Waterloo Place, London

The Catholic Sacrifice. Sermons Preached

at All Saints, Margaret Street. By the Rev. BERDMORE COMPTON, M.A., Vicar of All Saints, Margaret Street. Crown 8vo. 5s.

CONTENTS.

The Eucharistic Life—The Sacrifice of Sweet Savour—The Pure Offering— The Catholic Oblation—The Sacrificial Feast—The Preparation for the Eucharist—The Introductory Office—The Canon—Degrees of Apprehension—The Fascination of Christ Crucified—The Shewbread—Consecration of Worship and Work—Water, Blood, Wine—The Blood of Sprinkling —The Mystery of Sacraments—The Oblation of Gethsemane—Offertory and Tribute Money.

The Sayings of the Great Forty Days,

between the Resurrection and Ascension, regarded as the Outlines of the Kingdom of God. In Five Discourses. With an Examination of Dr. Newman's Theory of Development. By GEORGE MOBERLY, D.C.L., Bishop of Salisbury. Fifth Edition. Crown 8vo. 5s.

Plain Sermons, preached at Brighstone.

By GEORGE MOBERLY, D.C.L., Bishop of Salisbury. New Edition. Crown 8vo. 5s.

CONTENTS.

Except a Man be Born again—The Lord with the Doctors—The Draw-Net—I will lay me down in Peace—Ye have not so learned Christ—Trinity Sunday—My Flesh is Meat indeed—The Corn of Wheat dying and multiplied—The Seed Corn springing to new Life—I am the Way, the Truth, and the Life—The Ruler of the Sea—Stewards of the Mysteries of God—Ephphatha—The Widow of Nain—Josiah's Discovery of the Law—The Invisible World : Angels—Prayers, especially Daily Prayers—They all with one consent began to make excuse—Ascension Day—The Comforter—The Tokens of the Spirit—Elijah's Warning, Fathers and Children—Thou shalt see them no more for ever—Baskets full of Fragments—Harvest—The Marriage Supper of the Lamb—The Last Judgment.

Sermons preached at Winchester Col-

lege. By GEORGE MOBERLY, D.C.L., Bishop of Salisbury. 2 Vols. Crown 8vo. 6s. 6d. each. Sold separately.

Sermons.   By HENRY MELVILL, B.D., late
Canon of St. Paul's, and Chaplain in Ordinary to the Queen.
New Edition. 2 Vols.   Crown 8vo.   5s. each.   Sold separately.

CONTENTS OF VOL. I.

The First Prophecy—Christ the Minister of the Church—The Impossibility of Creature-Merit—The Humiliation of the Man Christ Jesus—The Doctrine of the Resurrection viewed in connection with that of the Soul's Immortality—The Power of Wickedness and Righteousness to reproduce themselves—The Power of Religion to strengthen the Human Intellect—The Provision made by God for the Poor—St. Paul, a Tent-Maker—The Advantages of a state of Expectation—Truth as it is in Jesus—The Difficulties of Scripture.

CONTENTS OF VOL II.

Jacob's Vision and Vow—The continued Agency of the Father and the Son—The Resurrection of Dry Bones—Protestantism and Popery—Christianity a Sword—The Death of Moses—The Ascension of Christ—The Spirit upon the Waters—The Proportion of Grace to Trial—Pleading before the Mountains—Heaven—God's Way in the Sanctuary.

" *Every one who can remember the days when Canon Melvill was the preacher of the day, will be glad to see these four-and-twenty of his sermons so nicely reproduced. His Sermons were all the result of real study and genuine reading, with far more theology in them than those of many who make much more profession of theology. There are sermons here which we can personally remember; it has been a pleasure to us to be reminded of them, and we are glad to see them brought before the present generation. We hope that they may be studied, for they deserve it thoroughly.*"—LITERARY CHURCHMAN.

" *The Sermons of Canon Melvill, now republished in two handy volumes, need only to be mentioned to be sure of a hearty welcome. Sound learning, well-weighed words, calm and keen logic, and solemn devoutness, mark the whole series of masterly discourses, which embrace some of the chief doctrines of the Church, and set them forth in clear and Scriptural strength.*"—STANDARD.

" *It would be easy to quote portions of exceeding beauty and power. It was not, however, the charm of style, nor wealth of words, both which Canon Melvill possessed in so great abundance, that he relied on to win souls; but the power and spirit of Him Who said, 'I,*

if I be lifted up, will draw all men to Me.'"—RECORD.

" *Messrs. Rivington have published very opportunely, at a time when Churchmen are thinking with satisfaction of the new blood infused into the Chapter of St. Paul's, Sermons by Henry Melvill, who in his day was as celebrated as a preacher as is Canon Liddon now. The sermons are not only couched in elegant language, but are replete with matter which the younger clergy would do well to study.*"—JOHN BULL.

" *Few preachers have had more admirers than the Rev. Henry Melvill, and the new edition of his Sermons, in two volumes, will doubtless find plenty of purchasers. The Sermons abound in thought, and the thoughts are couched in English which is at once elegant in construction and easy to read.*"—CHURCH TIMES.

. . . . " *As they are models of their particular style of oratory, they will be valuable helps to young preachers.*"—UNION REVIEW.

" *Henry Melvill's intellect was large, his imagination brilliant, his ardour intense, and his style strong, fervid, and picturesque. Often he seemed to glow with the inspiration of a prophet.*"—AMERICAN QUARTERLY CHURCH REVIEW.

Sermons on Certain of the Less

Prominent Facts and References in Sacred Story. By HENRY MELVILL, B.D., late Canon of St. Paul's, and Chaplain in Ordinary to the Queen. New Edition. 2 Vols. Crown 8vo. 5s. each. Sold separately.

CONTENTS OF VOL. I.

The Faith of Joseph on his Death-bed—Angels as Remembrancers—The Burning of the Magical Books—The Parting Hymn—Cæsar's Household—The Sleepless Night—The Well of Bethlehem—The Thirst of Christ—The second Delivery of the Lord's Prayer—Peculiarities in the Miracle in the Coasts of Decapolis—The Latter Rain—The Lowly Errand—Nehemiah before Artaxerxes—Jabez.

CONTENTS OF VOL. II.

The Young Man in the Linen Cloth—The Fire on the Shore—The Finding the Guest-Chamber—The Spectre's Sermon a truism—Various Opinions—The Misrepresentations of Eve—Seeking, after Finding—The Bird's Nest—Angels our Guardians in trifles—The appearance of failure—Simon the Cyrenian—The power of the Eye—Pilate's Wife—The Examination of Cain.

" *We are glad to see this new edition of what we have always considered to be Melvill's best sermons, because in them we have his best thoughts.* . . . *Many of these sermons are the strongest arguments yet adduced for internal evidence of the veracity of the Scriptural narratives.*"—STANDARD.

" *Polished, classical, and winning, these sermons bear the marks of literary labour. A study of them will aid the modern preacher to refine and polish his discourses, and to add to the vigour which is now the fashion, the graces of chastened eloquence and winning rhetoric.*"—ENGLISH CHURCHMAN.

" *The sermons of the lamented Melvill are too well known to require any commendation from us. We have here all the power of rhetoric, and the grace and beauty of style, for which the author has been distinguished, and which have contributed to render him a model to preachers, and given him a representative position in the history of the English pulpit.*"—WEEKLY REVIEW.

. . . " *Unusually interesting* . . . . *No one can read these sermons without deriving instruction from them, without being compelled to acknowledge that new light has been cast for him*

on numerous passages of Scripture, which he must henceforth read with greater intelligence and greater interest than before." . . .—EDINBURGH COURANT.

. . . . " *For skill in developing the significance of the ' less prominent facts of Holy Scripture' no one could compete with the late Canon Melvill, four volumes of whose discourses—two of them occupied entirely with his sermons on subjects of this class—are before us. His preaching was unique. He selected for the most part texts that are not frequently treated, and when he chose those of a more ordinary character, he generally presented them in a new light, and elicited from them some truth which would not have suggested itself to any other preacher. He was singularly ingenious in some of his conceptions, and wonderfully forcible and impressive in his mode of developing and applying them.*" . . . .—NONCONFORMIST.

" *The publishers of these well-known, almost classic sermons, have conferred a boon on all lovers of our pulpit literature by this beautiful, portable edition of some of the most brilliant and original discourses that have been delivered to this generation.*" . . . .—BRITISH QUARTERLY REVIEW.

Selection from the Sermons preached

during the Latter Years of his Life, in the Parish Church of Barnes, and in the Cathedral of St. Paul's. By HENRY MELVILL, B.D., late Canon of St. Paul's, and Chaplain in Ordinary to the Queen. New Edition. 2 Vols. Crown 8vo. 5s. each. Sold separately.

CONTENTS OF VOL. I.

The Parity of the consequences of Adam's Transgression and Christ's Death—The Song of Simeon—The Days of Old—Omissions of Scripture—The Madman in Sport—Peace, Peace, when there is no Peace—A very lovely Song—This is that King Ahaz—Ariel—New Wine and Old Bottles—Demas—Michael and the Devil—The Folly of Excessive Labour—St. Paul at Philippi—Believing a Lie—The Prodigal Son—The Foolishness of Preaching—Knowledge and Sorrow—The Unjust Steward—The Man born blind.

CONTENTS OF VOL. II.

Rejoicing as in Spoil — Satan a Copyist — The binding the Tares into Bundles — Two walking together—Agreeing with the Adversary—God speaking to Moses—Hoping in Mercy—Faith as a Grain of Mustard Seed—Mary's Recompense—War in Heaven—Glory into Shame—The Last Judgment—Man like to Vanity—God so Loved the World—Saul—And what shall this Man do?—The Sickness and Death of Elisha—Abiding in our Callings—Trinity Sunday.

The Mystery of the Temptation: a

Course of Lectures. By the Rev. W. H. HUTCHINGS, M.A., Sub-Warden of the House of Mercy, Clewer. Crown 8vo. 4s. 6d.

CONTENTS.

The Entrance into the Temptation—The Fast—The Personality of Satan—The First Temptation—The Second Temptation—The Third Temptation—The End of the Temptation.

Sermons on Special Occasions. By

DANIEL MOORE, M.A., Chaplain in Ordinary to the Queen, and Vicar of Holy Trinity, Paddington. Crown 8vo. 7s. 6d.

CONTENTS.

The Words of Christ imperishable—The Gospel Welcome—The Conversion of St. Paul—The Christian's Mission—Business and Godliness—Soberness and Watchfulness—The Joy of the Disciples at the Resurrection—The Saviour's Ascension—Jesus in the Midst—The Moral Attractions of the Cross—The Gospel Workmen—The Work of the Holy Spirit—The Doctrine of the Holy Trinity—The Law of Moral Recompenses—The Goodness of King Joash—The Tenderness of Christ—Christ our Example in Youth—Jacob in Life and in Death—The Spiritual Mind—Britain's Obligations to the Gospel, preached at St. Paul's Cathedral, at the Anniversary of the Sons of the Clergy—The Throne in Mourning, preached on occasion of the death of the Prince Consort—Prayer and Providence, preached after the Order for Public Prayer in relation to the Cattle Plague—The Unsearchableness of God, preached at Nottingham, at the Meeting of the British Association for the Advancement of Science.

The Age and the Gospel; Four Ser-

mons preached before the University of Cambridge, at the Hulsean Lecture, 1864. With a Discourse on Final Retribution. By DANIEL MOORE, M.A., Chaplain in Ordinary to the Queen, and Vicar of Holy Trinity, Paddington. Crown 8vo. 5s.

The Soul in its Probation: Sermons

Preached at the Church of S. Alban the Martyr, Holborn, on the Sundays in Lent, 1873. By the Rev. F. N. OXENHAM, M.A. 8vo. 5s.

The Permanence of Christianity.   Considered in Eight Lectures preached before the University of Oxford, in the year 1872, on the Foundation of the late Rev. John Bampton, M.A. By JOHN RICHARD TURNER EATON, M.A., late Fellow and Tutor of Merton College, Rector of Lapworth, Warwickshire. 8vo. 12s.

The Religion of the Christ: its Historic and Literary Development considered as an Evidence of its Origin. Being the Bampton Lectures for 1874. By the Rev. STANLEY LEATHES, M.A., Minister of St. Philip's, Regent Street, and Professor of Hebrew, King's College, London. 8vo. 12s.

"*These lectures are a noble contribution to the evidences of the Christian faith; and to those who have made themselves acquainted with the author's previous works on the witness to Christ borne by the Old Testament, by S. Paul, and by S. John, they will have a special value as consummating a cumulative line of argument which a very logical and a very reverent mind has exhibited with irresistible force.*" — BRITISH QUARTERLY REVIEW.

"*The Bampton Lectures of the present year are not only in themselves worthy of a most thoughtful study, but are admirably adapted to meet some of the foremost objections which are now being brought against 'the divine authority of the Holy Scriptures.' We earnestly recommend our readers to buy the book for themselves.*"—LITERARY CHURCHMAN.

"*A volume which ought to take its place beside the best standard works on the evidences of Christianity—a kind of literature in which the Church of England is peculiarly rich.*"—SCOTSMAN.

"*In these 'Eight Divinity Lectures to confirm the Christian Faith,' the will of the Rev. John Bampton has been profoundly carried out.*"—NOTES AND QUERIES.

"*There is a graceful ease in the style, a sustained continuity in the thought, a cumulative force in the argument, and a range of thoughtful exposition which are not often found in such close combination, and which give to the volume a solid merit.*"—WATCHMAN.

"*His Bampton Lectures are perhaps the most suggestive and elaborate of all his productions, and would of themselves win for him a high position as a writer on Christian evidence.*"—FREEMAN.

"*An argument which has wonderful freshness and point, which is compacted together into a glowing treatise and logical statement, which is not encumbered and stiff with learning, which is written in the language of daily life, which embraces the results of thorough study up to most recent writers, and which any one can read with profit. . . . The preface, in which Mr. Leathes sums up the arguments in his lucid way, which are more elaborately drawn out in the Lectures, is one of the finest specimens of clear, candid, temperate reasoning in modern literature.*"—NEW YORK INDEPENDENT.

"*With thoughtful minds it will carry great weight.*"—NEW YORK CHURCHMAN.

The Witness of the Old Testament to

Christ. Being the Boyle Lectures for the year 1868. By the Rev. STANLEY LEATHES, M.A., Minister of St. Philip's, Regent Street, and Professor of Hebrew, King's College, London. 8vo. 9s.

The Witness of St. Paul to Christ.

Being the Boyle Lectures for 1869. With an Appendix on the Credibility of the Acts, in Reply to the Recent Strictures of Dr. Davidson. By the Rev. STANLEY LEATHES, M.A., Minister of St. Philip's, Regent Street, and Professor of Hebrew, King's College, London. 8vo. 10s. 6d.

The Witness of St. John to Christ.

Being the Boyle Lectures for 1870. With an Appendix on the Authorship and Integrity of St. John's Gospel, and the Unity of the Johannine Writings. By the Rev. STANLEY LEATHES, M.A., Minister of St. Philip's, Regent Street, and Professor of Hebrew, King's College, London. 8vo. 10s. 6d.

Samaritans, and other Sermons, preached

in the Church of S. George the Martyr, Middlesex. By the Rev. GERARD LUDLOW HALLETT, B.C.L., Senior Curate, Deputy Minor Canon of Westminster, Chaplain to the National Hospital for the Paralysed and Epileptic, Lecturer of SS. Bene't and Peter, London. Second Edition. Crown 8vo. 3s.

Sermons, Doctrinal and Didactic, on

the Topics of the Day. By the Rev. THOMAS WILLIAMSON PEILE, D.D., sometime Fellow of Trinity College, Cambridge. Crown 8vo. 6s. 6d.

Faith and Practice: A Selection of

Sermons Preached in St. Philip's Chapel, Regent Street. By the Rev. FRANCIS PIGOU, M.A., Vicar of Doncaster, and Hon. Chaplain in Ordinary to the Queen. Small 8vo. 6s.

The Thirty-nine Articles of the Church

of England explained in a Series of Lectures. By the Rev.
R. W. JELF, D.D., late Canon of Christ Church, Oxford, and
sometime Principal of King's College, London. Edited by
the Rev. J. R. KING, M.A., Vicar of St. Peter's-in-the-East,
Oxford, and formerly Fellow and Tutor of Merton College.
8vo. 15s.

The Thirty-nine Articles of the Church

of England, illustrated with Notes. By the Venerable Archdeacon WELCHMAN. New Edition. 8vo. 2s. Or, inter-
leaved with blank paper, 3s.

Twelve Addresses at his Visitation

of the Cathedral and Diocese of Lincoln, in the year
MDCCCLXXIII. By CHR. WORDSWORTH, D.D., Bishop of
Lincoln. Crown 8vo. 3s. 6d.

The Maccabees and the Church; or,

The History of the Maccabees considered with reference to the
Present Condition and Prospects of the Church. Two Sermons
preached before the University of Cambridge. By CHR.
WORDSWORTH, D.D., Bishop of Lincoln. Small 8vo. 2s. 6d.

The Home Life of Jesus of Nazareth,

and other Sermons. By the Rev. AUGUSTUS GURNEY, M.A.,
Vicar of Wribbenhall, Kidderminster. Crown 8vo. 5s.

Warnings of the Holy Week, &c. Being

a Course of Parochial Lectures for the Week before Easter
and the Easter Festivals. By the Rev. W. ADAMS, M.A.,
Author of " Sacred Allegories," &c. Seventh Edition.
Small 8vo. 4s. 6d.

The Perfect Man ; or, Jesus an Example
of Godly Life. By the Rev. HARRY JONES, M.A., Rector
of S. George-in-the-East. Second Edition. Crown 8vo.
3*s.* 6*d.*

Life in the World; being a Selection
from Sermons preached at S. Luke's, Berwick Street. By
the Rev. HARRY JONES, M.A., Rector of S. George-in-the-
East. Second Edition. Crown 8vo. 5*s.*

Sermons on Various Subjects. By the
Rev. W. J. HALL, M.A., Rector of S. Clement's Eastcheap
with S. Martin's Orgar, and Minor Canon of S. Paul's Cathedral. Crown 8vo. 5*s.*

Sermons Preached in a Country Vil-
lage. By the Rev. T. K. ARNOLD, M.A., late Rector of
Lyndon. Post 8vo. 5*s.* 6*d.*

Six Short Sermons on Sin. Lent Lec-
tures at S. Alban the Martyr, Holborn. By the Rev. ORBY
SHIPLEY, M.A. Fifth Edition. Small 8vo. 1*s.*

The Way of Holiness in Married Life.
A Course of Sermons preached in Lent. By the Rev. HENRY
J. ELLISON, M.A., Hon. Canon of Christ Church, and Vicar
of New Windsor, Berks. Second Edition. Small 8vo. 2*s.* 6*d.*

Parochial Sermons preached in a Vil-
lage Church. Fourth Series. By the Rev. CHARLES A.
HEURTLEY, D.D., Margaret Professor of Divinity, and Canon
of Christ Church, Oxford. Crown 8vo. 5*s.* 6*d.*

Short Sermons on the Psalms in their

Order. Preached in a Village Church. By W. J. STRACEY,
M.A., Rector of Oxnead, and Vicar of Buxton, Norfolk, for-
merly Fellow of Magdalen College, Cambridge. Psalm
I—XXV. Crown 8vo. 5s.

The Christian Character; Six Sermons

preached in Lent. By JOHN JACKSON, D.D., Bishop of
London. Seventh Edition. Small 8vo. 3s. 6d.

Simple Sermons. By the Rev. W. H.

RANKEN, M.A., Fellow of Corpus Christi College, Oxford,
and Rector of Meysey Hampton, near Crickdale. Small 8vo.
5s.

Waterloo Place, London

7. Religious Education.

A Key to Christian Doctrine and Practice founded on the Church Catechism. By the Rev. JOHN HENRY BLUNT, M.A., F.S.A., Editor of "The Annotated Book of Common Prayer," &c. &c. Small 8vo. 2s. 6d.
Forming a Volume of "Keys to Christian Knowledge."

"*Of cheap and reliable text-books of this nature there has hitherto been a great want. We are often asked to recommend books for use in Church Sunday-schools, and we therefore take this opportunity of saying that we know of none more likely to be of service both to teachers and scholars than these 'Keys.'*"—CHURCHMAN'S SHILLING MAGAZINE.

"*This is another of Mr. Blunt's most useful manuals, with all the precision of a school book, yet diverging into matters of practical application so freely as to make it most serviceable, either as a teacher's suggestion book, or as an intelligent pupil's reading book.*"—LITERARY CHURCHMAN.

"*Will be very useful for the higher classes in Sunday-schools, or rather for the fuller instruction of the Sunday-school teachers themselves, where the parish priest is wise enough to devote a certain time regularly to their preparation for their voluntary task.*"—UNION REVIEW.

Household Theology: a Handbook of Religious Information respecting the Holy Bible, the Prayer Book, the Church, the Ministry, Divine Worship, the Creeds, &c. &c. By the Rev. JOHN HENRY BLUNT, M.A., F.S.A., Editor of "The Annotated Book of Common Prayer," &c. &c. New Edition. Small 8vo. 3s. 6d.

CONTENTS.

The Bible—The Prayer Book—The Church—Table of Dates—Ministerial Offices—Divine Worship—The Creeds—A Practical Summary of Christian Doctrine—The Great Christian Writers of Early Times—Ancient and Modern Heresies and Sects—The Church Calendar—A short explanation of Words used in Church History and Theology—Index.

Catechesis ; or, Christian Instruction

preparatory to Confirmation and First Communion. By CHARLES WORDSWORTH, D.C.L., Bishop of St. Andrews. New Edition. Small 8vo. 2s.

A Help to Catechizing. For the Use of

Clergymen, Schools, and Private Families. By JAMES BEAVEN, D.D., formerly Professor of Divinity in the University of King's College, Toronto. New Edition. 18mo. 2s.

Manual of Catechetical Instruction.

By E. B. RAMSAY, M.A., late Dean of Edinburgh. Ninth Edition. 18mo. 1s. 6d.

Catechetical Exercises on the Apostles'

Creed ; chiefly from Bp. Pearson. By EDWARD BICKER-STETH, D.D., Dean of Lichfield. New Edition. 18mo. 2s.

Questions Illustrating the Thirty-nine

Articles. By EDWARD BICKERSTETH, D.D., Dean of Lichfield. Fifth Edition. 12mo. 3s. 6d.

Your Duty and Mine. By the Rev.

Sir JAMES ERASMUS PHILIPPS, Bart., M.A., Vicar of Warminster, Author of "Seven Common Faults," &c. Second Edition. Small 8vo. 1s.

Seven Common Faults. By the Rev. Sir

JAMES ERASMUS PHILIPPS, Bart., M.A., Vicar of Warminster. Twelfth Edition. Small 8vo. 1s.

Theophilus Anglicanus; or, Instruc-
tion concerning the Principles of the Church Universal and the
Church of England. By CHRISTOPHER WORDSWORTH, D.D.,
Bishop of Lincoln. Tenth Edition. Small 8vo. 2s. 6d.

Elements of Instruction on the Church;
being an Abridgment of "Theophilus Anglicanus." By
CHRISTOPHER WORDSWORTH, D.D., Bishop of Lincoln.
Third Edition. 18mo. 1s. Or in Paper Cover, 6d.

A Glossary of Ecclesiastical Terms.
Containing Brief Explanations of Words used in Theology,
Liturgiology, Chronology, Law, Architecture, Antiquities,
Symbolism, Greek Hierology and Mediæval Latin; together
with some account of Titles of our Lord, Emblems of Saints,
Hymns, Orders, Heresies, Ornaments, Offices, Vestments and
Ceremonial, and Miscellaneous Subjects. By Various Writers.
Edited by the Rev. ORBY SHIPLEY, M.A. Crown 8vo. 18s.

Plain Sermons on the Latter Part of
the Catechism; being the Conclusion of the Series contained
in the Ninth Volume of "Plain Sermons." By the Rev. ISAAC
WILLIAMS, B.D., formerly Fellow of Trinity College, Oxford,
Author of "A Devotional Commentary on the Gospel Narrative," &c. 8vo. 6s. 6d.

An Abridgment of Scripture History;
consisting of Lessons selected from the Old Testament, for the
use of Schools and Families. By Mrs. TRIMMER. 12mo.
1s. 6d.

An Abridgment of the New Testament;
consisting of Lessons composed from the Writings of the Four
Evangelists, for the use of Schools and Families. By Mrs.
TRIMMER. 12mo. 1s. 4d.

8. Allegories and Tales.

Allegories and Tales. By the Rev. W.
E. HEYGATE, M.A., Rector of Brighstone. Crown 8vo. 5s.

" It is eminently original, and every one of its sixty-three short allegories is a story that the dullest child will read and the intelligent child will understand and enjoy. Grave thought, kindly raillery, biting sarcasm, grim humour, sincere indignation, wise counsel, a broad charity, and other characteristics, run through the allegories, many of which are highly poetical and good models of that style of composition."—EDINBURGH COURANT.

Mr. Heygate's volume contains about sixty short tales or allegories, all rife with good teaching, plainly set forth, and written in a very engaging and attractive style. As a present for children this book would be at once acceptable and beneficial. It can be highly commended."—CHURCH HERALD.

" There are both grace and precision about these 'Allegories and Tales,' which make them charming to read

either for young or for old. The stories are some of them quaint, some of them picturesque, all of them pleasant; and the moral they inclose shines out soft and clear as through a crystal. This is a book that may be recommended for a present, not only for young people, but for those of larger growth."—ATHENÆUM.

" The Rector of Brighstone has the gift of writing moral and spiritual lessons for the young in the most attractive fashion. His 'Allegories and Tales' are excellent specimens of stories, with a moral, in which the moral is not obtrusive and yet is not lost."—ENGLISH INDEPENDENT.

" A book of very great beauty and power. Mr. Heygate is a thoughtful, earnest and able writer, on whom more than any one is fallen in a striking manner the mantle of the great author of 'Agathos.'"—JOHN BULL.

Soimême; a Story of a Wilful Life.
Small 8vo. 3s. 6d.

" There is a very quiet, earnest tone in this story, which reconciles the reader to the lesson which it is intended to teach. It is essentially a story of character, and the heroine who is supposed to relate it is presented in a clearly defined and somewhat picturesque manner . . . To the thoughtful who are passing from youth to riper years, 'Soimême' will prove both attractive and useful."—PUBLIC OPINION.

" A vein of lofty, moral, and deep religious feeling runs through the whole tale, and the author neither proses nor preaches."—STANDARD.

" A very natural, unaffected, and

simple little story for young people—one which they will not only read but enjoy."—MORNING HERALD.

" The author promises to become a valuable accession to the ranks of our popular lady writers. 'Soimême' is a simple life-like story, charmingly told and gracefully written, and, what is better still, its tendencies are excellent. The lessons it teaches are of the highest order."—EUROPEAN MAIL.

" There are many clever little bits of description, and excellent maxims worth remembering. The scenery is all charmingly described."—MONTHLY PACKET.

Waterloo Place, London

The First Chronicle of Æscendune.

A Tale of the Days of Saint Dunstan. By the Rev. A. D. CRAKE, B.A., Chaplain of All Saints' School, Bloxham, Author of the "History of the Church under the Roman Empire," &c. &c. Crown 8vo. 3s. 6d.

" *The volume will possess a strong interest, especially for the young, and be useful, too, for though in form a tale, it may be classed among ' the side-lights of history.'* "—STANDARD.

" *History is strictly adhered to, and so clearly put before the mind, that all clouds, if clouds there were, as to the persons, occurrences, and state of public feeling at the time about which he writes, quickly and entirely disappear. The author has provided against criticism by a full preface and very lucid notes, which give the writer's authority for most of the chief facts of his narrative. Altogether the book shows great thought and careful study of the manners and customs of those early Saxon times.* "—JOHN BULL.

" *Mr. Crake, while carefully consulting both the earliest and latest authorities, from Florence of Worcester to Mr. E. A. Freeman, so as to make his tale harmonise in events and colouring with the actual facts, has taken care not to write too far above the level of his boy readers. We shall be glad when Mr. Crake takes up his pen once more, to give us a further instalment of the annals of the House of Æscendune.* "—CHURCH TIMES.

" *A very interesting and well written story of Saxon times—the times of Dunstan and the hapless Edwy. The author has evidently taken great pains to examine into the real history of the period (and the result is certainly favourable to the reputation of Dunstan). . . . We can scarcely imagine it possible that it should be anything* else than a great favourite." —LITERARY CHURCHMAN.

It is one of the best historical tales for the young that has been published for a long time."—NONCONFORMIST.

" *Written with much spirit and a careful attention to the best authorities on the history of the period of which he treats.*"—NATIONAL CHURCH.

" *The literary merit of the story is considerable. It is told with simplicity and animation; and some of the characters—particularly those of King Edwy and Elfric—are drawn with much force, while the plot is well-constructed, and the incidents are numerous and interesting.*"—SCOTSMAN.

" *The facts upon which the Chronicle is based have been carefully brought together from a variety of sources, and great skill has been shown in the construction of the narrative. The aim of the author is certainly a good one, and his efforts have been attended with a considerable amount of success.*"—ROCK.

" *The vein struck by the author in the 'First Chronicle,' if a comparatively fresh one, is also to some extent a hazardous one, for it is notoriously difficult to focus public interest at a point pre-mediæval; the chance is doubly doubtful in this volume, because intended for youth,—youth which is all for the hey-day of modern adventure. Yet Mr. Crake accomplishes his delicate task with singular grace and finish, and paints his early picture so attractively, that any boy of refined taste must be taken by the dramatic fascination of the story.*"—SUSSEX DAILY NEWS.

Alfgar the Dane, or the Second Chronicle of Æscendune. A Tale. By the Rev. A. D. CRAKE, B.A., Chaplain of All Saints' School, Bloxham, Author of the "History of the Church under the Roman Empire," &c. &c. Crown 8vo. 3s. 6d.

and at Oxford and Cambridge

The Hillford Confirmation. A Tale.
By M. C. PHILLPOTTS. New Edition. 16mo. 1s.

The Manor Farm. A Tale. By M. C.
PHILLPOTTS. Small 8vo. With Illustrations. 3s. 6d.

Sacred Allegories. The Shadow of the
Cross—The Distant Hills—The Old Man's Home—The King's
Messengers. By the Rev. WILLIAM ADAMS, M.A., late
Fellow of Merton College, Oxford. New Edition. With
numerous Illustrations. Small 8vo. 5s.
   The Four Allegories may be had separately, with Illustra-
tions. Crown 8vo. 2s. 6d. each. Also a Cheap Edition.
Small 8vo. 1s. each.

The Shepherd of Hermas. Translated
into English, with an Introduction and Notes. By CHARLES
H. HOOLE, M.A., Senior Student of Christ Church, Oxford.
Small 8vo. 4s. 6d.

Herbert Tresham; a Tale of the Great
Rebellion. By the Rev. JOHN MASON NEALE, D.D., late
Warden of Sackville College, East Grinsted. New Edition.
Small 8vo. 3s. 6d.

Semele; or, The Spirit of Beauty: a
Venetian Tale. By the Rev. J. D. MEREWEATHER, B.A.,
English Chaplain at Venice. Small 8vo. 3s. 6d.

9. History and Biography.

A Christian Painter of the Nineteenth

Century; being the Life of Hippolyte Flandrin. By the Author of "A Dominician Artist," "Life of S. Francis de Sales," &c. Crown 8vo. 7s. 6d.

Bossuet and his Contemporaries. By

the Author of "Life of S. Francis de Sales," "A Dominican Artist," &c. Crown 8vo. 12s.

"*The book as a literary work has rare merits, and as a chronicle of Church life in France at an eventful period it is invaluable in itself, and rendered more so by its well-timed appearance. Whether in his diocesan organisation, his direct spiritual work, or in his more public career, the life of Bossuet is one which deserves the careful study of English Churchmen.*" —JOHN BULL.

"*It contains so many interesting facts that it may be profitably read even by those who already know the man and the period.*"—SPECTATOR.

"*Here is a clear and good work, the product of thorough industry and of honest mind.*"—NONCONFORMIST.

"*A very interesting and well-timed publication.*"—STANDARD.

"*Bossuet's daily life, his style of preaching, his association with the stirring political, social, and ecclesiastical events of his time, are presented in a simple but picturesque way.*"— DAILY NEWS.

"*Should be read widely.*"—SCOTS-MAN.

"*All biography is delightful, and this story of Bossuet is eminently so.*" —NOTES AND QUERIES.

"*In the ten chapters that compose the work we have a rapid yet complete sketch of the life of Bossuet, accompanied by short and generally judicious criticisms of his works, which are arranged in chronological order, and thus play the part they ought to play in the biography of a man whose writings were his deeds.*"— ATHENÆUM.

"*We are always glad to welcome a fresh work from the graceful pen of the author of 'A Dominican Artist.' And the fact that not only is there no popular Life of Bossuet to be found in France, as we are told in the preface, but, so far as we are aware, no Life of him at all in English, gives an additional interest to the present volume.*" —SATURDAY REVIEW.

"*Une biographie générale et complète puisée aux meilleures sources, et toujours appuyée soit sur les œuvres même du grand évêque, soit sur les mémoires contemporains, soit sur les jugements des critiques modernes les plus autorisés. . . . C'est là un bon livre longuement médité, et qui ferait honneur à l'un de nos plus sérieux érudits.*"—POLYBIBLION (PARIS).

A Dominican Artist: A Sketch of the

Life of the Rev. Père Besson, of the Order of St. Dominic.
By the Author of "The Life of Madame Louise de France,"
&c.   New Edition.   Crown 8vo.   6s.

" *The author of the Life of Père Besson writes with a grace and refinement of devotional feeling peculiarly suited to a subject-matter which suffers beyond most others from any coarseness of touch. It would be difficult to find ' the simplicity and purity of a holy life' more exquisitely illustrated than in Father Besson's career, both before and after his joining the Dominican Order under the auspices of Lacordaire. . . . Certainly we have never come across what could more strictly be termed in the truest sense ' the life of a beautiful soul.' The author has done well in presenting to English readers this singularly graceful biography, in which all who can appreciate genuine simplicity and nobleness of Christian character will find much to admire and little or nothing to condemn.*"—SATURDAY REVIEW.

" *It would indeed have been a deplorable omission had so exquisite a biography been by any neglect lost to English readers, and had a character so perfect in its simple and complete devotion been withheld from our admiration. . . . . But we have dwelt too long already on this fascinating book, and must now leave it to our readers.*"—LITERARY CHURCHMAN.

" *A beautiful and most interesting sketch of the late Père Besson, an artist who forsook the easel for the altar.*"—CHURCH TIMES.

" *A book which is as pleasant for reading as it is profitable for meditation.*"—UNION REVIEW.

" *Whatever a reader may think of Père Besson's profession as a monk, no one will doubt his goodness ; no one can fail to profit who will patiently read his life, as here written by a friend, whose sole defect is in being slightly unctuous.*"—ATHENÆUM.

" *The life of the Rev. Père Besson, who gave up an artist's career, to which he was devotedly attached, and a mother whose affection for him is not inaptly likened to that of Monica for St. Augustine, must be read in its entirety to be rightly appreciated. And the whole tenour of the book is too devotional, too full of expressions of the most touching dependence on God, to make criticism possible, even if it was called for, which it is not.*"—JOHN BULL.

" *The story of Père Besson's life is one of much interest, and told with simplicity, candour, and good feeling.*"—SPECTATOR.

" *A beautiful book, describing the most saintly and very individual life of one of the companions of Lacordaire.*"—MONTHLY PACKET.

" *We strongly recommend it to our readers. It is a charming biography, that will delight and edify both old and young.*"—WESTMINSTER GAZETTE.

The Life of Madame Louise de France,

Daughter of Louis XV., also known as the Mother Térèse de
S. Augustin.   By the Author of "A Dominican Artist," &c.
New Edition.   Crown 8vo.   6s.

" *Such a record of deep, earnest, self-sacrificing piety, beneath the surface of Parisian life, during what we all regard as the worst age of French godlessness, ought to teach us all a lesson of hope and faith, let appearances be what they may. Here, from out of the court and* family of Louis XV. there issues this Madame Louise, whose life is set before us as a specimen of as calm and unworldly devotion—of a devotion, too, full of shrewd sense and practical administrative talent—as any we have ever met with.*"—LITERARY CHURCHMAN.

Waterloo Place, London

The Revival of Priestly Life in the

Seventeenth Century in France : a Sketch. By the Author of "A Dominican Artist," "Life of S. Francis de Sales," &c. Crown 8vo. 9s.

"*A book the authorship of which will command the respect of all who can honour sterling worth. No Christian, to whatever denomination he may belong, can read without quick* sympathy and emotion these touching sketches of the early Oratorians and the Lazarists, whose devotion we can all admire."*—STANDARD.

Life of S. Francis de Sales. By the

Author of "A Dominican Artist," &c. Crown 8vo. 6s.

"*It is written with the delicacy, freshness, and absence of all affectation which characterized the former works by the same hand, and which render these books so very much more pleasant reading than are religious biographies in general. The character of S. Francis de Sales, Bishop of Geneva, is a charming one; a more simple, pure, and pious life it would be difficult to conceive. His unaffected humility, his freedom from dogmatism in an age when dogma was placed above religion, his freedom from bigotry in an age of persecution, were alike admirable.*"—STANDARD.

"*The author of 'A Dominican Artist,' in writing this new life of the wise and loving Bishop and Prince of Geneva, has aimed less at historical or ecclesiastical investigation than at a vivid and natural representation of the inner mind and life of the subject of his biography, as it can be traced in his own writings and in those of his most intimate and affectionate friends. The book is written with the grave and quiet grace which characterizes the productions of its author, and cannot* fail to please those readers who can sympathize with all forms of goodness and devotion to noble purpose."*—WESTMINSTER REVIEW.

"*A book which contains the record of a life as sweet, pure, and noble, as any man by divine help, granted to devout sincerity of soul, has been permitted to live upon earth. The example of this gentle but resolute and energetic spirit, wholly dedicated to the highest conceivable good, offering itself, with all the temporal uses of mental existence, to the service of infinite and eternal beneficence, is extremely touching. It is a book worthy of acceptance.*"—DAILY NEWS.

"*It is not a translation or adaptation, but an original work, and a very charming portrait of one of the most winning characters in the long gallery of Saints. And it is a matter of entire thankfulness to us to find a distinctively Anglican writer setting forward the good Bishop's work among Protestants, as a true missionary task to reclaim souls from deadly error, and bring them back to the truth.*"—UNION REVIEW.

The Last Days of Père Gratry. By PÈRE

ADOLPHE PERRAUD, of the Oratory, and Professor of La Sorbonne. Translated by Special permission. By the Author of "Life of S. Francis de Sales," &c. Crown 8vo. 3s. 6d.

Henri Perreyve. By A. GRATRY, Prêtre

de l'Oratoire, Professeur de Morale Evangélique à la Sorbonne, et Membre de l'Académie Française. Translated, by special permission, by the Author of "A Dominican Artist," "Life of S. Francis de Sales," &c. &c. With Portrait. Crown 8vo. 7s. 6d.

"*A most touching and powerful piece of biography, interspersed with profound reflections on personal religion, and on the prospects of Christianity. . . . For priests this book is a treasure. The moral of it is the absolute necessity of 'recollectedness' to the higher, and especially the true priestly life.*"—CHURCH REVIEW.

"*The works of the translator of Henri Perreyve form, for the most part, a series of saintly biographies which have obtained a larger share of popularity than is generally accorded to books of this description. . . . The description of his last days will probably be read with greater interest than any other part of the book; presenting as it does an example of fortitude under suffering, and resignation, when cut off so soon after entering upon a much-coveted and useful career, of rare occurrence in this age of self-assertion. This is, in fact, the essential teaching of the entire volume. . . . The translator of the Abbé Gratry's work has done well in giving English readers an opportunity of profiting by its lessons.*'—MORNING POST.

"*Those who take a pleasure in reading a beautiful account of a beautiful character would do well to procure the Life of 'Henri Perreyve.' . . . We* would especially recommend the book for the perusal of English priests, who may learn many a holy lesson from the devoted spirit in which the subject of the memoir gave himself up to the duties of his sacred office, and to the cultivation of the graces with which he was endowed.*"—CHURCH TIMES.

"*It is easy to see that Henri Perreyve, Professor of Moral Theology at the Sorbonne, was a Roman Catholic priest of no ordinary type. With comparatively little of what Protestants call superstition, with great courage and sincerity, with a nature singularly guileless and noble, his priestly vocation, although pursued, according to his biographer, with unbridled zeal, did not stifle his human sympathies and aspirations. He could not believe that his faith compelled him 'to renounce sense and reason,' or that a priest was not free to speak, act, and think like other men. Indeed, the Abbé Gratry makes a kind of apology for his friend's free-speaking in this respect, and endeavours to explain it. Perreyve was the beloved disciple of Lacordaire, who left him all his manuscripts, notes, and papers, and he himself attained the position of a great pulpit orator.*"—PALL MALL GAZETTE.

Walter Kerr Hamilton, Bishop of Salisbury.

A Sketch by HENRY PARRY LIDDON, D.D., Canon of St. Paul's, and Ireland Professor of Exegesis in the University of Oxford. Second Edition. 8vo. 2s. 6d., or with the Funeral Sermon, "Life in Death," 3s. 6d.

𝔚aterloo 𝔓lace, 𝔏ondon

Life of S. Vincent de Paul. With Introduction by the Rev. R. F. WILSON, M.A., Prebendary of Salisbury and Vicar of Rownhams, and Chaplain to the Bishop of Salisbury. Crown 8vo. 9s.

"*A most readable volume, illustrating plans and arrangements, which from the circumstances of the day are invested with peculiar interest.*"—ENGLISH CHURCHMAN.

"*All will be pleased at reading the present admirably written narrative, in which we do not know whether to admire more the candour and earnestness of the writer or his plain, sensible, and agreeable style.*"—WEEKLY REGISTER.

"*We trust that this deeply interesting and beautifully written biography will be extensively circulated in England.*"—CHURCH HERALD.

"*We heartily recommend the introduction to the study of all concerned with ordinations.*"—GUARDIAN.

"*We are glad that S. Vincent de Paul, one of the most remarkable men produced by the Gallican Church, has at last found a competent English biographer. The volume before us has evidently been written with conscientious care and scrupulous industry. It is based on the best authorities, which have been compared with praiseworthy diligence; its style is clear, elegant, and unambitious; and it shows a fine appreciation of the life and character of the man whom it commemorates.*"—SCOTTISH GUARDIAN.

"*Mr. Wilson has done his work admirably and evidently* con amore, *and he completely proves the thesis with which he starts, viz., that in the life of the Saint there is a homeliness and simplicity, and a general absence of the miraculous or the more ascetic type of saintliness.*"—JOHN BULL.

John Wesley's Place in Church History

determined, with the aid of Facts and Documents unknown to, or unnoticed by, his Biographers. With a New and Authentic Portrait. By R. DENNY URLIN, of the Middle Temple, Barrister-at-Law, &c. Small 8vo. 5s. 6d.

A History of the Holy Eastern Church.

The Patriarchate of Antioch. By the Rev. JOHN MASON NEALE, D.D., late Warden of Sackville College, East Grinsted. A Posthumous Fragment. Together with Memoirs of the Patriarchs of Antioch, by Constantius, Patriarch of Constantinople; translated from the Greek, and three Appendices. Edited, with an Introduction, by the Rev. GEORGE WILLIAMS, B.D., Vicar of Ringwood, late Fellow of King's College, Cambridge. 8vo. 10s. 6d.

History of the Church under the

Roman Empire, A.D. 30-476. By the Rev. A. D. CRAKE, B.A., Chaplain of All Saints' School, Bloxham. Crown 8vo. 7s. 6d.

"*A compendious history of the Christian Church under the Roman Empire will be hailed with pleasure by all readers of ecclesiastical lore. . . . The author is quite free from the spirit of controversialism; wherever he refers to a prevalent practice of ancient times he gives his authority. In his statement of facts or opinions he is always accurate and concise, and his manual is doubtless destined to a lengthened period of popularity.*"—MORNING POST.

"*It is very well done. It gives a very comprehensive view of the progress of events, ecclesiastical and political, at the great centres of civilisation during the first five centuries of Christianity.*"—DAILY NEWS.

"*In his well-planned and carefully written volume of 500 pages Mr. Crake has supplied a well-known and long-felt want. Relying on all the highest and best authorities for his main facts and conclusions, and wisely making use of all modern research, Mr. Crake has spared neither time nor labour to make his work accurate, trustworthy, and intelligent.*"—STANDARD.

"*Really interesting, well suited to the needs of those for whom it was prepared, and its Church tone is unexceptionable.*"—CHURCH TIMES.

"*As a volume for students and the higher forms of our public schools it is admirably adapted.*"—CHURCH HERALD.

"*We cordially recommend it for schools for the young.*"—ENGLISH CHURCHMAN.

"*Mr. Crake gives us in a clear and concise form a narrative of the Church history during the period with which it is most important that the young should first be made acquainted. The different events appear to be described with a judicious regard to their relative importance, and the manual may be safely recommended.*"—JOHN BULL.

"*The facts are well marshalled, the literary style of the book is simple and good; while the principles enunciated throughout render it a volume which may be safely put into the hands of students. For the higher forms of grammar-schools it is exactly the book required. Never ponderous, and frequently very attractive and interesting, it is at once readable and edifying, and fills efficiently a vacant place in elementary historical literature. Furthermore its type is clear and bold, and it is well broken up into paragraphs.*"—UNION REVIEW.

"*It retells an oft-told tale in a singularly fresh and perspicuous style, rendering the book neither above the comprehension of an intelligent boy or girl of fourteen or upwards, nor beneath the attention of an educated man. We can imagine no better book as an addition to a parochial library, as a prize, or as a reading book in the upper forms of middle-class schools.*"—SCOTTISH GUARDIAN.

Church Memorials and Characteristics;

being a Church History of the six First Centuries. By the late WILLIAM ROBERTS, Esq., M.A., F.R.S. Edited by his Son, ARTHUR ROBERTS, M.A., Rector of Woodrising, Norfolk. 8vo. 7s. 6d.

A Key to the Knowledge of Church
History (Ancient). Edited by the Rev. JOHN HENRY BLUNT,
M.A., F.S.A., Editor of "The Annotated Book of Common
Prayer," &c. &c. Small 8vo. 2s. 6d.
Forming a Volume of "Keys to Christian Knowledge."

"*It offers a short and condensed account of the origin, growth, and condition of the Church in all parts of the world, from A.D. 1 down to the end of the fifteenth century. Mr. Blunt's first object has been conciseness, and this has been admirably carried out, and to students of Church history this feature will readily recommend itself. As an elementary work 'A Key' will be specially valuable, inasmuch as it points out certain definite lines of thought, by which those who enjoy the opportunity may be guided in reading the statements of more elaborate histories. At the same time it is but fair to Mr. Blunt to remark that, for general readers, the little volume contains* everything that could be consistently expected in a volume of its character. There are many notes, theological, scriptural, and historical, and the 'get up' of the book is specially commendable. As a text-book for the higher forms of schools the work will be acceptable to numerous teachers.*"—* PUBLIC OPINION.

"*It contains some concise notes on Church History, compressed into a small compass, and we think it is likely to be useful as a book of reference.*"—JOHN BULL.

"*A very terse and reliable collection of the main facts and incidents connected with Church History.*"—ROCK.

A Key to the Knowledge of Church
History (Modern). Edited by the Rev. JOHN HENRY BLUNT,
M.A., F.S.A., Editor of "The Annotated Book of Common
Prayer," &c. &c. Small 8vo. 2s. 6d.
Forming a Volume of "Keys to Christian Knowledge."

The Reformation of the Church of
England; its History, Principles, and Results. A.D. 1514-1547.
By the Rev. JOHN HENRY BLUNT, M.A., F.S.A., Editor of
"The Annotated Book of Common Prayer," &c. &c. Third
Edition. 8vo. 16s.

Perranzabuloe, the Lost Church Found;
or, The Church of England not a New Church, but Ancient,
Apostolical, and Independent, and a Protesting Church Nine
Hundred Years before the Reformation. By the Rev. C. T.
COLLINS TRELAWNY, M.A., late Rector of Timsbury, Somerset.
New Edition. Crown 8vo. 3s. 6d.

History of the English Institutions.

By PHILIP V. SMITH, M.A., Barrister-at-Law, Fellow of King's College, Cambridge. Crown 8vo. 3s. 6d.

Forming a Volume of "Historical Handbooks," edited by OSCAR BROWNING, M.A., Fellow of King's College, Cambridge, Assistant Master at Eton College.

[See RIVINGTON'S SCHOOL CATALOGUE.]

History of French Literature, adapted

from the French of M. Demogeot. By C. BRIDGE. Crown 8vo. 3s. 6a.

Forming a Volume of "Historical Handbooks," edited by OSCAR BROWNING, M.A., Fellow of King's College, Cambridge, Assistant-Master at Eton College.

[See RIVINGTON'S SCHOOL CATALOGUE.]

The Roman Empire. From the Death

of Theodosius the Great to the Coronation of Charles the Great, A.D. 395 to A.D. 800. By A. M. CURTEIS, M.A., Assistant-Master at Sherborne School, late Fellow of Trinity College, Oxford. With Maps. Crown 8vo. 3s. 6d.

Forming a Volume of "Historical Handbooks," edited by OSCAR BROWNING, M.A., Fellow of King's College, Cambridge, Assistant-Master at Eton College.

[See RIVINGTON'S SCHOOL CATALOGUE.]

History of Modern English Law. By

Sir ROLAND KNYVET WILSON, Bart., M.A., Barrister-at-Law, late Fellow of King's College, Cambridge. Crown 8vo. 3s. 6d.

Forming a Volume of "Historical Handbooks," edited by OSCAR BROWNING, M.A., Fellow of King's College, Cambridge, Assistant-Master at Eton College.

[See RIVINGTON'S SCHOOL CATALOGUE.]

The Annual Register: a Review of Public

Events at Home and Abroad, for the Years 1863 to 1874. 8vo. 18s. each.

Life of Robert Gray, Bishop of Cape

Town and Metropolitan of Africa. Edited by his Son, the
Rev. CHARLES GRAY, M.A., Vicar of Helmsley, York.
With Portrait and Map. 2 Vols. 8vo.

Life, Journals, and Letters of Henry

ALFORD, D.D., late Dean of Canterbury.   Edited by his
WIDOW.   With   Portrait   and   Illustrations.   New   Edition.
Crown 8vo.   9s.

"The Life of Dean Alford will have a far more general interest than that of many more conspicuous theologians. . . . His life is written by his widow, and we need scarcely say that it was a difficult and delicate task for a wife to undertake. On the whole, Mrs. Alford has acquitted herself admirably. . . . His life was the best commentary on his character, and the remarks we have made or quoted as we have gone along leave us little more to add. Those who desire thoroughly to appreciate a valuable life and a beautiful character we refer to the volume itself."—TIMES.

"It was a beautiful life he lived; and touchingly beautiful in its unadorned simplicity is the record given to us in this volume by his life-long companion, who from his early boyhood had shared his every thought. . . . The real value of the memoir is that it gives us so attractive a portrait of its subject. Of this too much can hardly be said. . . . The goodness, the piety, the calm thankfulness, the ready submission, the charity breathing in every line, is unmistakeable. And it is this that makes the book so attractive."—GUARDIAN.

"We have here the simple and loving record of a happy, industrious, and holy life. . . . To have known and valued Henry Alford will long be a source of heartfelt satisfaction to many others, besides those immediate friends whose names are linked with his in this beautiful and touching Life by his widow."—SATURDAY REVIEW.

"Here is a book of rare interest, the editing of which bears evidence not only of loving affection, as was natural, but of great care; and happily so many of Dean Alford's letters are given that one has a real insight into his own feelings."—JOHN BULL.

"No elaborate memoir from the pen of even his most intimate friend could give a truer insight or reflect more clearly the beautiful traits of Alford's inner character, with all the subdued and Christian sweetness which seems to have characterized the late Dean of Canterbury from his very earliest years, than these daily 'Experiences,' indited by his own hands."—SCOTSMAN.

"We must refer our readers to the volume for its incidents, and for very much that will enhance their admiration and their thankfulness to God that such a life has been lived. The memoir has been compiled by his widow in a spirit in perfect sympathy with his own."—BRITISH QUARTERLY REVIEW.

Life and Correspondence of Samuel

JOHNSON, D.D., Missionary of the Church of England in Connecticut, and First President of King's College, New York.
By E. E. BEARDSLEY, D.D. With Portrait. 8vo. 12s.

and at Oxford and Cambridge

Historical Narratives. From the Russian.

By H. C. ROMANOFF, Author of "Sketches of the Rites and Customs of the Greco-Russian Church," &c. Crown 8vo. 6s.

Sketches of the Rites and Customs of

the Greco-Russian Church. By H. C. ROMANOFF. With an Introductory Notice by the Author of "The Heir of Redclyffe." Second Edition. Crown 8vo. 7s. 6d.

"The volume before us is anything but a formal liturgical treatise. It might be more valuable to a few scholars if it were, but it would certainly fail to obtain perusal at the hands of the great majority of those whom the writer, not unreasonably, hopes to attract by the narrative style she has adopted. What she has set before us is a series of brief outlines, which, by their simple effort to clothe the information given us in a living garb, reminds us of a once-popular child's book which we remember a generation ago, called 'Sketches of Human Manners.'"—CHURCH TIMES.
"The twofold object of this work is 'to present the English with correct descriptions of the ceremonies of the Greco-Russian Church, and at the same time with pictures of domestic life in Russian homes, especially those of the clergy and the middle class of nobles;' and, beyond question, the author's labour has been so far successful that, whilst her Church scenes may be commended as a series of most dramatic and picturesque tableaux, her social sketches enable us to look at certain points beneath the surface of Russian life, and materially enlarge our knowledge of a country concerning which we have still a very great deal to learn."—ATHENÆUM.

Fables respecting the Popes of the

Middle Ages. A Contribution to Ecclesiastical History. By JOHN J. IGN. VON DÖLLINGER, D.D., D.C.L. Translated by the Rev. ALFRED PLUMMER, M.A., Master of University College, Durham, late Fellow of Trinity College, Oxford. 8vo. 14s.

Curious Myths of the Middle Ages.

By S. BARING-GOULD, M.A., Author of "Origin and Development of Religious Belief," &c. With Illustrations. New Edition. Crown 8vo. 6s.

Reflections on the Revolution in

France, in 1790. By the Right Hon. EDMUND BURKE, M.P. New Edition, with a short Biographical Notice. Crown 8vo. 3s. 6d.

The Campaigns of Napoleon. The Text

(in French) from M. THIERS' "Histoire du Consulat et de l'Empire," and "Histoire de la Révolution Française." Edited with English Notes, for the use of Schools, by EDWARD E. BOWEN, M.A., Master of the Modern Side, Harrow School. With Maps. Crown 8vo.

ARCOLA. 4s. 6d.   MARENGO. 4s. 6d.
JENA. 3s. 6d.   WATERLOO.

Egypt's Record of Time to the Exodus

of Israel, critically investigated; with a comparative Survey of the Patriarchal History and the Chronology of Scripture; resulting in the Reconciliation of the Septuagint and Hebrew Computations, and Manetho with both. By the Rev. W. B. GALLOWAY, M.A., Vicar of St. Mark's, Regent's Park, Author of "Physical Facts and Scriptural Record." 8vo. 15s.

A History of England for Children.

By GEORGE DAVYS, D.D., formerly Bishop of Peterborough. New Edition. 18mo. 1s. 6d.

With twelve Coloured Illustrations. Square Crown 8vo. 3s. 6d.

10. Miscellaneous.

The Knight of Intercession, and other
Poems. By the Rev. S. J. STONE, M.A., Pembroke College, Oxford. Third Edition, revised and enlarged. Small 8vo. 6s.

Yesterday, To-Day, and for Ever: A
Poem in Twelve Books. By E. H. BICKERSTETH, M.A., Vicar of Christ Church, Hampstead. Tenth Edition. Small 8vo. 6s.

A Presentation Edition with red borders. Small 4to. 10s. 6d.

"We should have noticed among its kind a very magnificent presentation edition of 'Yesterday, To-day, and For Ever,' by the Rev. E. H. Bickersteth. This blank verse poem, in twelve books, has made its way into the religious world of England and America without much help from the critics. It is now made splendid for its admirers by morocco binding, broad margins, red lines, and beautiful photographs."—TIMES.

"The most simple, the richest, and the most perfect sacred poem which recent days have produced."—MORNING ADVERTISER.

"A poem worth reading, worthy of attentive study; full of noble thoughts, beautiful diction, and high imagination."—STANDARD.

"In these light miscellany days there is a spiritual refreshment in the spectacle of a man girding up the loins of his mind to the task of producing a genuine epic. And it is true poetry. There is a definiteness, a crispness about it, which in these moist, viewy, hazy days is no less invigorating than novel."—EDINBURGH DAILY REVIEW.

"Mr. Bickersteth writes like a man who cultivates at once reverence and earnestness of thought."—GUARDIAN.

The Two Brothers, and other Poems. By
EDWARD HENRY BICKERSTETH, M.A., Vicar of Christ Church, Hampstead. Second Edition. Small 8vo. 6s.

Waterloo Place, London

A Year's Botany. Adapted to Home

Reading. By FRANCES ANNA KITCHENER. Illustrated by the Author. Crown 8vo. 5s.

CONTENTS.

General Description of Flowers—Flowers with Simple Pistils—Flowers with Compound Pistils—Flowers with Apocarpous Fruits—Flowers with Syncarpous Fruits—Stamens and Morphology of Branches—Fertilization—Seeds—Early Growth and Food of Plants—Wood, Stems, and Roots—Leaves—Classification—Umbellates, Composites, Spurges, and Pines—Some Monocotyledonous Families—Orchids—Appendix of Technical Terms—Index.

[See RIVINGTON'S SCHOOL CATALOGUE.]

An Easy Introduction to Chemistry.

For the Use of Schools. Edited by the Rev. ARTHUR RIGG, M.A., late Principal of the College, Chester; and WALTER T. GOOLDEN, B.A., late Science Scholar of Merton College, Oxford. New Edition, considerably altered and revised. With Illustrations. Crown 8vo. 2s. 6d.

[See RIVINGTON'S SCHOOL CATALOGUE.]

A Shadow of Dante. Being an Essay

towards studying Himself, his World, and his Pilgrimage. By MARIA FRANCESCA ROSSETTI. With Illustrations. Second Edition. Crown 8vo. 10s. 6d.

" The ' Shadow of Dante' is a well-conceived and inviting volume, designed to recommend the ' Divina Commedia' to English readers, and to facilitate the study and comprehension of its contents."—ATHENÆUM.

" And it is in itself a true work of art, a whole finely conceived, and carried out with sustained power."—GUARDIAN.

" We find the volume furnished with useful diagrams of the Dantesque universe, of Hell, Purgatory, and the ' Rose of the Blessed,' and adorned with a beautiful group of the likenesses of the poet, and with symbolic figures (on the binding) in which the taste and execution of Mr. D. G. Rossetti will be re-

cognised. The exposition appears to us remarkably well arranged and digested; the author's appreciation of Dante's religious sentiments and opinions is peculiarly hearty, and her style refreshingly independent and original."—PALL MALL GAZETTE.

" The result has been a book which is not only delightful in itself to read, but is admirably adapted as an encouragement to those students who wish to obtain a preliminary survey of the land before they attempt to follow Dante through his long and arduous pilgrimage. Of all poets Dante stands most in need of such assistance as this book offers."—SATURDAY REVIEW.

and at Oxford and Cambridge

Hymns and other Verses.   By WILLIAM
BRIGHT, D.D., Canon of Christ Church, and Regius Professor of Ecclesiastical History in the University of Oxford. Second Edition. Small 8vo. 5s.

Parish Musings; or, Devotional Poems.
By JOHN D. B. MONSELL, LL.D., late Vicar of Egham, and Rural Dean. New Edition. Small 8vo. 5s.
Also a Cheap Edition. Cloth limp, 1s. 6d.; or in cover, 1s.

Miscellaneous   Poems.   By   HENRY
FRANCIS LYTE, M.A. New Edition. Small 8vo. 5s.

The Elegies of Propertius.   Translated
into English Verse, by CHARLES ROBERT MOORE, M.A. Small 8vo. 2s. 6d.

The Iliad of Homer.   Translated by J. G.
CORDERY, late of Balliol College, Oxford, and now of H.M. Bengal Civil Service. Two Vols. 8vo. 16s.

English Nursery Rhymes.   Translated
into French. By JOHN ROBERTS, M.A., Fellow of Magdalen College, Cambridge. Square 16mo. 2s. 6d.

Physical Facts and Scriptural Record;
or, Eighteen Propositions for Geologists. By the Rev. W. B. GALLOWAY, M.A., Vicar of St. Mark's Regent's Park, Author of "Egypt's Record of Time," &c. 8vo. 10s. 6d.

Immanuel: Thoughts for Christmas and
other Seasons, with other Poems. By A. MIDDLEMORE
MORGAN, M.A. Small 8vo. 6s.

Mazzaroth; or, the Constellations. By
FRANCES ROLLESTON, Keswick. Royal 8vo. 12s.

Rivington's Devotional Series.

IN ELEGANT BINDINGS, SUITABLE FOR PRESENTS.

"TO many persons there is something repulsive in a devotional volume unbound, and Messrs. Rivington have now turned their attention to the binding of their Devotional Library in forms that, like the books themselves, are neat, handsome, good, and attractive."—*The Bookseller.*

THE CHRISTIAN YEAR, recently issued in this series, may be had in the under-mentioned plain and handsome bindings.

The Christian Year.

16MO. ELEGANTLY PRINTED WITH RED BORDERS.

	£ s. d.
CALF *or* MOROCCO *limp, blind tooled*	0 5 0
THE SAME, ILLUSTRATED WITH A CHOICE SELECTION OF PHOTOGRAPHS	0 9 0
THE SAME, ILLUSTRATED WITH STEEL ENGRAVINGS .	0 6 6
CALF *or* MOROCCO *limp, blind tooled, red cross on side* .	0 5 6
MOROCCO *superior*	0 6 6
POLISHED MOROCCO, *limp, elegant, gilt cross* . .	0 7 0
POLISHED MOROCCO, *gilt, elegant,* ILLUSTRATED WITH A CHOICE SELECTION OF PHOTOGRAPHS . .	0 17 6
RUSSIA *limp, gilt cross*	0 8 0
RUSSIA *limp, gilt lines and gilt cross,* ILLUSTRATED WITH A CHOICE SELECTION OF PHOTOGRAPHS . .	0 13 0
TURKEY MOROCCO, *limp circuit* . . .	0 7 6
RUSSIA, *limp circuit*	0 9 0

The Christian Year.

CHEAP EDITION, WITHOUT THE RED BORDERS.

FRENCH ROAN, *red inlaid or gilt outline cross* . .	0 1 6
THE SAME, ILLUSTRATED WITH STEEL ENGRAVINGS .	0 2 6
FRENCH MOROCCO, *gilt extra*	0 2 0

The Imitation of Christ is also kept in the above-mentioned styles at the same prices.

The other Volumes of "The Devotional Series," viz.:—

Taylor's Holy Living	Wilson's Lord's Supper
Taylor's Holy Dying	De Sales' Devout Life

Herbert's English Poems and Proverbs

Can be had in a variety of elegant bindings.

Index.

𝔚𝔞𝔱𝔢𝔯𝔩𝔬𝔬 𝔓𝔩𝔞𝔠𝔢, 𝔏𝔬𝔫𝔡𝔬𝔫 .